MUSCOVY'S SOLDIERS

The Emergence of the Russian Army 1462-1689

Michael Fredholm von Essen

'This is the Century of the Soldier', Falvio Testir, Poet, 1641

Helion & Company

Helion & Company Limited
Unit 8 Amherst Business Centre
Budbrooke Road
Warwick
CV34 5WE
England
Tel. 01926 499 619
Fax 0121 711 4075
Email: info@helion.co.uk
Website: www.helion.co.uk
Twitter: @helionbooks
Visit our blog at http://blog.helion.co.uk/

Published by Helion & Company 2018
Designed and typeset by Serena Jones
Cover designed by Paul Hewitt, Battlefield Design (www.battlefield-design.co.uk)
Printed by Henry Ling Limited, Dorchester, Dorset

ISBN 978-1-912390-01-06

British Library Cataloguing-in-Publication Data.
A catalogue record for this book is available from the British Library.

For details of other military history titles published by Helion & Company
Limited, contact the above address, or visit our website: http://www.helion.co.uk

We always welcome receiving book proposals from prospective authors.

Contents

List of Illustrations & Maps

Illustrations

Maps

Introduction

This book aims to describe and analyse the emergence of the early modern Russian army, before the military reforms introduced by Tsar Peter the Great around the turn of the eighteenth century brought it fully in line with developments in Western Europe. It will show that Tsar Peter's reforms, although decisive, rested on a legacy of previous reforms, beginning with those of Tsar Ivan IV, known in English as 'the Terrible'. Yet, the origin of the early modern Russian, or Muscovite, army can be found in the East, not the West. Muscovy was a Christian, European principality, but it was also one of the successor states to Chinggis Khan's Mongol empire.

The close association during the Middle Ages with the Mongol Golden Horde and its Tatar successor states, often led by descendants of Chinggis Khan, had transformed the Muscovite military system into a Eurasian one. In the sixteenth and seventeenth centuries, close links with the steppe around the Volga, the North Caucasus, and Siberia brought further Oriental influences into the Muscovite military system. For the same reason, the Ottoman Empire served as a source of military and administrative inspiration for Muscovy before Western Europe came to assume this role. Both Russian and Western scholars have long had an interest in exploring how the Muscovite army assimilated Western techniques and structures and how important West European influences were in relationship to Muscovite traditions.[1] It is time to look beyond the West European influences and see what else constituted the Muscovite military system. Many other Muscovite institutions and customs, too, derived from the Mongols, yet the close relationship is nowhere more visible than in the Muscovite military system.

The oriental influences were a mark of adaption and not, it needs to be said, a sign of backwardness. However, at this period of time Muscovy was backward in at least two dimensions: the material and the intellectual. The material dimension was caused by shortages in economic resources which resulted in state poverty. In combination with a difficult climate and geography, state poverty interfered with Moscow's ability to sustain a prolonged war. The intellectual dimension was caused by a lack of schooling and technical training which meant that for the introduction of any new technology, such as artillery, fortifications, but also new concepts of

---

1   See, e.g., Christopher Duffy, *Russia's Military Way to the West: Origins and Nature of Russian Military Power 1700–1800* (Knighton, Powys: Terence Wise, 1994; first published by Routledge & Kegan Paul, 1981), p.xi.

military tactics and organisation, foreign expertise was needed. But foreign mercenaries were expensive, which militated against the already high level of state poverty.[2] Muscovy was not unique in this position, and other states grappled with the same problems, yet these particular shortcomings affected Muscovy's military performance.

This book does not aim to be a general history of Muscovy, which in any case would be impossible within the present format. Nor does it aim to provide a comprehensive military history of Muscovy, with details on all battles and campaigns. What the book hopes to achieve is to describe all aspects of the Muscovite army – recruitment, organisation, weapons, training, and tactics – that are relevant for an understanding of how the Muscovite army emerged and modelled itself on first the East, then the West, in the formative period of time before Muscovy became a truly European great power. The book also aims to explain some of the strategies employed during campaigns against Muscovy's Western and Eastern enemies and the reasons for their adoption by the Muscovite military leadership.

The early modern Muscovite army emerged from contacts, and conflicts, with the Mongols and Tatars on the Eurasian steppes, the hill peoples of the Caucasus, and the forest tribes of Siberia, yet held its own against militarily highly developed adversaries such as Sweden, Poland, the Ottoman Empire, and Manchu-held China. For a full appreciation of the Muscovite military system, we need to examine how these adversaries rated the Muscovite army. For the sixteenth century, there are German records, written by those who fought against, or equally often, within the Muscovite army. Examples included Albert Schlichting, a German in Polish service who fell into Muscovite captivity, after which he in 1571 wrote the anti-Muscovite treatise *De Moribus et Imperandi Crudelitate Basilij Moschoviae Tyranni Brevis Enarratio*, and Heinrich von Staden (b.1545), who was in Muscovite military service but when out of the country, in 1578 wrote a treatise on Muscovy which included notes on how to conquer it. With regard to the seventeenth century, there are significant Swedish records. Sweden indeed left records of its ongoing intelligence operations against Muscovy. The results of these activities included a treatise on the Muscovite state and its institutions written in 1666 by a defector, Grigoriy Kotoshikhin (d. 1667). An official in Muscovy's ambassadors' chancellery, Kotoshikhin defected to first Poland, then, in 1665, to Sweden. The treatise was his ticket to a salary in the Swedish capital Stockholm. Unfortunately, Kotoshikhin already in 1667, in a state of drunkenness, killed his landlord, for which he was executed. There is also the Swedish military intelligence handbook on the Muscovite army from 1673/1674, produced by a Swedish intelligence officer, Erik Palmquist (c.1650–1676?). Together, these documents give an outstanding view of how Sweden assessed Muscovy as a state and military opponent.

---

2   William C. Fuller, Jr., *Strategy and Power in Russia 1600–1914* (New York: The Free Press, 1992), pp.xvii–xviii. Fuller also identifies a third dimension, the administrative one which was the effect of inadequate socio-political organisation. However, Muscovy made a virtue out of necessity and embarked upon another type of political and social organisation than western Europe which, Fuller argues, under Tsar Peter indeed resulted in military advantages. *Ibid.*, pp.xix, 83–4.

While the Mongol legacy of the early Muscovite army has been noted elsewhere,[3] the real and continuous impact of Oriental influences has not yet been detailed. Besides, the detailed information on the Muscovite army in 1673/1674 which can be found in Palmquist's military handbook has never been fully used in English-language works. By the second half of the seventeenth century, Muscovy had already carried out comprehensive military reforms and had an army that, although not up to date according to the highest Western standards, still was able to fight with some success against both Western and Eastern adversaries. A foundation for the full application of Western military reform had been laid, which in due time Tsar Peter could take advantage of. The book accordingly ends with 1689, when Tsar Peter's reign began, Muscovy's border in the east with Manchu China was negotiated and delimited in the Nerchinsk Treaty, and Muscovy indeed could be said finally to have become Russia.[4]

The appreciation that Tsar Peter's conquests rested on a legacy of previous reforms was perhaps best expressed in the Triumphal Arch erected in memory of the Nystad peace treaty, signed after the Great Northern War of 1700–1721 between Russia and Sweden, the victory in which put Russia on the path to great power status. The Arch depicted Tsars Ivan IV and Peter I, with the respective accompanying words *Incipit* ('He began') and *Perficit* ('He finished'). However, before Peter came his undeservedly forgotten father, Tsar Aleksey Mikhailovich, a humane and moderate ruler who laid the ground for many of his son's subsequent achievements, by introducing the new formation army which relied on nationwide conscription and adopted West European organisation and armament.

---

3 Charles J. Halperin, *Russia and the Golden Horde: The Mongol Impact on Medieval Russian History* (Bloomington: Indiana University Press, 1987); Donald Ostrowski, *Muscovy and the Mongols: Cross-Cultural Influences on the Steppe Frontier, 1304–1589* (Cambridge: Cambridge University Press, 1998).

4 The present book can without exaggeration be said to be long in the making. In 1979, when I worked as a student trainee in the Army Museum (Armémuseum), Stockholm, the museum librarian, Margaret Tainsh Beskow, first introduced me to Erik Palmquist's handbook. At the same time, Arne Danielsson, who was in charge of the Swedish State Trophy Collection, introduced me to the many Russian colours and standards that formed part of the collection. In part based on Palmquist's information, I wrote a short paper on the streltsy for a hobbyist association. Two decades later, I expanded the paper which was then published as Michael Fredholm von Essen, 'From Muscovy to Russia: The Emergence of the Russian Army, 1462–1689,' *Arquebusier* 24: 4 (1998), pp.2–11. I already then intended to expand the article into a book, a project which eventually took place, but only after another twenty years.

1

The Army of Muscovite Russia

Ivan III, Grand Prince of Muscovy

The core territory that would become Russia was the immense lowland that constituted the east European plain west of the Ural mountains. Rising imperceptibly eastwards towards the Urals, the plain was divided by slow and winding rivers, chief among them the Volga, Don, and Dnieper, with almost insignificant gradients and few rapids. Flowing southwards, the Volga eventually reached the Caspian Sea, while the Don and Dnieper flowed into the Black Sea. The northern parts of the east European plain were forested, while in the south the forest was eventually replaced by, first, the forest-steppe, and then, the broad expanse of the steppe proper that also reached eastwards north of the Caucasus and into Inner Asia. Likewise, the forested north continued to the east, beyond the Ural range, throughout Siberia all the way to the Pacific coast. Further to the north, conditions were arctic, with permafrost and tundra instead of forestlands along the shores of the Arctic Ocean right across the continent.

Medieval Russia was divided into a number of independent and semi-independent principalities and republics. There was no Russia as such, nor was there a unified Russian nation. The term Russian can be used in a linguistic sense, however, for the various regional dialects that in time would become modern Russian. Even so, the territory, in particular to the north and north-east, was primarily inhabited by Finno-Ugrian peoples, including the Komi west of the Ural range and the Samoyed (Nenets) in the tundra region that encompassed the northern reaches of the Urals. There were Finno-Ugrian peoples further to the south as well, including the Cheremis (Mari) and Mordvins who lived in the Urals interspersed with Turkic-speaking peoples such as the Chuvash, Bashkirs, and Tatars.

In the fourteenth century, Moscow, ruled by a Grand Prince (*velikiy knyaz'*), gained a leading role among these principalities and tribes, a feat achieved chiefly by accepting tributary status towards the Golden Horde (or to be more precise, the Qipchaq Khanate), the regional successor state of the Mongol empire once created by Chinggis Khan. Nonetheless, relations between Moscow and the Horde were not always friendly. In 1481, after a brief confrontation at the Ugra River in 1480, the Grand Prince Ivan III (1440–

1505; r. 1462–1505) of Moscow declared independence. Among foreigners, his principality henceforth became known as Muscovy, and its inhabitants, Muscovites. Muscovy was a Slavic, Orthodox Christian principality but even more, it was one of several successor states to the Golden Horde. Moreover, numerous Tatar princes swore allegiance to Muscovy, and they were included in the Muscovite nobility. Moscow could not have declared its independence had its rulers not already established a system of alliances with Inner Asian rulers to the rear of the Horde, in a process facilitated by the fact that the Horde during the previous three decades had lost most of its earlier influence. Ivan declared himself an independent ruler, but he did not renounce or withdraw from the culture and traditions of the steppe.

Grand Prince Ivan in 1472 married Zoë (Sophia) Palaeologus, the last Byzantine emperor's niece (Ivan's first wife had died in 1467). After this union, Ivan adopted the Byzantine double-headed eagle on the seal of Moscow and as his standard, to signal that Moscow was the spiritual heir of Constantinople. Ivan also added, by his own authority, the title of sovereign over the whole of Russia and he and his subjects henceforth referred to him as Tsar (that is, the short form of Caesar).[1] Long after the death of Ivan, from the 1520s onwards, this resulted in the concept of Moscow as the 'Third Rome', after Constantinople which was then deemed to have been the 'Second Rome'.[2] Before this, however, the Church and its links to Constantinople strived to be a strong counter-current to Muscovy's Inner Asian legacy, inherited from the Mongols. There was already a common religious belief among Orthodox Christian Muscovites that they were the last true believers in the world, the last Christian bastion, with Muscovy being – in the words of Archbishop Vassian Rylo of Rostov in a 1480 letter to Ivan III – a New Israel that was predestined to lead its people to the Kingdom of Heaven. Although these sentiments did not result in a crusading ideology, since dogma exclusively focused on existing Orthodox Christians, not the conversion of new ones, the Church created and sustained a feeling of exceptionalism, which henceforth often came to characterise Russian views of their destiny and, for this reason, their actions. This feeling also served to enhance the status of the ruler, who from his traditional position as leader of the army through religious sentiments was endowed with the absolute personal power of a Moses, whose task it was to lead God's chosen people. Rylo also condemned the Tatars as godless and evil, and condemned peaceful negotiations with them. The Church was firmly against anything that might suggest links to the Mongol and Tatar past, and criticised the Tsar for upholding such connections.[3] For this reason, there were frequent tensions between the secular and spiritual powers in Muscovy. However, since it was the churchmen who wrote the history of Muscovy, much of this can only be found by reading between the lines of the Church chronicles, comparing their recommendations to what the Tsars actually did.

Ivan consolidated Muscovy into what would become a new, Russian-speaking state, which he indeed can be described as having created. In 1478,

---

1   Ostrowski, *Muscovy and the Mongols*, p.178.

2   *Ibid.*, p.246.

3   *Ibid.*, pp.164–5.

1. Road made of round logs pushed into the ground, a corduroy road. (Anthonis Goeteeris, 1619)

he took control over Novgorod, which extended Muscovy's borders, or at least influence, to the Gulf of Finland in the west as well as northwards all the way to the Arctic Ocean. Yet Muscovy remained a medieval land power, without either a merchant or military navy. Moreover, Muscovy remained an Inner Asian state, with an Inner Asian army.

Ivan's main adversary was not any of the other, less powerful Russian-speaking principalities but the Horde, which was then known as the Great Horde. In 1502, Ivan allied with the Khan of the Crimean Khanate, another Mongol successor state (founded by a Mongol prince in 1441), and the two defeated the remnant of the Horde by the river Tikhaya Sosna. This led to the disintegration of the Horde as a state, which paved the way for a future Russia to emerge under Ivan's successors.

Muscovy encompassed a large territory, highways were non-existent and roads were rare and, when they existed at all, in poor condition. Some consisted of a causeway of round logs pushed into the ground perpendicular to the direction of the road so as to provide footing when inclement weather resulted in muddy roads, which was common. Such log roads (used throughout northern Europe and in later times known in English as corduroy roads) could be many miles long. As individual logs were frequently broken or rotten to the core, loose adjacent logs rolled and shifted back and forth, and the roads were difficult and dangerous to get across, in particular for horses. In summer, most travel accordingly took place by river. Merchandise was in summer transported almost exclusively by water. It was easier to move overland in winter. During winter conditions, sledges could negotiate the frozen ground far easier than any cart in summer. This did not mean that winter travel was without risk. Sledges customarily travelled in large caravans, of up to possibly 1,000 sledges at a time, so as to avoid bandit attacks.

State messengers could make good use of the post service, which had been introduced by the Mongols.[4] In winter, the post service could cover the distance between Moscow and Novgorod in about a week or less. However, the post service did not link to the Baltic Sea ports and trade centres such as Narva and Reval (present-day Tallinn, the northernmost member of the Hanseatic League) in Estonia, and Dorpat (present-day Tartu) and Riga in Livonia. There were very few villages on the route from Novgorod to Narva, and travel in winter was not only faster, but also shorter since a more direct route could be used. Travel from Novgorod to Narva would take at least three or four days. In summer, the only reasonable road with access to a Baltic port was that between Pskov and Riga. Again several days would be needed.

The other option for access to Western Europe was to go by the Arctic route, by way of Vologda and Arkhangel'sk on the White Sea. From Moscow, one first travelled overland to Yaroslavl', then overland or by river to Vologda, which became one of the major transit centers of Muscovy's foreign trade, after which the route continued to Arkhangel'sk. By then, most foreign trade was conducted with England, the Netherlands, and other countries in the West via Arkhangel'sk. Vologda also became a centre for the trade with Siberia. In winter, the journey from Moscow to Vologda might take six days.[5] In summer the same journey might require eight days. By river transport, travel from Vologda to Arkhangel'sk took around 11 days.[6] However, travel in the opposite direction, upstream, would take up to five weeks.[7]

A seventeenth-century Swedish intelligence officer, Erik Palmquist, noted that road conditions could be inferred from the type of trees that thrived in that particular terrain, the roads being "mostly good and dry where there is pine or spruce forest. But where birch, aspen or alder grows, they are good for very little, being deep in mud." He also noted that "it seems as if the Russians, as a matter of principle, allow the roads leading into the country, and especially those nearest the borders, to deteriorate to such a degree through lack of maintenance that it becomes, if not impossible, then at least extremely difficult, for foreigners to enter the country."[8]

The Muscovite Military System

The close association with the Golden Horde had transformed the Muscovite military system. By the late fifteenth century, the Muscovite army consisted almost exclusively of cavalry, organised along Mongol lines. The

4   *Ibid.*, p.47.

5   Anthony Jenkinson, *Voyages* (1589), in Lloyd E. Berry and Robert O. Crummey (eds.), *Rude & Barbarous Kingdom: Russia in the Accounts of Sixteenth-Century English Voyagers* (Madison: University of Wisconsin Press, 1968), p.52.

6   Issac Massa, *A Short History of the Beginnings and Origins of These Present Present Wars in Moscow under the Reign of Various Sovereigns down to the Year 1610* (Toronto: University of Toronto Press, 1982), p.196.

7   Sir Thomas Randolph, *Account* (1589), in Berry and Crummey, *Rude & Barbarous Kingdom*, p.67.

8   Erik Palmquist, *Några observationer angående Ryssland, sammanfattade av Erik Palmquist år 1674* (Moscow: Lomonosov, 2012), p.99.

Muscovites' chief weapon was the Inner Asian composite bow, which like the accompanying bowcase and quiver was of Mongol type. In sixteenth- and seventeenth-century Muscovy, a complete set of cavalryman's armament, including a bow in its bowcase and a quiver full of arrows, was known as *saadak*. Those who could afford it wore mail or scale armour of traditional Turco-Mongol type, with metal plates, joined by straps, to protect the chest, back, arms, and legs, such a suit of armour being known as *zertsalo* ('mirror'). If this was beyond their means, Muscovite cavalry instead often wore a short-sleeved, high-collared, densely padded hemp coat (*tegilyay*, from the corresponding Mongol term), a type of armour which indeed grew more common in this period until metal armour fell out of use among all except the highest and most wealthy nobility. Sometimes the *tegilyay* included iron bands or even armour plate fastened inside. A related type of armour was the brigandine (*kuyak*, again from the corresponding Mongol term), a garment of cloth or leather reinforced with metal plates from both sides, of the type commonly used by Mongols. Like Tatars and Mongols, those Muscovites who could afford it wore silk garments under their armour.[9] The conic, spiked iron helmet, too, was of Mongol, or to be more specific, Turco-Persian type. It was known as *misyurka* (from *Misr*, Arabic for 'Egypt'). Originally quite tall, helmets over time gradually grew more flattened. Some who could not afford an iron helmet instead wore a padded cloth or brigandine (*kuyak*) helmet with a metal nasal sewn on.

Over time, the use of not only armour, but lance and shield as well, disappeared, and the cavalryman became a mounted archer with only a sword, a dagger, and perhaps an axe hanging at the saddle-bow as sidearm. By the sixteenth century, only a few Muscovite cavalrymen carried handguns or muskets. A horseman carried both his whip and sabre fastened to his hands with straps, so that he could drop them both when shooting the bow.

Giles Fletcher (1546–1611), an English diplomat in Muscovy, described the Muscovite mounted archer: "The common horseman hath nothing else but his bow in his case under his right arm and his quiver and sword hanging on the left side, except some few that bear a case of dags or a javelin or short staff along their horse side."[10] But the nobles presented a different and considerably more splendid view. Fletcher continued:

> The under captains will have commonly some piece of armour besides, as a shirt of mail or such like. The general with the other chief captains and men of nobility will have their horse very richly furnished, their saddles of cloth of gold, their bridles fair bossed and tasseled with gold and silk fringe, bestudded with pearl and precious stones, themselves in very fair armour, which they call *bulatnyy* [of Damascus steel], made of fair shining steel, yet covered commonly with cloth of gold and edged round with ermine fur, his steel helmet on his head of a very great price, his sword, bow, and arrows at this side, his spear in his hand, with another

---

9   Richard Chancellor, *Voyages* (1589), in Berry and Crummey, *Rude & Barbarous Kingdom*, p.28.
10   Giles Fletcher, *Of the Russian Commonwealth* (1591), in Berry and Crummey, *Rude & Barbarous Kingdom*, p.183.

2. Clockwise from top left: Muscovite mounted archers in *tegilyay*, one with his sabre fastened to a strap, another with whip in hand (Sigismund von Herberstein, 1549); Muscovite cavalryman on foot, in a brigandine helmet with metal nasal and with his sabre fastened to a strap so that he can drop it when shooting the bow (Viskovatov, 1841); Muscovite cavalryman, armed with bow and the set of darts or javelins known as *djid*, a term from the Caucasus (Viskovatov, 1841). Overleaf: Muscovite *saadak* set, including bow case and quiver (Viskovatov, 1841).

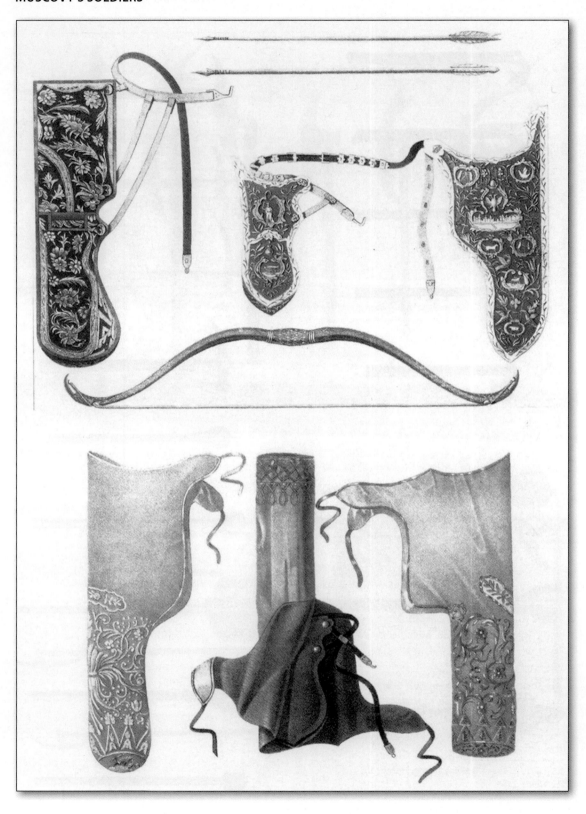

fair helmet and his *shestopyor* or horseman's scepter [six-flanged mace] carried before him.[11]

Fletcher noted that both weapons and tactics were of eastern origin: "Their swords, bows, and arrows are of the Turkish fashion. They practice like the Tatar to shoot forwards and backwards as they fly and retire."[12] In other words, the Muscovite, an excellent mounted archer, commonly employed the Parthian shot as a tactical device.

The contemporary English merchant George Turberville (1540?–1610?) noted the same. In a letter in verse, written in 1568 or 1569, he described the Muscovite bow further:

> Their bows are very short, like Turkish bows outright,
> Of sinews made with birchen bark in cunning manner dight.
> Small arrows, cruel heads, that fell and forked be,
> Which being shot from out those bows, a cruel way will flee.[13]

Muscovite cavalrymen rode horses in the Mongol style, with short stirrups that allowed them to stand clear of the saddle. They used Mongol saddles and stirrups, and relied on a Mongol-style short whip instead of spurs. Horses were unshod. Many rode midsize Noghai horses acquired from the Tatars of this name who controlled vast territories north of the Caucasus. This was indeed the most common horse breed in Muscovy.[14] The Noghai was a small but sturdy steppe breed, of up to 14½ hands (145 cm). It was not suitable for heavy shock cavalry but could endure extended journeys, foraging on the way. Turberville reckoned that they easily rode 80 km per day, which corresponds with known travel times.[15] In fact, the Noghai influenced Muscovite horsemanship to the extent that even the whip became known as a *nagayka*, from the Russian pronunciation of Noghai.

Within the Grand Prince's own domain, the Muscovite population traditionally fell into two categories: those who performed military service (*sluzhilyye lyudi*) and those who paid taxes (*tyaglyye lyudi*). The latter included the Church, except in the frequent cases when Church representatives made themselves exempt from taxes for spiritual reasons. Among those who performed military service, the upper-level members, the boyars (*boyarin*, pl. *boyare*) or nobility, were, above all, a warrior elite akin to the princely retinues of the Middle Ages. They early on were granted temporary rights to collect their own 'feedings' (*kormleniye*, pl. *kormleniya*), in lieu of salaries, from the taxpayers they governed on behalf of their sovereign. But not all servicemen belonged to this category. Those who performed military service were subdivided into a socially inferior group of men who had been recruited into service or had contracted to serve in exchange for payment

---

11 *Ibid.*, pp.183–4. Spelling slightly amended.
12 *Ibid.*, p.184.
13 George Turberville, *Letter* (1589), in Berry and Crummey, *Rude & Barbarous Kingdom*, p.82.
14 Ostrowski, *Muscovy and the Mongols*, p.124.
15 George Turberville, *Letter* (1589), in Berry and Crummey, *Rude & Barbarous Kingdom*, p.82.

3. Muscovite boyar and noble. (Sigismund von Herberstein, 1549)

('contract servicemen', *sluzhilyye lyudi po priboru*) and the more prestigious 'hereditary servicemen' (*sluzhilyye lyudi po otechestvu*) who themselves were divided into provincial or middle service rank and the Moscow-ranked or upper service rank. All hereditary servicemen served on the basis of land ownership, either an inherited patrimonial freehold (*votchina*, pl. *votchiny*; 'in the family') or a service land grant (*pomest'ye,* pl. *pomest'ya*) which was conditional on lifelong and unlimited military service. Service landholders of the later category were known as *pomeshchiki*. The land grant privilege, too, was heritable; however, although a son was entitled to a land grant, it would not necessarily be the same land that his father had held. The service landholding system, which came into general use in the 1500s, was the result of the persistent problem of how the Muscovite government could mobilise and use resources that were both limited and scattered over a vast territory, without at the same time allowing centrifugal forces to break up the recently unified Muscovite state. The land grant system, like the previous 'feeding' rights, may have been adopted from the similar system employed within the Horde.[16] There was a common understanding that in times of war, "should anyone show himself to be courageous in battle and stain his hands with the blood of the enemy, he would be honoured with gifts, both movable and immovable."[17] The immovable gift would be a land grant.

The Grand Prince relied primarily on his own retinue, the household or 'court' (*dvor*). His retainers (*dvoryanin*, pl. *dvoryane*, in this period possibly best translated as 'household retainers'), based in Moscow and originally often bondsmen, in time received service land grants from the Grand Prince to support themselves. The Grand Prince's retinue grew in numbers, and by the end of the reign of Ivan III's predecessor, Vasiliy II (r. 1425–1462), it probably numbered no less than 5,000 men, all cavalry. The retinue was, in effect, a standing army, albeit one that depended on individual prowess, not unit training. It was commanded by a quartermaster-general (*okol'nichiy*), a title perhaps of Mongol origin that by then had become one of the highest ranks within the *dvor*.

---

16 Ostrowski, *Muscovy and the Mongols*, pp.48–9, 54.

17 J.L.I. Fennell (ed.), *Prince A.M. Kurbsky's History of Ivan IV* (Cambridge: Cambridge University Press, 1965), p.23.

On campaign, the Grand Prince's *dvor* was augmented by provincial retainers, generally from, and as groups named after, the towns held by Moscow. Such a man was known as a 'son of a boyar' (*syn boyarskiy*, pl. *deti boyarskiye*). Unlike many court retainers, they were originally free men. The relationship was not necessarily one of kinship, since the term also could refer to a dependent of a noble household. Registered in the towns and dependent on service land grants for their upkeep, they served in town contingents. Each was obliged to bring his own armed serving men, provided for and armed at his expense. Such men, too, might be bondsmen in status, but others were relatives who lacked the means to serve independently. Either way, the majority was probably professional warriors. They were also usually well armed. Since it was only a wealthy hereditary serviceman who could afford to bring his own armed men, he could also afford to arm them properly. The result would be a large cavalry army, consisting of men of different categories: members of the Grand Prince's personal retinue (*dvoryane*), nobles (*boyare*), hereditary servicemen (*deti boyarskiye*), and serving men (*sluga*, pl. *slugi*) in the attending retinues. From the sixteenth century onwards, there was little difference between the court retainers and the sons of boyars. They were often referred to, collectively, as *dvoryane i deti boyarskiye*.

The Grand Prince could also count on the assistance of his relatives and numerous vassal princes and boyars, each of whom would bring his own, frequently considerable *dvor*. Unlike the boyars, the vassal princes were often recent arrivals at the Muscovite court, men from other principalities who had taken service with Muscovy as it emerged as the leading regional power.

An army, if not led by the Grand Prince himself, was commanded by the most senior ranking prince or noble. The Grand Prince's own troops were also, in particular if the Grand Prince was absent, commanded by military officers known as voivodes (*voyevoda*, pl. *voyevody*). *Voyevoda* merely means military leader, and the title, originally used for the leader of a traditional princely retinue (*druzhina*) or a general levy of commoners (*opolcheniye*), was in the cavalry army used for the commander or deputy commander of a division (*polk*, often incorrectly translated as regiment since this is the modern meaning of the term) within a Muscovite army.

Infantry existed in the form of town cossacks (*gorodovyye kazaki*). By 1502, town cossacks already formed part of the garrison of Ryazan', but these are unlikely to have been the first. Town cossacks were not cossacks in the later sense but recruited soldiers stationed in garrisons in towns and along the borders in the south and east. Some were, no doubt, of Tatar origin, since the term cossack was Tatar in origin and implied somebody who for one reason or another had left the service of his ruler. Contracted for service among free commoners, their contingents were generally named after the town in which they served. They lived with their families, were paid monetary wages, received land for their upkeep, and were exempt from paying taxes. Their term of service was not fixed. Town cossacks served on foot or occasionally as cavalry and brought their own weapons. In time, some became provincial hereditary servicemen (*sluzhilyye lyudi po gorodovomu spisku*).

In addition, the Grand Prince could technically still raise a general levy of commoners (*opolcheniye*) for campaign duty. However, the Mongol style of fighting had diminished the value of infantry, reducing it to town garrison

4. Top to bottom: Muscovite shields, from the late sixteenth century onwards only used in Siberia; Muscovite suits of armour of the *zertsalo* ('mirror') type. (All Viskovatov, 1841)

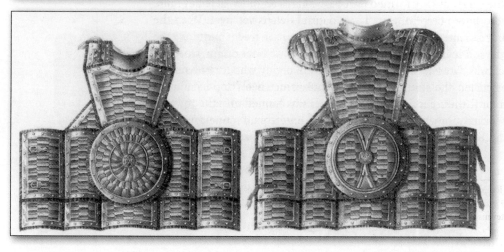

duty. From the fifteenth century, infantry again grew in importance, but the character of the commoners called out had changed. By the time of Vasiliy II and Ivan III the old city militia was replaced with townsmen and free farmers of taxpaying background with a hereditary obligation to serve as conscripted labourers in times of war (men known as *ratniki*, *pososhnyye lyudi*, or from the seventeenth century, *datochnyye lyudi*, meaning 'donated men'). These men served in the host (*pososhnaya rat'*, named after the tax assessment units – *sokha*, pl. *sokhi* – according to which they were levied) and did so as foot as well as 'horse' (*konevoy*), the latter men who drove the many horse-drawn carts, wagons, or sledges necessary for supplying the army. However, these men were usually not expected to take part in combat. Although some of the foot served as infantry, the majority were only involved in physical labour, that is, the construction and repair of forts, siege equipment and weapons, bridges, and roads. The 'horse' were only used for the transportation of men, supplies, and the artillery train and did not fight except in self-defence. The host was assembled upon order from the Grand Prince and was commanded by voivodes and headmen (*golovy*). Numbers could be substantial, typically counted in the thousands in each Muscovite army.[18]

The host fell under the authority of the *okol'nichiy* and was frequently called up for service in the border areas and during sieges. Rural farmers, too, were occasionally raised for these purposes. Besides providing general support when under siege, the host was primarily associated with the supply train. Muscovy was slow to establish a logistical arm. Carts and wagons were not always sufficient. For transportation purposes, riverboats played a major role because of Russia's network of large rivers. In particular heavy artillery was almost invariably moved by river.

Having said this, one legacy of the Mongol military system was that Muscovite cavalry often preferred not to encumber itself with a baggage train. In 1477, Ivan III preferred to release half of each division of his army to forage near Novgorod so that a baggage train would not be needed. As an additional bonus, this put severe psychological pressure on the defendants, as they saw their property being systematically lost.[19]

Another device taken over from the Mongol military system was the concept of the wagenburg, the use of one's wagons as a mobile defensive line on the steppe, where there often was no natural defensive cover. With the introduction of firearms, the Muscovites developed the wagenburg concept into the *gulyaygorod* ('walking town'), made up of a circle of wagons, from the sixteenth century fortified with about two-metre high mantlets and similar devices constructed of planks or logs and mounted on wheels or sledges, with holes bored for the musket-barrels. The timber was framed to clasp together one piece within another, as when building a log cabin.[20] The wagenburg was an old tradition on the Russian steppes, and it will be demonstrated that

---

18 John L.H. Keep, *Soldiers of the Tsar: Army and Society in Russia, 1462–1874* (Oxford: Clarendon, 1985), p.57.

19 Carol B. Stevens, *Russia's Wars of Emergence 1460-1730* (London: Routledge, 2013), p.45.

20 Giles Fletcher, *Of the Russian Commonwealth* (1591), in Berry and Crummey, *Rude & Barbarous Kingdom*, p.186.

the practice survived into the late seventeenth century, even after the new innovation, the *gulyaygorod*, had become obsolete. However, because of the cavalry nature of the Muscovite army, the use of a wagenburg or *gulyaygorod* was defensive, not offensive. The gulyaygorod was essentially a fortified camp. It was first mentioned in 1522 in an encounter with Tatars on the Oka River.[21]

Following steppe fashion, Muscovites used copper kettledrums attached to the drummer's saddle for signalling. Moreover, Fletcher noted, they had kettledrums that were so big that they were:

> [Carried] upon a board laid on four horses that are sparred together with chains, every drum having eight strikers or drummers, besides trumpets and shawms [a wind instrument of the oboe class] which they sound after a wild manner much different from ours. When they give any charge or make any invasion, they make a great halloo or shout altogether as loud as they can, which, with the sound of their trumpets, shawms, and drums, maketh a confused and horrible noise. So they set on first discharging their arrows, then dealing with their swords, which they use in a bravery to shake and brandish over their heads before they come to strokes.[22]

From the fifteenth century onwards, Tatar allies formed important contingents within the Muscovite army. The Tatars served under their own chiefs, and each group was generally allotted a town and its district (*vyyezd*) for subsistence. A typical example was the Tatar Khanate of Kasimov, which emerged when the two brothers Kasim and Yakub went to Moscow in 1445. The two brothers were the sons of a Chinggisid Khan of the Golden Horde, Ulugh Muhammad. The latter had in 1437 been ousted as Khan of the Golden Horde by his younger brother. As a result, Ulugh Muhammad instead founded the Kazan' Khanate from other remnants of the Golden Horde (a process that began in 1437 and ended only in 1445). Muscovy still remained a client state of the Horde. Kasim and Yakub were therefore endowed with a small town on the Oka River, which henceforth became known as Kasimov. However, then Ulugh Muhammad was murdered by the eldest of his three sons, Mahmud, who made himself the Khan of Kazan'. Because of the fallout between the brothers due to the patricide, Kasim and Yakub entered Muscovite service with their men and domain in 1447. As a result, the Khanate of Kasimov henceforth functioned as a client state of Muscovy.[23] Little is known about its military forces; however, the Kasimov Tatars regularly contributed strong contingents of Tatar cavalry to the Muscovite army and played a significant role in the Muscovite military system. From a military point of view, the Kasimov Tatars probably differed little from other Inner Asian Tatars.

As noted, Muscovy bought most of her cavalry horses from the Noghai Tatars. The Noghai, too, had split from the Golden Horde in the fifteenth

---

21   Richard Hellie, *Enserfment and Military Change in Muscovy* (Chicago: University of Chicago Press, 1971), p.164.

22   Giles Fletcher, *Of the Russian Commonwealth* (1591), in Berry and Crummey, *Rude & Barbarous Kingdom*, p.185.

23   See, e.g., Ostrowski, *Muscovy and the Mongols*, p.54; Bulat R. Rakhimzyanov, 'The Debatable Questions of the Early Kasimov Khanate (1437–1462)', *Russian History* 37:2 (2010), pp.83–101.

century. At the height of its power in the fifteenth and sixteenth centuries, the Noghai Horde united the Turkic nomads who had formed part of the Golden Horde, creating a nomad state that stretched from the Crimea to Siberia and into present-day Kazakhstan. Ivan III concluded an alliance with the Noghai Horde around 1475, that is, already before his confrontation with the Great Horde on the Ugra River, and it was no doubt this alliance that made him confident enough to face off the Great Horde.

The Mongol Legacy of the Muscovite Army

By the fifteenth century, the Muscovite military system had been thoroughly transformed by more than two centuries of Mongol rule. Moscow had copied, and made its own, numerous political, military, and social institutions borrowed from the Mongols. These included, in addition to the organisation and armament of the army, the Mongol system of taxation and civilian administration, the diplomatic forms and customs of Inner Asia, the post service, and some aspects of criminal law. Moscow had become part of an Inner Asian community of shared customs and institutions. Muscovites thereby gained an excellent understanding of Inner Asian culture, diplomatic conventions, protocol, and steppe politics and dynamics.[24] Muscovite foreign policy towards the steppe powers generally was considerably more adroit than its policy towards the other European powers, which were less well understood in Moscow due to the physical distance and comparable isolation of Muscovy, the latter a factor that was augmented by Muscovy remaining attached to its own version of Orthodox Christianity that stayed aloof from both the Catholic and Lutheran creeds. Furthermore, the most prominent noble families in Muscovy, such as the Mstislavskiys, Shuyskiys, and Bel'skiys, all regularly intermarried with the Tatar nobility. Indeed, by 1600, at least 60 princes of Mongol ancestry, together with their families and retainers, had gone into Muscovite service. Estimates of the Mongol component of Muscovite nobility varies, but based on surnames, as many as 17 percent might then have been of Mongol, Tatar, Caucasian, or Siberian ancestry. In fact, the real number may have been higher, since many adopted Russian names when they converted to Orthodox Christianity.[25]

Muscovite princes and nobles had also regularly participated, as Mongol subjects, in the Mongol campaigns against Muscovy's neighbours. Such campaigns, in which Muscovite princes took part, might penetrate into distant countries, including into Lithuania (which controlled vast territories in present-day Belarus with inhabitants that in time would develop into what was referred to as White Russians, that is, 'western Russians' since the colour white denoted the western direction in steppe tradition), Poland (which in addition to the Polish heartland also controlled territories with a population that in time would become known as first Little Russians, then Ukrainians), and Hungary. Mongol campaigns also penetrated deep into the Caucasus, including into present-

---

24 Halperin, *Russia and the Golden Horde*, p.90.
25 Ostrowski, *Muscovy and the Mongols*, pp.55–8.

5. Muscovite helmet types, ranging from the misyurka to the brigandine helmet. (Viskovatov, 1841)

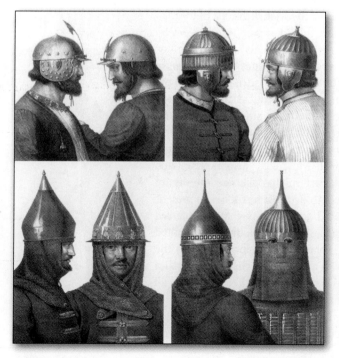

day Azerbaijan.[26] There is little doubt that on these occasions, if not before, when the Muscovite nobles themselves were subjugated, they learnt from the successful Mongol practices of war. The Russian princes had an obvious interest in uplifting their own military capacity to the level that by then was the most advanced of what was available and of proven success, and for them, there was no doubt that this was the Mongol art of war.

It has already been described how the early Muscovite soldiers were armed and equipped in the Mongol fashion. However, even the clothes worn by Muscovites at the time were of Inner Asian origin, ranging from the *caftan*, a long narrow gown, to the high, soft boots associated with equestrian nomads.

On the tactical level, an early Muscovite army fundamentally operated as a Mongol one. The Muscovite military system relied on the Mongol division of armies into five tactical units: an advance guard, a main force, left and right wings, and a rearguard. The army generally formed up in either a small array, consisting of three divisions, or a large array, of five. The small array consisted of the centre or great division (*bol'shoy polk*), the right wing or arm (*pravaya ruka*), and the left wing or arm (*levaya ruka*). To this were added, in the large array, the vanguard (*peredovoy polk*) and the rearguard (*storozhevoy polk*). Each was commanded by a voivode, selected from among the princes and boyars. The size of the divisions varied greatly, from 300 to more than 15,000 men.[27] Most common were probably divisions

26 Halperin, *Russia and the Golden Horde*, pp.78–9.
27 A.V. Chernov, *Vooruzhennye sily Russkogo gosudarstva v XV-XVII vv.: S obrazovaniya tsentralizovannogo gosudarstva do reform pri Petre I* (Moscow: Voyennoye Izdatel'stvo Ministerstva Oborony Soyuza SSR, 1954), ch. 1. Available from Biblioteka Khronosa web site <www.hrono.ru/libris/lib_ch/chrnv00.html>, accessed on 25 January 2018.

consisting of some 2,000 to 5,000 men, but the great division in particular might be considerably stronger. The great division was commanded by the 'great voivode' (*bol'shoy voyevoda*), who in the absence of the Grand Prince at the same time served as commander-in-chief of all Muscovite forces. Each voivode had a subordinate voivode within his division. The order of seniority was the great division which held primacy, followed by the right arm division, the vanguard division, the rearguard division, and the left arm division, in this order, which is confirmed by the elite service registers that have survived from the sixteenth century. It follows that this was also the order of seniority of the divisional voivodes.

The Muscovite army organisation was based on the old Inner Asian division into units of nominally ten, hundred, and thousand men. Organisationally, the great division was divided into 'thousands' (*tysyachi*), 'hundreds' (*sotni*, sing. *sotnya*), 'half-hundreds' (*polusotni*), and 'tens' (*desyatki*), respectively commanded by 'leaders of thousand' (*tysyatskiye*, or *voyevody*), 'headmen' (*golovy*), 'leaders of fifty' (*pyatidesyatniki*), and 'leaders of ten' (*desyatniki*).

The great division was the main force of the army while on the march and in battle formed its centre in the line. Every army could have its own great division. Along with the five main divisions, there might (at least from the mid-sixteenth century) also be a light cavalry reconnaissance division (*yertaul'nyy polk*; from Turco-Mongol *yortaghul*, 'raiding party') commanded by another voivode (*voyevoda yertaul'nyy*), and possibly a force of artillery (*naryad*), commanded by an artillery voivode (*voyevoda ot naryada*). Other voivodes commanded any units of non-Russian troops, such as Tatars. The *gulyaygorod*, when one was used, was commanded by an officer known as the *voyevoda gulyavyy*.

On the battlefield, the Muscovite army had embraced Mongol tactics. Highly mobile horse archers were used for harassing slow-moving enemy forces. When confronted with enemy cavalry, the Muscovite cavalry aimed first to engage with archery, then withdraw in feigned flight until the pursuing enemy could be attacked in the flank by other Muscovite cavalry or rashly followed all the way into the range of fire of the Muscovite artillery or arquebusiers, or into an ambush by the infantry. Raiding and looting were frequently used as a weapon of terror, to reduce the enemy population's will to fight. Many of the enemies of Muscovy concluded, wrongly, that the raiding served no other purpose than destruction. This was not quite true, although it has to be admitted that a number of campaigns consisted of little but the raiding, looting, and burning of border villages.

The Muscovite Grand Princes had also learnt from the Mongol administrative system. By adopting the Mongol system of tribute and tax collection, the Muscovite rulers were able to extract more revenue from their subjects than ever before. Moscow continued to collect the full amount of tribute even after its rulers stopped handing it over to the Golden Horde.[28]

Another Mongol legacy was the post service. This was a means for the ruler to receive and send messages, but it was also a means to keep outlying

---

28 Halperin, *Russia and the Golden Horde*, p.89.

regions under control and observation. The system relied on post stations (*yam*, pl. *yama*) and couriers and stage coaches for transportation of messages and goods. Tsar Ivan III in his testament to his successors urged them to retain the post service due to its great value.

Incidentally, the Mongol imperial tradition, too, survived in Muscovy, and it did so for longer than the casual observer might have suspected, since for religious reasons, this survival was anathema to the churchmen. Accordingly, little of it was mentioned in the books and treatises produced by them. However, from time to time the Mongol tradition shone through in the actions of Muscovite rulers and in texts produced by non-churchmen. As late as in 1667, Grigoriy Kotoshikhin, a Muscovite official who had defected to Sweden, explained in his manual to the Muscovite state, a comprehensive treatise that he produced for the Swedes as his ticket out, in the very first passage of the first chapter that the ruler of Muscovy was a Tsar (that is, emperor) by virtue of Ivan IV's conquest of three imperial Mongol successor states, the Khanates of Kazan', Astrakhan', and Sibir' (more on which below), through which he had assumed the right to the title of emperor.[29] This understanding of the right to Mongol imperial rule having passed to the Tsars was indeed significant, since in his role as the White Tsar (*belyy tsar'*, the colour white implying the geographical west), the ruler of Muscovy was entitled to the *yasak*, fur tribute, from the Inner Asian tribes formerly ruled by the Mongols. Indeed, already from 1465 onwards, Muscovite raiding parties were sent beyond the Urals to claim *yasak*. For this reason, Moscow recruited Finno-Ugrian Komi tribesmen from west of the Ural range as auxiliaries, since they had local knowledge of where rival tribes with access to fur could be found.[30] In Inner Asian cosmology, the colour white represented the west. In other words, the White Tsar was the Emperor of the West and accordingly a legitimate heir of the imperial family of Chinggis Khan, despite not being of Chinggisid blood himself. As late as in the seventeenth century, the Kalmyk Mongols addressed Tsar Aleksey Mikhailovich as the White Tsar.[31]

The remaining respect for the Chinggisid line also explains an otherwise inexplicable episode in the history of Tsar Ivan IV. In 1575–1576, Ivan temporarily abdicated his throne in favour of Simeon Bekbulatovich (d. 1616), a Chinggisid who had adopted Christianity and was Muscovy's client Khan of the Kasimov Tatars. The Khan of Kasimov was customarily referred to as Tsarevich,[32] that is, the son of a tsar, a prince, and was allowed revenue from Muscovite towns including Serpukhov and his residence Yur'yev on the southern defensive line, the Oka River. Although Ivan retained a considerable degree of influence during his period of abdication, addressed Simeon as Grand Prince, and, in fact, can be said to have ruled from behind the throne,[33] Simeon was not killed, like so many other of Ivan's discarded favourites, but was eventually awarded the rule of the

---

29 Grigori Carpofsson Cotossichin [Kotoshikhin], *Beskrifning om muschofsche rijkets staat* (Stockholm: Ljus, 1908; first published in 1669), p.5.

30 James Forsyth, *A History of the Peoples of Siberia: Russia's North Asian Colony 1581–1990* (Cambridge: Cambridge University Press, 1994), p.28.

31 Ostrowski, *Muscovy and the Mongols*, p.181.

32 Cotossichin, *Beskrifning*, p.68.

33 V.P. Adrianova-Peretts (ed.), *Poslaniya Ivana Groznogo* (St. Petersburg: Nauka, 2005), pp.195, 372; Ostrowski, *Muscovy and the Mongols*, pp.21, 187–8.

important towns of Tver' and Torzhok and in 1577 took part in the invasion of Livonia with his Tatar troops. The two English contemporary observers Giles Fletcher and Jerome Horsey interpreted Ivan's abdication as a means to cancel all charters of privilege previously granted to bishoprics and monasteries. There is, perhaps unsurprisingly, no surviving church documentation that proves this, but Fletcher's and Horsey's interpretation is in line with the known rivalry between Ivan and the Church. Moreover, following steppe tradition any such grant of privilege would have to be renewed by the new ruler, and there are no such surviving charters issued by Simeon.[34] It is likely that the whole purpose of the abdication was that Simeon would not renew the privileges. From Ivan's point of view, to abdicate in favour of a Chinggisid did not dilute his power, and as an additional boon, increased his acceptance with the Tatars.

Lingering respect for Chinggisid traditions and the adoption of Mongol institutions continued to play a role in Russia until at least the time of Tsar Peter I (1672–1725, r. 1689–1725). However, it was not Mongol political customs that resulted in the eventual Russian unification, centralisation, and absolutism under Moscow. For this, the Orthodox Christian concept of Moscow as a New Israel and, ultimately, as the 'Third Rome', and imperial Byzantine church traditions played the by far greater role. As will be shown, the introduction of enserfment among Muscovite peasants also had nothing to do with the Mongols but was an effect of the need for labour to sustain the then military system of the Muscovite state and, to a lesser extent, to favour major monasteries.

Artillery

Gunpowder was used early by the Muscovites (who perhaps acquired the technology, through their Mongol suzerains, from China as early as around 1300), and cannons known variously as *pushki* and *tyufyaki* were definitely part of the Moscow garrison by 1382, since they were then used against the Golden Horde army led by Tokhtamysh. Artillery was perhaps introduced from the east and the west at the same time, as these two words appear to be of respectively Czech and Turkic origin. With the new technology also arrived the concept of handheld firearms and light field artillery (*pishchal'*, pl. *pishchali*, a word which appeared in the late fourteenth century and derived from the Czech language), which appeared at roughly the same time.[35] The Muscovites soon surpassed the Mongols in both the quality and, in particular, the extensive use of artillery and firearms.

Fortress artillery early on consisted of small-calibre, forged and welded iron guns (*tyufyaki*), which by the late fifteenth century were about 40–120 cm long and used for firing clusters of multiple small shot or stones. With a calibre of 50–75 mm, they were primarily employed as fortress artillery and not much used in the field.

True cannons (*pushki*), designed for high-trajectory firing, soon became a speciality of Muscovy. By the late fifteenth century, the old forged and

---

34 Giles Fletcher, *Of the Russian Commonwealth* (1591), in Berry and Crummey, *Rude & Barbarous Kingdom*, p.166.

35 George Vernadsky, *The Mongols and Russia* (New Haven: Yale University Press, 1953), pp.365–6.

welded iron cannons were gradually replaced with bronze cannons cast in Muscovy, by primarily German and Italian gun-founders such as Rudolfo 'Aristotele' Fioravanti degli Alberti (c.1420–c.1486), a Bolognan military engineer and architect who arrived about 1475. By 1488, Italian specialists had established a cannon foundry in Moscow, where they also produced gunpowder. The Italians introduced large cast bronze guns (with a calibre of up to 90 mm). Bronze cannons were more durable than the old forged iron cannons and were faster to produce. However, since iron was cheaper than imported bronze, forged iron artillery continued to be produced into the sixteenth century. Ivan III brought artillery to lay siege to Novgorod in 1478, which contributed to Novgorod's decision to surrender. Ivan also brought artillery to besiege Kazan' in 1482, to annex Tver' in 1485, in 1493 against Serpensk, and in 1496 against Vyborg. In 1507 artillery was used in the battle of Orsha, and in 1514 Ivan's successor brought artillery to lay siege to Smolensk. Fioravanti accompanied Ivan's artillery in the campaigns against Novgorod, Kazan' and Tver'.[36] Cast bronze cannons may have been used in the successful siege of Fellin (present-day Viljandi) in Livonia in 1481. The oldest surviving such gun dates from 1485.

Like in many early armies, there is some confusion about the technical vocabulary used for the new gunpowder weapons. As noted, the Russian term for both handheld firearms and light artillery was *pishchal'*. Is is accordingly not always easy to know if a reference in a text refers to a handheld firearm or a light artillery piece. Despite the term also being applied to light field artillery, most *pishchali* were used from fortress walls. Light guns became common early in the fifteenth century, and are recorded in Moscow at the latest by 1451. The use of such pieces as wall guns (*zatinnyye pishchali*) continued into the seventeenth century, when they were 20–30 mm in calibre. Wall guns were fixed to the walls they were meant to defend.

Gunpowder weapons fired stone or iron balls, iron case-shot, and eventually also explosive grenades. The biggest fired 30 kg balls. Calibres ranged from about 30 mm (for fortress types) to about 250 mm (for siege guns). Lengths varied from 0.8 to more than 6 metres; weight of the gun from 20 to 7,500 kg.

Most artillery was used as wall (fortress) guns. A limited number was used for siege operations, and at this early time few were ever taken on campaign. Field artillery developed only slowly. Judging from contemporary illustrations, Muscovite artillery was more commonly mounted on simple sleds than wheeled gun carriages well into the sixteenth century. The barrel of the gun was fixed by iron cramps to the wooden gun carriage. In the field, cannons were primarily used in conjunction with the *gulyaygorod*.

Artillerymen (known as *pushkar'*, pl. *pushkari*, and *zatinshchik*, pl. *zatinshchiki*, respectively, depending on whether they manned cannon or wall guns) always formed a prominent part of Muscovy's armies. Portable handguns (*pishchali*) were used in the 1480 River Ugra confrontation, described in the Vologda-Perm' Chronicle. Ivan III deployed handheld *pishchali* and archery fire to prevent the Tatars of the Great Horde from crossing the river. The

---

36   See, e.g., Chernov, *Vooruzhennye sily*, ch. 1.

chronicle noted: "Our forces, using arrows and arquebuses, killed many Tatars; their arrows were falling among our forces but did not hurt anyone. They pushed the Tatars away from the river."[37] What seems to have happened is that since firearms had a longer effective range than Tatar bows (we will encounter this characteristic again, below), the Tatars found themselves unable to reach the Muscovites before taking casualties, which they were unwilling to do. Most likely, handheld firearms, 1.4–1.7 metres in length and with a calibre of 30–40 mm, were in use earlier than 1480. However, because of the inconsistent technical vocabulary, this cannot be proven with any degree of certainty.

Fortifications

Another military field in which the Muscovites surpassed their Mongol suzerains was fortifications. The cities and towns of Muscovy were habitually fortified, since raids were commonplace and nomad horsemen in particular typically lacked the capability to carry out a proper siege. Medieval forts were generally built of wood, commonly a stockade or palisade (*tyn*), 2–5 metres high, consisting of timber driven directly into the ground or on top of an earthen rampart. To make the rampart even more difficult for an intruder, tree branches, too, were often driven into the ground. Additional protection was provided by an outer moat or natural obstacle such as a river or gully. A vertical palisade was referred to as a standing barrier (*stoyachiy ostrog*). Often built on a rampart, with the timber driven into the ground to provide a vertical wall, in elaborate forts it had log scaffolding on the inside so as to provide a fighting platform. But the palisade could also be driven into the ground in a slanting manner, inclined inwards, which made the palisade more difficult to scale. This was known as a slanting barrier (*kosoy ostrog*). Such a barrier, too, was built on a rampart, often with scaffolding on the inside.[38]

Such town fortifications were generally secure in the face of Tatar marauders. Tatars seldom employed artillery, particularly not during raiding. Over time, the wooden palisades would develop into elaborate structures, with towers and fighting platforms built in the style of timber block houses.

More important fortifications were built of stone. Commonly built in major cities such as Moscow, Novgorod, and Pskov, they primarily consisted of a combination of brickwork and stone, with walls 10–20 metres high and 2–12 metres thick. The walls were additionally fortified with battlements and towers. Traditional fortifications were polygonal, depending on the terrain for its choice of shape. From 1492 onwards, fortresses were instead designed, in so far as the terrain allowed, following new European patterns to be regular in shape, that is, with straight walls between the towers which allowed for both frontal and flanking fire. The Moscow Kremlin, built by Italian architects in 1485–1495, was the first of the new model built in Muscovy. It was followed, among others, by those in Novgorod, Pskov, and Ivangorod, the latter built by Italian architects in 1492 on the bank of the Narova River, opposite the

---

37 Basil Dmytryshyn (ed.), *Medieval Russia: A Sourcebook, 900-1700* (Hinsdale, Illinois: The Dryden Press, 2nd edn. 1973), p.192. Spelling of words slightly amended.
38 Konstantin Nossov, *Russian Fortresses 1480–1682* (Oxford: Osprey Fortress Series 39, 2006), p.14.

Livonian fortress of Narva and intended as a rival trading port to those used by Livonia and the Hanseatic League. The trade aspect was important, which Tsar Ivan III emphasised by also closing down the latter's headquarters in Novgorod. The Italian designs were new to Muscovy; however, they were based on Milanese fortresses, the design of which already from the 1490s were overtaken in Western and Central Europe by more modern ones based on angled bastions.

The construction of Ivangorod by West European architects was particularly appropriate, since the Livonians and Lithuanians, unlike most Tatars, employed siege artillery. However, they did so to a more limited extent than the Muscovites. As a consequence, the Muscovite response when its fortresses were threatened by attack from these adversaries was primarily to reinforce the existing walls, by either making them thicker or by covering them with earth and turf. From the sixteenth century onwards, all new towns were built by orders of the Tsar and according to decrees that established standards for fortifications. This meant that from this period onwards, European designs became standard for newly erected fortresses throughout the territories under the control of the Tsar.

The Muscovite towns typically consisted of two parts, a walled 'city' (*gorod*), which housed soldiers, administrators, and clergy, and a 'trading quarter' (*posad*), which often was located outside the wall and which housed the town market, merchants, and artisans. For this reason, a town was principally a military and administrative centre, not a place of commerce. A town was under the control of a commandant who answered to the Tsar and whose primary responsibility was tax collection and defence. The commandant was, among other duties, responsible for the recruited contract servicemen (*sluzhilyye lyudi po pribory*) who served as town garrison in exchange for wages. Although paid, the pay was commonly insufficient and most also worked in shops or farms outside the fortified section of the town to make ends meet.

The town garrison typically consisted of arquebusiers and artillerymen. However, in wartime both peasants and townsmen were conscripted for military service, although mostly, as noted, for support functions. Some served as conscripted labourers (*pososhnyye lyudi*), tasked with the construction of field fortifications, disposal of the dead, and so on. Others served as coachmen in transportation units (based on the post service, consisting of men known as *yamshchiki*) that provided carts and sledges. Yet others were called up for the construction or improvement of city walls. While called up, these men were paid by the state so that they could support themselves. At times, every third or fourth adult male of a certain region might be called up.[39]

---

39   Alexander Filjushkin, *Ivan the Terrible: A Military History* (London: Frontline Books, 2008), p.20.

2

The Reformed Army of Ivan IV

Ivan IV, the Terrible

The first great reformer of the Muscovite army, and for that matter, the Muscovite state, was Ivan IV (1530–1584, r. 1533–1584). In 1550, having just turned 20, Ivan began to carry out what would become a comprehensive reform of the Muscovite military system.

Ivan IV was the grandson of Ivan III and the son of Vasiliy III (1479–1533, r. 1505–1533). Young Ivan grew up in a brutal environment, which goes some way in explaining why he became known (in English) as 'the Terrible'.[1] His Russian nickname (*Groznyy*) in reality meant the Dreaded or Threatening, which in sixteenth-century Russian did not have a negative connotation per se but rather suggested awe-inspiring authority, a person who was respected and worthy of respect.[2] In English, Ivan 'the Terrifying' would perhaps have been a better cognomen. A brilliant reformer and an intellectual of sorts, Ivan IV nonetheless was a ruthless ruler who carried out brutal and no doubt excessive purges among the Muscovite nobility and within his own court. However, Ivan retained enough of his popularity among the Muscovite population to be remembered in folklore,[3] and for reasons that will be shown, his subsequent bad reputation was primarily the result of vicious propaganda by his political opponents. Ivan's popularity with the Muscovite population was acknowledged even by his enemies, including Reinhold Heidenstein (c.1553–1620), a Prussian sometime diplomat in Poland who at other times was in Polish service. In 1584 or 1585 Heidenstein observed:

> Those who study the history of his reign should be all the more surprised that in spite of his cruelty the people should love him so strongly with the love which

---

1 See, e.g., Ivan's own account of his early life, in J.L I. Fennell (ed.), *The Correspondence between Prince A.M. Kurbsky and Tsar Ivan IV of Russia 1564–1579* (Cambridge: Cambridge University Press, 1955), pp.69–101.

2 Carolyn Johnston Pouncy (ed.), *The Domostroi: Rules For Russian Households in the Time of Ivan the Terrible* (Ithaca: Cornell University Press, 1994), p.63, n.5.

3 Maureen Perrie, *The Image of Ivan the Terrible in Russian Folklore* (Cambridge: Cambridge University Press, 2002), pp.45–55.

6. Above, left: Ivan IV, reconstruction based on his skull by Soviet forensic specialist Mikhail Gerasimov. Right: Ivan IV, the painting known as the Copenhagen portrait, reputed to be the most life-like contemporary depiction.

other sovereigns can acquire only by indulgence and kindness, and that this extraordinary devotion to their sovereign could last so long. And it must be observed that the people not only do not murmur against him, but even during the war displayed incredible staunchness in defending and protecting fortresses; and of deserters there were very few. On the contrary, during this same war there were many who preferred to remain loyal to the Tsar even at great risk to themselves, rather than accept the greatest rewards for treachery.[4]

In 1557, the English merchant Anthony Jenkinson (1530–1611), too, had concluded that "no prince in Christendom is more feared of his own than he is, nor yet better beloved."[5] One reason for this was the religious sentiments that had come to define the Muscovite population. Heidenstein noted:

> They regard as barbarians, or infidels, all those who differ from them in the matter of faith … according to the rules of their religion; and regarding loyalty to the sovereign as obligatory, as loyalty to God, they exalt the staunchness of those who remain loyal to their oath of allegiance to the Prince to their last, and they say that their souls, on leaving their bodies, go straight to Heaven.[6]

Ivan was proclaimed Grand Prince of Muscovy at the age of three. His mother died when he was seven. At 16, he assumed personal control of the

---

4   Cited in R. Wipper, *Ivan Grozny* (Moscow: Foreign Languages Publishing House, 1947), pp.202–3.
5   Jenkinson cited in Richard Hakluyt (ed.), *The Discovery of Muscovy: From the Collections of Richard Hakluyt - With The Voyages of Ohthere and Wulfstan from King Alfred's Orosius* (London: Cassell & Company, 1889), p.144.
6   Cited in Wipper, *Ivan Grozny*, p.203.

government. Since many autocratic, landed princes and boyars opposed his power, Ivan built an alternative power base among the Moscow merchants, who came to depend on his power. Ivan also struggled with the growing power, wealth, and independence of the Church. Ivan assumed the title of Tsar and was crowned in 1547 by the Metropolitan of Moscow. In 1549, as part of a political reform to strengthen his rule against both princes and churchmen, Ivan established and summoned a new institution, a national assembly or council of representatives of the land (*zemskiy sobor*, 'land assembly'), with participants selected from those loyal to him. The national assembly was likely a reversion to Tatar practices. In all but name, it was the same institution as the steppe nomads' *quriltai*, or decision-making assembly, a key institution within the Golden Horde which, in the past, the Russian princes often attended.[7] But Ivan knew that military strength, too, was required, and one year later, the national assembly was followed by the first of his wide-ranging military reforms.

Ivan conquered the neighbouring Kazan' Khanate in 1552. By 1556 he had also conquered Astrakhan', on the Caspian Sea, destroying the Astrakhan' Khanate in the process. At the same time, in 1554–1557, he fought the Muscovite-Swedish War (which begun with a series of destructive but probably unsanctioned raids, by both parties, across the common border). Because of his many conquests, Ivan IV was the first ruler who formally assumed the title 'Tsar over the whole of Russia' (*Tsar' vseya Rusi*). Although his grandfather Ivan III had used this title as early as in the Moscow-Lithuanian Treaty of 1494, he had never been so recognised abroad.

Then followed the Livonian War of 1558–1583, involving the Livonian Order of the Knights of the Sword, Poland, Grand Duchy of Lithuania, Muscovy, Sweden, and Denmark in various constellations. This coincided with the Muscovite-Lithuanian War of 1561–1570, the first Muscovite-Ottoman War over Astrakhan' in 1569, and what in Sweden became known as the Twenty-five Years War with Muscovy of 1570–1595, with active combat operations taking place in 1570–1583 and, after Ivan's death, in 1590–1592.

In 1571, Muscovite troops entered the steppe to push the border southwards into the *Dikoye Polye* ('Wild Field'). In the same year, the Crimean Khanate sent an army that successfully raided Moscow itself. In 1572, the Crimean Khanate attempted another attack, but was defeated in the battle of Molodi (more on which below).

Meanwhile, the Livonian War simmered on. Muscovy's main adversary had become the Polish-Lithuanian Commonwealth (the *Rzeczpospolita*), formally known as the Crown of the Kingdom of Poland and the Grand Duchy of Lithuania. The Commonwealth was formally established by the Union of Lublin in July 1569, even though the two countries had been in a de facto personal union since 1386, with both ruled by a common monarch who simultaneously was King of Poland and Grand Duke of Lithuania. Ivan again invaded Livonia in 1577. Meanwhile, the Twenty-five Years War between Muscovy and Sweden of 1570–1595 simmered on, too.

---

7   Ostrowski, *Muscovy and the Mongols*, pp.21, 185–6.

7. Muscovite hereditary serviceman (left) and Tatar noble (right), showing their similarity in dress and armament. (Sigismund von Herberstein, 1549)

Moſcouita habitu militari.   *Tartarus gentili more armatus*

Understanding the need for military and administrative reform, the difficulties caused by the economic poverty of the state which he ruled, and the necessity of new alliances, Ivan from the outset favoured the immigration of foreign military professionals and craftsmen and welcomed European merchants. However, from about 1560 persecution mania set in, and by 1570 he mistrusted everyone. Despite personal religiosity, Ivan considered the Church a particular rival for power. In addition, the Church and the monasteries controlled vast amounts of land, which Ivan needed in order to provide land grants to hereditary servicemen. In 1569, Ivan had the Metropolitan of Moscow strangled. The inhabitants of Novgorod, close to his western borders, were denounced to him for treason, and in 1570, Ivan ravaged the city and massacred many of its inhabitants, in effect replacing its hereditary servicemen with new men from other, more assimilated Muscovite territories. Violence also continued at home. In 1580, Ivan struck and killed his favourite son.

In 1582, the conquest of the Khanate of Sibir' began, and although this principality, east of the Ural range, was conquered in 1583, the process of taking control of its territory was not concluded until 1598, long after Ivan's death.

Ivan's Military Reforms

Ivan IV inherited a traditional Muscovite, Tatar-style army. As noted, those who performed military service were subdivided into a socially inferior group of recruited men who had contracted to serve in exchange for payment (*sluzhilyye lyudi po priboru*) and the more prestigious hereditary servicemen (*sluzhilyye lyudi po otechestvu*). In the sixteenth century, the old system of *kormleniye* ('feeding') was phased out, and henceforth all hereditary servicemen served on the basis of land ownership, either an inherited freehold (*votchina*) or a land grant (*pomest'ye*) which was conditional on lifelong and unlimited military service. However, over time many freehold estates were withdrawn, and in a process effectively begun under Ivan III the Muscovite government instead parcelled out land grants in exchange for service.

By this process, the traditional nobility was transformed into a service nobility. They became the servitors of the state, whose rank and prestige no longer depended on lineage alone but also on what office they occupied. Yet the noble servitors,[8] the hereditary servicemen, were divided into a number of subdivisions, including the Moscow-ranked ones who served in the capital (the upper service rank), with extensive lands and numerous peasants at their disposal, and those who served in the provinces (the middle service rank), with limited lands and few or no peasants, and accordingly were deemed to be of lower social standing. Some have described these two groups as, respectively, 'upper service' and 'middle service' soldiers.[9] Others have instead referred to them as 'nobility' and 'hereditary servicemen'. This terminology is also used here, in particular the term hereditary serviceman which conveys the importance of the individual's rank of military service and lineage, yet does not imply an exalted aristocrat and accordingly gives a better understanding of his position in society.[10]

Despite Tsar Ivan's reduction of many freehold estates, nobles still at times managed to turn the individual land grant into a freehold. However, even so, it was granted to the family, not the noble personally, and the freehold estate, too, was held on conditional terms in return for military service.

By tradition, at the age of about 15, the son of a hereditary serviceman would be enrolled for service by undergoing the military initiation (*verstan'ye*, pl. *verstan'ya*). For some, entry into service might be delayed until an age as late as 18, while others might begin service already at 14. The name of the young serviceman would be recorded in one of the elite service registers or deployment books (*razryadnyye knigi*) that were sent to the military deployments chancellery (*Razryadnyy prikaz*) in Moscow, which best can be described as a ministry of defence. Due to its key importance, foreigners sometimes referred to it as the state chancellery. The oldest service registers date from the 1470s.[11] The young servicemen, now initiated (*verstannyy*, pl.

---

8   The term used in Keep, *Soldiers of the Tsar*.
9   The terms used in Hellie, *Enserfment and Military Change*.
10   Carol Belkin Stevens, *Soldiers on the Steppe: Army Reform and Social Change in Early Modern Russia* (DeKalb: Northern Illinois University Press, 1995), p.xi.
11   Keep, *Soldiers of the Tsar*, p.35.

8. Muscovite nobleman (Gottbergska stamboken, 1592; possibly derived from a woodcut depicting the Great Embassy of Ivan IV to Emperor Maximilian II in 1576).

verstannyye), were divided into different ranks (*stat'i*) according to their family background which also determined what kind of military position they could receive. The elite who were Moscow-ranked (*sluzhilyye lyudi po moskovskomu spisku*) were divided into ranks with elaborate titles, in descending order *stol'niki*, *stryapchiye*, *dvoryane moskovskiye*, and *zhil'tsy*. But most servicemen were provincials. The three provincial grades were, in descending order, *vybornyy* ('selected'), *dvorovoy* ('court-ranked'), and *gorodovoy* ('town-ranked').[12] As inititated servicemen, they henceforth had the right to receive land grants in exchange for military service as a means for them to support themselves.

Individuals were appointed according to an elaborate order of precedence (*mestnichestvo*). Originally a system to reconcile and integrate the often conflicting status claims of the original Muscovite servicemen and those Tatars and others who had joined and taken service with Muscovy later, the basic assumption was that a serviceman could only be appointed to positions that were commensurate with those occupied by his ancestors. For instance, somebody whose ancestor had held higher rank than the ancestor of another could not be appointed to a position subordinate to the other. This frequently

---

12   Chernov, *Vooruzhennye sily*, ch. 3; Keep, *Soldiers of the Tsar*, pp.22, 32.

caused difficulties, since appointments thereby were subordinated genealogy, and often led to considerable disunity of command. On the other hand, the system also promoted greater loyalty to the new identity as members of Muscovy's hereditary service class. It was not only Tatars and others of an eastern origin who had joined the Muscovite service class in large numbers. According to some estimates, in the seventeenth century as many as 49 per cent of the Muscovite nobility had surnames that indicated a Polish, Lithuanian, or west European origin.[13] The order of precedence system was probably originally derived from Mongol traditions.[14]

The elite service registers listed appointments to military command, together with the size of the division commanded, for both campaign and garrison duty. In the 1560s, the earliest period for which reasonably complete records exist, such sources indicate that the maximum strength of the hereditary serviceman cavalry was some 30,000 to 35,000. By the seventeenth century, this number had fallen to some 15,000 to 20,000. However, the deployment books, although generally very detailed, do not give the full story, since they did not record the sometimes considerable number of serving men brought by each hereditary serviceman. Nor did they necessarily record other types of troops such as streltsy, cossacks, or Tatars (see below). They also did not include any muster rolls for provincial troops available for mobilisation. Moreover, because their primary purpose was to support the order of precedence system, they focused on the past, not the present, and included no data on the number and disposition of current military forces.[15] This means that only estimates are available for Muscovy's total military strength. Estimates range from 50,000 to 100,000 at the time of Ivan IV in the mid-sixteenth century, with considerable less by the end of the century, due to deaths, the then escalating financial crisis of the hereditary service system (more on which below), and the corresponding, increased rate of desertions.[16]

A nobleman commonly spent far more time on campaign than on his estate. This was a problem, since his absence often resulted in the estate being ruined by lack of competent management, corruption, or the loss of labour caused by peasants moving elsewhere. Reasons for peasants abandoning an estate were manifold, including the ravages of wars, better opportunities somewhere else, or indeed at times forced removal by more powerful estate holders elsewhere. In most cases, peasant departures were not clandestine operations but well planned, with entire peasant families departing with livestock, belongings, agricultural tools, and seeds at a time when the nobleman was absent on service. They also did not usually move very far, in most cases no longer than from one province to the next. Entrepreneurial

13 Ostrowski, *Muscovy and the Mongols*, p.58.

14 *Ibid.*, pp.47–8.

15 Marshall Poe, 'Muscovite Personnel Records, 1475–1550: New Light on the Early Evolution of Russian Bureaucracy', *Jahrbücher für Geschichte Osteuropas* 45:3 (1997), pp.361–78.

16 Filjushkin, *Ivan the Terrible*, p.22. Hellie, *Enserfment and Military Change*, pp.267–73, attempts to summarise what is known about the numbers of the Muscovite military forces in the sixteenth and seventeenth centuries.

peasants, however, would leave and move on to the southern frontier, where there was virgin land and plenty of opportunities, including finding official employment. Those who fled greater distances, such as to the frontier, were usually well-to-do who could afford both the journey and taking advantage of any opportunity that materialised upon arrival. Those who were guilty of crimes, or were more adventurous still, could push on further, beyond the border, and join the free cossack communities.

The hereditary servicemen were not only intended to be self-supported financially and logistically, they were also fundamentally self-trained. This meant that their personal, martial capacity varied considerably, with those of a military bent being far more proficient than those who merely served to uphold family tradition and safeguard their land grant. Moreover, they were generally not proficient in operating as a unit, since they hardly ever trained in formation. Although it can be assumed that those hereditary servicemen who spent their life on campaign would develop a certain proficiency, regardless of personal circumstances, there was no military training in times of peace, beyond the occasional roll call for muster purposes. There were also no tactical exercises and manoeuvres.

The traditional system of hereditary service favoured the highest ranks of society, the traditional nobility consisting of boyars and princes. Ivan IV accordingly reformed the Muscovite army with regard to recruitment, armament, and organisation, with the chief purpose to strengthen the state against these powerful individuals. Through a number of administrative and military reforms, Ivan restricted the power and privilege of the nobles, and enabled the rise to high positions of skilled individuals of non-noble background.

Ivan's military reform work began in 1550 with three drastic measures. First, Ivan formulated a decree (*ukaz*) that restricted the nobility's right to inherit military posts, and instead ordered that competence rather than birth should be decisive whenever commanders were appointed. In effect, he attempted to abolish the order of precedence (*mestnichestvo*) by commanding that important campaigns be fought without resort to precedence (*bez mest*). This reform was strongly resisted by the nobility and only fully accomplished more than a century later. Second, to secure the loyalty of a new generation of commanders, Ivan in 1550 distributed land grants around Moscow to 1,000 army officers among the servicemen most loyal to himself, forming what became known as the 'sovereign's division' (*gosudarev polk*), also known as the 'selected thousand' (*izbrannaya tysyacha*). These men, 1,078 in number,[17] primarily recruited among the lower levels of hereditary servicemen, received land grants around Moscow, and were hence known as the Moscow retainer (*dvoryane*) division, in contrast to the provincial *dvoryane*.[18] This, together with a reform of the central administration, was the first step in the organisation of a centralised system of army command. Third, as a foundation on which to rest his power, Ivan also raised Muscovy's first standing corps of infantry matchlockmen (*strel'tsy*, more on whom below). With the

---

17   Keep, *Soldiers of the Tsar*, p.29.
18   Chernov, *Vooruzhennye sily*, ch. 2.

exception of various princely retinues, the streltsy were Russia's first standing military units. As a strong infantry formation of uniformly armed matchlockmen, they were a vast improvement over existing forces in most situations that went beyond those of traditional Tatar raiding.

Ivan IV also reformed the mustering of the traditional noble and hereditary serviceman cavalry. In 1556, he issued a new code of military service (*Ulozheniye o sluzhbe*) that obligated each land grant-holder henceforth to appear in person and for each allotment of 100 populated *chetverti* of land (1 *chetvert'*, or quarter, being 1.35 acres) bring one serving man, with a horse and full armour, and with two horses for a distant campaign.[19] Service was to be with "with horses, men, and weapons". The number of such serving cavalrymen to be raised depended on the size of his land grant, with the nobility providing many while poorer hereditary servicemen only being obliged to provide one or two. Since the elite service registers only noted the servicemen, not their armed serving men, the

number of serving men can only be estimated, but even given the significant and growing number of poor hereditary servicemen, the total number of serving men was likely not lower than the number of servicemen and might have been considerably higher. The mustered troops were assigned to either campaign service ('division service,' *polkovaya sluzhba*) or garrison service ('town service,' *gorodovaya sluzhba*). They were not paid or supplied by the state, since the land grant was expected to provide for all their necessary supplies while on campaign. Fletcher noted: "Every man is to bring sufficient for himself to serve his turn for four months, and, if need require, to give order for more to be brought unto him to the camp from his tenant that tilleth his land or some other place."[20]

9. Ryndy bodyguards. (Erik Palmquist, 1674)

In Moscow, the lowest rank of hereditary servicemen was, as noted, known as *zhilets* (pl. *zhil'tsy*). This rank was reportedly introduced by Ivan IV as part of his military reform of the hereditary servicemen, with the purpose of raising provincial servicemen to Moscow rank as a means to create a military force loyal to himself.[21] The *zhil'tsy* were so named since

19 Chernov, *Vooruzhennye sily*, ch. 2; Hellie, *Enserfment and Military Change*, p.38; Keep, *Soldiers of the Tsar*, p.30.
20 Giles Fletcher, *Of the Russian Commonwealth* (1591), in Berry and Crummey, *Rude & Barbarous Kingdom*, p.184.
21 Aleksandr Vasil'yevich Viskovatov, *Istoricheskoye opisaniye odezhdy i vooruzheniya rossiyskikh" voysk"*, Vol. 1 (St. Petersburg: Voyennaya tipografiya, 1841), pp.87–88.

10. Muscovite berdysh poleaxes and 'embassy' axes carried by *ryndy.* (Viskovatov, 1841)

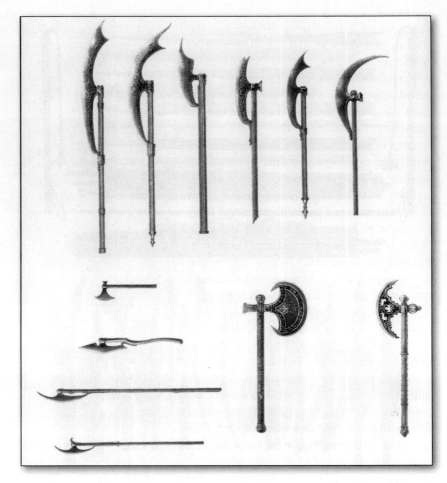

they lived close to the Tsar (the term derived from the Russian verb *zhit'*, 'to live', the implication being something of a live-in serviceman). The *zhil'tsy* served on guard duty at the palaces, taking their turns by forties every night, and also served as an honorary guard for the tsar when he was travelling. They were hereditary servicemen who were promoted into the position from the provincial rank of *vybornyy* ('selected'). They did not necessarily have lands near Moscow but lived and served there a quarter of the year at a time. Three hundred such men (in his day, Fletcher said 200[22]) were promoted to serve for three years as *zhil'tsy*. In time of war, they constituted a part of the sovereign's divison. Their total number seems to have fluctuated. By the middle of the seventeenth century, there were about 1,500 *zhil'tsy*.[23] In the 1660s, Kotoshikhin mentioned that they were 2,000.[24]

The Tsar was protected by four ceremonial bodyguards (*rynda*, pl. *ryndy*), selected young men who wore a uniform consisting of a tall white fur hat, a long white velvet or satin gown lined with ermine, boots, and

---

22   Giles Fletcher, *Of the Russian Commonwealth* (1591), in Berry and Crummey, *Rude & Barbarous Kingdom*, p.240.

23   Chernov, *Vooruzhennye sily*, ch. 3; Hellie, *Enserfment and Military Change*, p.23.

24   Cotossichin, *Beskrifning*, p.31.

two gold chains crossed over the chest. They were armed with ceremonial axes, of a type called an 'embassy' axe since it primarily was ceremonial, decorated with gold and silver. The *ryndy* were selected, apparently by the Tsar personally, among *deti boyarskiye* and the appointment, once made, could not be refused.[25] In 1664, Palmquist described their dress as "silver-embroidered white coats lined with white fox skin, and wearing white fox-skin caps flecked with flack; they have two large gold chains crossed over their chests and bear silver axes."[26] The *ryndy* institution had been devised by Tsar Vasiliy III, Ivan's father. When accompanying the Tsar on campaign, they and their own attendants, who were referred to as *podryndy* (sub-*ryndy*), wore armour.[27] On campaign, they were armed with bow, lance, a set of darts or javelins (known as *djid*, a term from the Caucasus), and a bear spear (a heavy spear with a leaf-shaped head, known as *rogatina*, pl. *rogatiny*). In times of peace they carried the aforementioned axe and a six-flanged mace (*shestopyor*).[28] The custom to have four *ryndy* standing close to the Tsar survived throughout the seventeenth century and was attested to by many foreign visitors to his court.

The noblemen in Moscow who served as initiated hereditary servicemen were generally no more than some 2,600 to 3,300. However, they were comparatively rich, which allowed them to muster many fighting men. It is likely that the sovereign's division often reached a strength of some 20,000 men.[29]

Not many service registers have survived from the time, since they were all ordered destroyed in 1682 (see below). Reviews and musters of line troops were early on not always recorded in writing and, even when recorded, such accounts, too, have often been lost.[30] Yet some information is available. In 1556, 174 hereditary servicemen were obliged to attend the muster in Serpukhovskiy district. Of this number, 92 showed up, and they brought 668 serving men with them, that is, about seven per noble. As for the 82 who did not show up, all but two had legitimate reasons for not coming. Four were ill, eight were held captive abroad, three had taken up posts in local administration, and the rest already served in town garrisons, as embassy escorts abroad, and so on. Only two failed to show up without legitimate cause. Some brought more fighting men than required; they then received payments according to the type of arms and equipment they had provided to their men. Yet, not all were accepted for duty. Of the 668 fighting men provided, 164 were declared unfit for service. Some of these had no horses. There was also a shortage of pack horses. In addition, only 210 of the men were fully armoured.[31]

Ivan retained the traditional organisation of the army into divisions (*polki*), hundreds (*sotni*), and so on. He retained the title of voivode for

---

25 *Ibid.*, pp.68, 74, 75.

26 Palmquist, *Några observationer*, p.249.

27 Ulla Birgegård (ed.), *J.G. Sparwenfeld's Diary of a Journey to Russia 1684–87* (Stockholm: Kungl. Vitterhets Historie och Antikvitets Akademien, Slavica suecana Series A, Vol. 1, 2002), p.151.

28 Viskovatov, *Istoricheskoye opisaniye* 1, pp.86–7.

29 Hellie, *Enserfment and Military Change*, pp.268–72; Filjushkin, *Ivan the Terrible*, p.29.

30 Poe, 'Muscovite Personnel Records', pp.361–78.

31 Filjushkin, *Ivan the Terrible*, pp.26–9.

division commander and the *okol'nichiy*, the latter a grade that endured throughout the seventeenth century. Ivan also took measures to regularise military service through administrative procedures. Muster rolls had to be completed for all forces. Although some of the departments of central administration (*prikazy*) had been formed more than half a century earlier, Ivan during the 1550s gave them their final shape.

Ivan also created the first Muscovite 'regimental' artillery (*naryad*, pl. *naryady*). As noted, the artillery had long formed part of Muscovy's military organisation, but as a separate formation. Ivan took part of the old artillery division and formed units known as *naryady* ('patrols') of artillery that, in times of war, were attached to the individual divisions of the army. Each division accordingly received its own artillery support.

The old cavalry army was otherwise retained, together with the Tatar contingents from the central regions of the Muscovite state. Ivan also retained the town cossack infantry as well as the host of labourers and workmen.

Ivan's reform encouraged the nobles to serve the Tsar, improved the recruitment of territorial troops, strengthened their discipline, and enabled the number of available troops to grow, over time, into some 80,000 to 100,000 men. Russian scholars are fond to point out that unlike Western Europe, which in the sixteenth century mainly relied on mercenaries as soldiers, Ivan IV created a national army.

A recurring problem for the servicemen was the need to maintain their land grants while on campaign. As noted, a peasant might choose to take employment elsewhere, move south, or even find himself forcibly removed to the estate of a more powerful neighbour. This wreaked havoc on a serviceman's ability to support himself. Ivan III had limited peasants' right of departure already in 1497, for this very reason. Eventually, the loss of labour became such a problem that Ivan IV, by the very end of his reign, introduced a system of temporary prohibition on the transfer or voluntary removal of peasants from their estate. In 1580, Ivan issued a code (*Ulozheniye*) which restricted the conveyance of peasants from one estate to another to St. George's Day. Moreover, the following year, 1581, was declared interdicted, that is, peasants were not allowed to leave the land to which they were attached at all. The interdiction remained in force until 1586. In addition, Ivan in 1581 ordered a census to be carried out, during which the names of all peasants should be listed with the estate on which they served. The census was completed in 1592. The interdiction and the census, when taken together, represented the introduction of enserfment in Muscovy, and this was the direct result of the need to guarantee the availability of labour on the land grants so that servicemen could support themselves while on military duty. It has been suggested that the demand that peasants be tied to the land originated with the servicemen of the Novgorod region, which by then was thoroughly devastated and depopulated by the events of the Livonian War.[32] Subsequent Muscovite governments followed the practice initiated by Ivan IV and had interdicted years alternated with free years. This

---

32 Wipper, *Ivan Grozny*, p.229.

practice, which also favoured a number of powerful monasteries,[33] continued until the day of transfer on St. George's Day was abolished in 1607. Nonetheless, peasants continued to leave for a variety of reasons. The introduction of enserfment in Muscovy cannot be said to have been completed until the introduction of a new legal system, the code of the land assembly (*Sobornoye ulozheniye*) of 1649, which made the boundaries between social strata more rigid and granted serfholders an indefinite period to pursue their runaway serfs, thus creating the legal basis for the permanent establishment of serfdom. Serfdom, with its unintended negative consequences for the development of Muscovy's and, later, Russia's political and social organisation, was accordingly the solution to urgent labour shortages that hampered the hereditary servicemen's ability to carry out their military duties.

11. Strelets. (Erik Palmquist, 1674)

Streltsy

In 1510, a unit of 1,000 infantry matchlockmen (*pishchal'niki*) was raised, which subsequently took part in the siege of Pskov. However, as always with Muscovite units, it was disbanded immediately after the campaign for which it was formed. Raised again at a later time, the matchlock unit participated in the siege of Smolensk in 1512, after which it was again disbanded. Matchlockmen were also raised from Novgorod.[34] Within a generation, at the latest by 1530, infantry armed with muskets (*pishchali*) became know as 'shooters', streltsy (*strelets*, pl. *strel'tsy*) instead of *pishchal'niki*.[35] Under the new name, infantry would become a key ingredient of Muscovy's armed forces.

The creation of a standing corps of infantry matchlockmen was arguably the most important part of Ivan's military reforms. Ivan's first streltsy appeared in 1546 and 1547. It is not known whether these constituted a truly new type of troops or merely were the latest reincarnation of the type used already since the 1530s, if not before. However, there is no evidence that they then constituted a standing corps of infantry, so a continuation of past practices seems most likely.[36] However, in 1550 Ivan raised streltsy of a different type. This was

33 Hellie, *Enserfment and Military Change*, pp.237, 240.
34 Chernov, *Vooruzhennye sily*, ch. 1; Hellie, *Enserfment and Military Change*, p.160.
35 Filjushkin, *Ivan the Terrible*, p.32.
36 A.V. Chernov, 'Obrazovanie streletskogo voyska', *Istoricheskiye zapiski*, t.38 (Moscow, 1951), pp.281–90, on pp.283–4. At the time when Chernov was writing, socialist doctrine left him no choice but to attempt to justify Karl Marx's erroneous statement that the streltsy were formed already in 1545, so this specific part of Chernov's argument can be disregarded.

intended as a standing corps of infantry matchlockmen. Ivan probably based his new corps on what he had heard about the Ottoman janissaries, and the Muscovite streltsy soon acquired a role similar to the Ottoman corps. First, Muscovy had long-standing relations with the Ottoman Empire due to its Inner Eurasian connections. Second, and most likely, the immediate source of the idea was a certain Ivan Peresvetov, who had learned about Ottoman military institutions during six years of service in Hungary and Poland, and who in 1549 or thereabouts submitted books and petitions to Ivan suggesting various reforms. One of them was the formation of a 20,000 strong standing infantry army equipped with firearms to be used in conjunction with mobile fortifications, the *gulyaygorod*, to defend Muscovy against the Tatars and to enable a more active foreign policy.[37] It does appear likely that Ivan's new standing corps in fact was organised, and possibly also armed, differently from the already existing types of matchlockmen. Moreover, and of greater importance, Ivan's streltsy were selected men, and full-time soldiers. Unlike the noble cavalry and previous infantry units, they were not disbanded at the end of a campaign.

The first six streltsy regiments of the corps each consisted of 500 men. Each streltsy regiment (early on referred to as a *stat'ya* and, later, a *prikaz*) was divided into five companies of about 100 men each, a company accordingly being known as a *sotnya* (hundred) like the corresponding unit in the traditional cavalry. The regiment was commanded by a headman (*golova*), under whom served a deputy (*podgolova*),[38] below whom were commanders of respectively 100 men (*sotniki*), 50 men (*pyatidesyatniki*), and 10 men (*desyatniki*).[39] Soon some streltsy regiments increased in numbers, so that a regiment could consist of from 500 to 1,000 streltsy. The streltsy corps trained regularly, and each regiment had its integral artillery, consisting of from six to eight cannons.

As heads of the regiments were appointed hereditary servicemen: Grigoriy Zhelobov syn Pusheshnikov (head of the first regiment), Matvey Ivanov syn Rzhevskiy (head of the second regiment, he simultaneously held a court rank derived from the word for deacon, *d'yak*), Ivan Semyonov syn Cheremisinov-Karaulov (head of the third; his name suggests a Cheremis ethnic background), Vasiliy Funikov syn Pronchishchev (head of the fourth), Fyodor Ivanov syn Durasov (head of the fifth), and Yakov Stepanov syn Bundov (head of the sixth).[40] The regimental numbers were most likely arbitrary, since regiments were named after their commanders. The troops were recruited from free townsmen and farmers. Recruits were to be "young and quick", and vouched for by somebody in authority, a group of elders, or the whole male population of an existing streltsy cantonment.[41] The streltsy lived in cantonments, separated from the rest of the town, by law, fortifications, and/or natural obstacles. They were paid with food supplies

---

37 Chernov, *Vooruzhennye sily*, ch. 2; Hellie, *Enserfment and Military Change*, p.165.
38 Cotossichin, *Beskrifning*, p.73.
39 Chernov, *Vooruzhennye sily*, ch. 2.
40 Chernov, 'Obrazovanie streletskogo voyska', p.285.
41 Chernov, *Vooruzhennye sily*, ch. 3.

and money, and service was for life. It was also hereditary. Despite being regarded as standing forces and maintained by the state, Muscovy could not afford to pay continuous wages. As a result, the streltsy were to be maintained in part by wages, and in part by trade privileges and land grants. Each strelets received a plot of land on which he built a house for himself and his family, at his own expense but for which he received a government subsidy. Since service was hereditary, his family could remain after the soldier's death but it was expected that a male relative would take his place in the regiment. In addition, service came with a number of privileges, for instance the right to bring goods into town without paying a toll. Such privileges in time caused the streltsy increasingly to identify and ally with their town's other small traders. In contrast to the hereditary servicemen who generally came from a rural background, the streltsy were closely associated with the towns in which they were based. And despite the ambition to build a standing force, individual streltsy had to engage in trades to support themselves and their families, just like poor hereditary servicemen who had to engage in agriculture, with or without serfs as labour, for the very same reason.

What really characterised the streltsy, beyond their new form of organisation and the fact that they at regular intervals engaged in unit training of sorts (usually shooting contests), was that they were uniformly armed and clothed. The streltsy received their arms and equipment from the state. Moscow streltsy received an annual subsidy in the form of cloth for their uniform (provincial streltsy only received this stipend every third or fourth year).[42] As a result, a streltsy regiment would present a uniformed appearance. As daily dress, the Moscow streltsy wore heel-length caftans made of grey, black, or brown cloth with wide sleeves that narrowed at the wrist. They also wore hats, trimmed with fur, and the usual Muscovite boots. In battle, they were equipped with helmets and, at least early in the period, probably chain mail or other armour under their caftans. Exactly what kind of helmet was issued to the streltsy corps remains unclear. Based on an early reconstruction, it has been suggested that they used special round helmets with narrow brims.[43] However, no such helmet has been preserved, and it is more likely that the streltsy received the same types of helmets as other troops, that is, Turco-Mongol or Turco-Persian ones early in the period and imported, simple morions later. Some Moscow streltsy also had a full dress uniform consisting of a similar but better-quality caftan of red cloth with gilded braiding on the chest, together with a whitish belt and heeled boots with turned-up toes. Uniforms may have changed in colour but not in style. By the end of the sixteenth century, certain regiments wore yellow or blue caftans. Some regiments wore silver braiding instead of gilded.

Streltsy were divided according to their garrison town into 'selected' (*vybornoye*) or Moscow-ranked streltsy and town streltsy (*gorodovoye*), stationed elsewhere. In times of peace, the streltsy served in garrisons or as part of the border defensive lines. At war, both Moscow and town

---

42 Cotossichin, *Beskrifning*, pp.80, 95, 96.
43 Viskovatov, *Istoricheskoye opisaniye* 1, pl. 106.

12. Berdysh poleaxe. (Erik Palmquist, 1674)

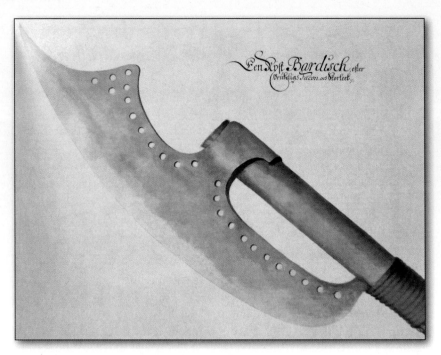

streltsy participated in campaigns and battles. The streltsy were under the administration of a special government office (*Streletskiy prikaz*) commanded by a voivode. The office was first mentioned in 1571 but may have been established earlier.[44]

A selected group of streltsy, the 'streltsy at the stirrup' (*stremyannyye strel'tsy*), served mounted, or more likely, as an early form of dragoons who were supposed to follow the Tsar on horseback but stay at his side, fighting dismounted. Established by Ivan IV, they were reportedly armed with bows as well as matchlock muskets. These men, 2,000 strong and dressed in red, formed the Tsar's primary bodyguard, unlike the aforementioned *zhil'tsy* and *ryndy*, who had more ceremonial duties.[45]

Local streltsy units were also raised. So had, for instance, in the early seventeenth century the strategically important Novodevichiy monastery an independent, and large, garrison of 300–350 streltsy.

By the end of the sixteenth century, there were possibly as many as 20–25,000 streltsy, of whom about 7,500–10,000 garrisoned Moscow.[46]

The main armament of the streltsy was the matchlock musket, "with a plain and straight stock, somewhat like a fowling piece; the barrel is rudely and unartifically made, very heavy, yet shootheth but a very small bullet."[47] The calibre was indeed often small, the muskets varying in calibre from 14 mm to 18 mm. In addition to his musket, the strelets carried a sabre, and

---

44 Filjushkin, *Ivan the Terrible*, p.34.

45 Giles Fletcher, *Of the Russian Commonwealth* (1591), in Berry and Crummey, *Rude & Barbarous Kingdom*, p.180; Cotossichin, *Beskrifning*, p.95.

46 Chernov, *Vooruzhennye sily*, ch. 3.

47 Giles Fletcher, *Of the Russian Commonwealth*, in Berry and Crummey, *Rude & Barbarous Kingdom*, p.184.

the *berdysh* (perhaps derived from Polish *berdysz*), a poleaxe with a 40–100 cm long head mounted on a pole (in exceptional cases up to two metres long). It was used as a musket rest as well as for hand-to-hand combat, in particular against horsemen. The berdysh appeared in the fifteenth century and remained in common use throughout the seventeenth century. When not in use, the weapon was carried slung in a shoulder-loop, or, according to Fletcher who saw them, fixed on each soldier "at his back" which some have interpreted as thrust through the belt on the man's back.[48] The berdysh later developed into a weapon of honour; by the eighteenth century the berdysh and halberd were so used by the palace guard (*dvortsovoy strazh*) and police (*politseyskiye-budochniki*).

Ivan IV may have armed a few streltsy with what some later scholars interpreted as pikes. However, this particular streltsy weapon, known as a 'spear' (*kop'yo*) among the Muscovites, almost certainly was nothing more than a regular spear. If the streltsy 'spear' indeed was a real pike, which seems quite unlikely, it was used on the western front only. There is no evidence that any streltsy functioned as pikemen before the 1690s.[49] No pikes were used on the southern or eastern border, where mounted Tatar archers were the most common adversaries. Against such enemies, the use of pikes would have been suicidal.

Although the streltsy occasionally were called up in units for military training, this fundamentally consisted of training in marksmanship only. There were no tactical exercises, nor manoeuvres. Moreover, and this was a feature of the streltsy as much as of other troop types, the Muscovite army fundamentally failed to address the need for continuous training. The key reason for this was that the Muscovite economy simply was unable to sustain a large, standing army. The persistent lack of funding meant that the men had to be effectively demobilised when no longer needed, and then switched to individual trades to support themselves. With few exceptions, such as some of the Moscow streltsy, the streltsy units were standing forces on paper only. They could be mobilised, but to prepare them for campaign duties, training often would have to start all over from scratch, at least if they were expected to operate at full capacity.

Oprichniki

In early 1564, Ivan came into serious conflict with a group of powerful princes and boyars, led by Prince Kurbskiy, who promptly defected to the Grand Duchy of Lithuania with which Muscovy was at war. Ivan accordingly developed further his plan to raise a personal military force, loyal to himself alone, to safeguard his power. But this would bring an economic cost, which Ivan could not cover due to Muscovy's limited economic resources. In particular, he needed inhabited farmland for distribution to this hereditary servicemen. At the same time, Ivan's persecution mania developed. In 1565, he accordingly

---

48   *Ibid.*
49   Roberto Palacios-Fernandez, 'Moskovskiye strel'tsy', *Zeughaus* 1 (1992), pp.8–15, on p.15.

13. *Oprichnik* on horseback, engraved on a metal candle-holder from Aleksandrovskaya Sloboda, dated to the sixteenth or seventeenth century.

embarked upon a radical policy. He set aside about half of the realm as his private domain (*oprichnina*), which he ruled personally and in which he established a new administration and a separate, private army.

It is likely that the introduction of the *oprichnina* was yet another attempt by Ivan to stem the growing wealth and influence of the Church, which controlled a significant share of available farmland, by reverting to Tatar institutions. Its background was Mongol practice that entailed the setting aside of a portion of an estate for a deceased noble's widows and orphans, and there were reports that it indeed was Ivan's Circassian wife, Mariya Temryukovna, who first suggested the plan to establish an *oprichnina*. Ivan welcomed those loyal to himself into the *oprichnina*, in the same manner that a khan would welcome new retainers. Their religion was irrelevant, and he also allowed Germans and other foreigners into the *oprichnina*.[50] As for the other half of Muscovy, it remained the 'land' (*zemshchina*), which constituted everything that Ivan did not bring into the *oprichnina*.

The *oprichnina* was not created on a whim. Ivan had already in 1563–1564 carried out a thorough survey of the provinces, including the old hereditary lands of the nobility. He may already then have planned to include them in his personal domain, unless their owners voluntarily joined him. For when Ivan established the *oprichnina* in 1565, he invited and organised the best of his cavalry into a personal corps, with the outspoken purpose to maintain internal order and destroy the enemies of the Tsar. This corps, often known merely as the *oprichniki*, became Ivan's chief support in his struggle against the nobles, princes, and churchmen who opposed him. It was essentially a continuation of the selected force that Ivan had established by land grants already in 1550. However, unlike the selected force, the *oprichnina* was in some ways similar to a political party with an armed wing. The *oprichnina* was a state within the state, being in effect a revolution from the top, and like all revolutions, it resulted, for those affected by it, in a reign of terror. Because the oppression unleashed by Ivan's *oprichniki* was based on another steppe nomad principle, that of collective guilt. According to this legal principle, the family, retainers, and even servants of a traitor were regarded as equally guilty, hence subject to the same punishment as the guilty individual. The legal principle of collective guilt had reached Muscovy from the Mongols, who themselves may have borrowed it from Chinese practices.[51]

Ivan recruited his *oprichniki* chiefly among nobles and sons of hereditary servicemen, just as the earlier 'selected thousand'. Originally 1,000 men, by

---

50 Ostrowski, *Muscovy and the Mongols*, pp.21, 192–3.
51 *Ibid.*, pp.195–6.

the 1570s their numbers had grown to 5,000 or 6,000. They were allotted land grants for their subsistence as well as wages from the Tsar, and swore fealty to the Tsar alone. Many had not previously owned freeholds, so found themselves bound to Ivan as their main source of income. However, many landed men, too, realised that there were advantages in freely surrendering their lands to the Tsar and joining the *oprichnina*, which became the new elite. Each of its members who previously had been the proprietor of a hereditary freehold, without obligations, henceforth had to accept the conditional land grant introduced in its stead. Others who joined were foreigners previously without lands, such as Heinrich von Staden, a German soldier of fortune in Muscovite service.

Most *oprichniki* served as cavalrymen. They were organised in the standard division organisation of the time, commanded by voivodes such as the boyar Aleksey Danilovich Basmanov, Prince Afanasiy Ivanovich Vyazemskiy, the noble Grigoriy 'Malyuta' Luk'yanovich Skuratov-Bel'skiy and others. Their chief duty was to function as the Tsar's personal troops, as an internal security force tasked to maintain order and administer punishment to those who choose not voluntarily to surrender their lands and autonomy to the Tsar. For this purpose, they were used in a number of bloody repressions. However, *oprichniki* also took part in border defence and served on military campaigns. For this purpose, streltsy and artillery, too, formed part of these forces, which became the Tsar's personal army. On these occasions the divisions of the *oprichniki* (great division, vanguard division, and so on) were joined to the corresponding divisions of the ordinary army. Their military role was significant. In 1568, the force guarding the southern frontier of Muscovy consisted only of *oprichniki*, organised into a great division, vanguard division, and rearguard division at Mtsensk; and right and left arm divisions and a light cavalry reconnaissance division in Kaluga. No less than 1,280 streltsy of the *oprichniki* participated in the campaign of 1577. Eventually, the *oprichnina* included some 15,000 streltsy and cossacks.[52]

The *oprichniki* wore black caftans as uniforms, in many cases rode black horses, and each had a severed dog's head and a broom attached to his saddle, to emphasise their doglike loyalty to the Tsar and their readiness to sweep any treason out of the country. Their uniform enhanced the impact of their terror and no doubt contributed to their reputation and *esprit de corps* of personal loyalty to the Tsar above all else.

However, the fear engendered by the terror of the *oprichniki* caused problems when unity was required, such as when Muscovy was faced with serious Tatar attacks. In 1571, the Crimean Tatars raided deep into Muscovite territory and even burned the outskirts of Moscow. As a result, in 1572 Ivan dropped the term *oprichnina*, which by then had acquired a bad name due to the violence and purges. Henceforth the *oprichniki* no longer played the role of instrument of repression. However, the Tsar's personal domain remained in existence in the form of the court (*dvor*) which continued to play a key role in centralising the Muscovite government. And Ivan's persecution

---

52 Chernov, *Vooruzhennye sily*, ch. 2; Stevens, *Russia's Wars of Emergence*, p.89.

mania and mistrust of others could not be abolished as easily as the political institution that he had created. There would be more victims to his violent mood swings, including, as mentioned, his own son and heir in 1580.

Artillery and Fortifications

Artillery remained a particular Muscovite strength, and fortresses continued being protected by large numbers of cannons during the reign of Ivan IV and beyond. The cannon with probably the largest bore of its day was cast in Moscow soon after the death of Ivan. In 1586, Andrey Chokhov (c. 1545–1629) cast the Tsar Cannon (*Tsar'-pushka*) of bronze, preserved in the Kremlin until this day but since 1835 mounted on an ornamental carriage. The cannon barrel alone weighs nearly 40 tonnes and is 5.34 metres long. Its calibre is 890 mm. The Tsar Cannon was positioned to defend one of the main gates of the Kremlin when the Tatars threatened Moscow in 1591, but in the end the great cannon did not get the opportunity to fire a single shot. Another, arguably more useful, type of fortress artillery was the aforementioned *tyufyaki* which were used for firing clusters of small shot or stones. About a metre long, with a calibre of 50–75 mm, they were from this time onwards primarily employed as fortress artillery.[53]

But the real progress in artillery under Ivan IV was the development of field artillery. By the 1520s, horse-drawn, wheeled gun carriages became available, which made field artillery a more successful proposition than in the past. As noted, Ivan IV introduced *naryady* of distinct field artillery in 1552, with two to four light cannons (95–105 mm in calibre) dedicated to each division.

The period also saw other innovations in artillery, including multi-barrelled ones such as the organ gun (*soroka*). Its barrels, up to 100 or more in number, were fixed side by side, and/or in several tiers. Guns with the barrels fixed in a revolving drum appeared, too.[54]

Artillerymen (*pushkari* and *zatinshchiki*) were recruited contract servicemen (*po priboru*) who served in exchange for payment. Like other groups of early modern Muscovite soldiers, artillerymen lived in separate neighbourhoods. They were paid in cash and provisions and also received land so that they could support their families. However, they were not numerous. A small fortress might only have from five to 50 artillerymen. The artillerymen were regarded as specialist troops. In times of war, other soldiers were conscripted or ordered to assist with the artillery. As a result, most fortresses and towns had far more cannon than could be manned by the specialist artillerymen alone. When the Muscovites left Livonia, the Polish monk Abbé John Piotrowski noted about the fortresses that they abandoned: "We were all amazed to find in all the fortresses numerous cannon and an abundance of powder and cannon balls, more than we ourselves could

---

53   Hellie, *Enserfment and Military Change*, p.153.
54   V.M. Krylov, et al., *The Military-Historical Museum of Artillery, Engineer and Signal Corps: The Guide* (St. Petersburg: The Military-Historical Museum of Artillery, Engineer and Signal Corps, 2008), p.52.

collect in our own country."[55] Fletcher was impressed, too, based on what he heard and saw: "It is thought that no prince of Christendom hath better store of munition than the Russe emperor."[56]

Fortresses were further developed along European lines during the reign of Ivan IV. As far as is known, the first bastioned fortress appeared immediately after his time, namely the one at Ladoga in 1585–1586. This was soon followed by bastions in fortresses elsewhere. In the seventeenth century, bastions were also built in Moscow, Novgorod, Rostov, and other major cities.[57] Later on, modern bastions were built elsewhere as well, including the fortress at Terki in the Terek River delta in the Caucasus, which in the seventeenth century was greatly improved by a Dutch military engineer, Niclas van Salen.[58]

Cossacks

By the sixteenth century, there were two main categories of cossacks in the Muscovite army: town or service cossacks and free cossacks. The town cossacks were, as before, voluntary recruits who served as infantry in exchange for payment. In the army, they were regarded as holding a position below that of streltsy and artillerymen. They were paid in a similar way, receiving some cash and provisions but also a little land so that they could sustain their families. Like streltsy and artillerymen, they were settled in towns in their own distinct neighbourhood. A town cossack unit was headed by a headman (*golova*). His unit was subdivided into hundreds, and further on, into tens. Town cossacks could be mustered for both town and campaign duty. But there were also wealthy cossacks who instead served as cavalrymen and, as a result, might receive a personal land grant, in effect becoming a hereditary serviceman. They were not many, by the turn of the seventeenth century constituting no more than 12–15 percent of all service cossacks.[59]

Although important especially along the borders, the number of town or service cossacks was never great. Until the end of the seventeenth century, their numbers reached no more than an estimated 5,000–10,000 men. Their military role and organisation changed little until they lost their importance and were enlisted into the new formation regiments during the military reforms of the 1680s.

Moscow also regularly solicited the services of the free cossacks who lived along the Don, Volga, and Dniepr rivers. Since these technically were not subjects of the Tsar, and accordingly neither servicemen nor taxpayers,[60] relations with them were increasingly often handled by the ambassadors'

55 Cited in Wipper, *Ivan Grozny*, p.224.

56 Giles Fletcher, *Of the Russian Commonwealth* (1591), in Berry and Crummey, *Rude & Barbarous Kingdom*, p.186.

57 Nossov, *Russian Fortresses*, p.12.

58 Palmquist, *Några observationer*, pp.100, 278.

59 Chernov, *Vooruzhennye sily*, ch. 4.

60 I.D. Belyayev, *O russkom voyske v tsarstvovaniye Mikhaila Feodorovicha i posle ego, do preobrazovaniy, sdelannykh Petrom Velikim: Istoricheskoye izsledovaniye* (Moscow: Universitetskaya tipografiya, 1846), p.17.

chancellery (*Posol'skiy prikaz*), which functioned as Muscovy's foreign ministry. From the reign of Ivan IV, free cossack units were frequently hired to serve in the southern Russian steppes, in particular as a defence against Tatar raids. The cossacks were paid in cash and also received weapons and food supplies.

There was a certain degree of fluidity between the various types of cossacks, and categories were not always neatly fixed. An example of the variety of cossacks within a typical Muscovite army is provided by the campaign that ended with the battle of Molodi in 1572, for which the service records mention cossacks of several types. In this campaign, the great division included 2,000 cossacks who were described as 'mercenary cossacks' which would suggest that they were free cossacks in the service of Muscovy. The right arm division included 500 'mounted cossack arquebusiers' which would seem to be a different category. As for the other divisions, they included 650 cossack 'arquebusiers' from various Muscovite towns in the vanguard division, 350 cossack 'arquebusiers' from other Muscovite towns in the rearguard division, and 300 cossack 'arquebusiers' from specifically Smolensk in the left wing division.[61] There is little doubt that all the latter were town cossack infantry and accordingly quite different bodies of men as compared to the free, mercenary cossacks who in this case almost certainly served as cavalry.

The origin of the free cossacks was as obscure and opaque as many of the individual cossacks themselves. The Don had for long been the home of a variety of peoples who did not recognise the rule of any Russian prince. Following the Mongol conquest, Tatars became a prominent population group of the steppe and forest-steppe. However, the population also came to include large numbers of resettled inhabitants as the result of Mongol and Tatar raiding. As Slavic and Turkic ethnic elements merged, a new distinct cossack culture emerged. The name cossack derived from a Turkic word, *qazaq*, meaning 'seceder' or 'wanderer', by which was meant freebooters outside the control of the Khan. The first cossacks of this variety may have been men who had lost their position and affiliations during the disintegration of the Golden Horde, and then turned to mercenary employment instead. A cossack owed allegiance to neither khan nor sultan, prince nor tsar. In a Russian context, the term cossack was used for what fundamentally was a soldier of fortune and frontiersman. They might be renegade Tatars who served against the incursions of others of their kind, or they might be individuals who enlisted for full- or part-time military service in exchange for payment in money or in kind, without being either a hereditary serviceman or obliged by his community. Cossacks served as either infantry or cavalry under their own leaders, their chief being known as hetman (*ataman*). He organised his band into a retinue (*druzhina*).

Yet the early inhabitants were not destined to form more than a minor share of the cossack population. The first cossack settlements (*stanitsa*, pl. *stanitsy*) on the Don emerged only in the 1530s or 1540s. The settlements were fortified and attracted many Muscovite deserters and outcasts. Many

---

61   V.I. Buganov, *Dokumenty o srazhenii pri Molodyakh v 1572 g.* <www.vostlit.info/Texts/Dokumenty/Russ/XVI/1560-1580/Schlacht_Molodi/text.htm>. First published in *Istoricheskiy arkhiv* 4, (1959).

were criminals escaping from the law, while others were fugitive peasants from central Muscovy (and Poland or Lithuania, although most of the latter ended up at the lower Dnieper where other cossack settlements appeared) in search of better opportunities. Numbers grew rapidly from the 1550s onwards, as an increasing number of migrants from the north trickled south, abandoning their own ruined estates or those of others on which they had served, hoping to find better opportunities as cossacks. As political and social dislocation in the heartland increased, so did the numbers of migrants. They made a living from horse-rearing, hunting, and fishing, but also from robbery and, sailing their riverboats down the Volga to the Caspian, from piracy. Although less romantic occupations, eventually some took up farming and salt production as well.

The cossacks used riverine crafts such as the *chayka* ('seagull'), which was commonly used by Ukrainian cossacks in the sixteenth and seventeenth centuries. Such a vessel could be 20 metres long, with a width of 3–4 metres, and carry a fighting crew of some 50 to 70 men, in addition to 2–6 small cannons (falconets).[62] Although primarily designed for riverine transport, such craft carried sails and were sufficiently seaworthy to carry out raids along the shores of the Black Sea and the Caspian Sea. Similar craft, but for obvious reasons without falconets, had been used in the region for raiding purposes since the third century AD, by groups such as Goths, Heruls, Slavs, and Vikings.

The Don cossacks became the origin of many other groups of cossacks, including the first Volga cossacks, from whom in turn emerged the Yaik (Ural) cossacks, the Terek cossacks, and the Siberian cossacks. Cossack boatmen sailed the Volga already before Muscovy annexed Astrakhan' and its surrounding territory. Their piratical activities caused problems for trade, so by 1577 Muscovy sent troops to pacify the Volga and remove all cossacks. While some of the Volga cossacks returned to the Don, others joined the recently emerged Yaik cossacks on the Yaik (now Ural) River. Others instead set out across the Caspian Sea and sailed up the Terek River, where there since 1560 or at least 1567 already was a Muscovite outpost. They settled below the Caucasus mountains as the Terek cossacks in about 1578. The Terek cossacks were soon engaged in frontier fighting with the various peoples of the Caucasus – Kabardians, Circassians, Chechens, and Noghai, from whom they took up many customs including what in time would become known as the 'traditional' cossack dress of *cherkesska* and *burka* (more on which below), as well as new recruits and wives. Indeed, it was little but their Christian Orthodox faith that set them apart from the neighbouring Caucasian tribes. Yet others instead sailed up the Volga and its tributary the Kama to the Urals, where they in the service of the Stroganov merchant family began to push into Siberia (which will be described in a later chapter).

Moscow began military co-operation with the Don cossacks in 1549. Ivan IV regarded the Don cossacks as a suitable tool to apply pressure, by raiding, on the Crimean Khanate. Henceforth, whole cossack groups

---

62 Based on a reconstruction in the Odessa Maritime Museum, in turn based on a contemporary depiction. Michael Fredholm von Essen, 'Cossack Chaika', *Arquebusier* 25:2 (1999), p.19.

(*stanitsy*) from the Don, Volga, and Terek Rivers entered Muscovite service. They usually served in the role of a frontier force. Despite ups and downs in the relationship, cossacks acquired a lasting presence in the Muscovite army. Their exact numbers were never known, but by the end of the seventeenth century, the Don cossacks could field some 14,000 men.[63]

In 1586, Muscovite regular troops returned the mouth of the Terek. The Terek cossacks continued their activities but henceforth did so in the service of Moscow. The Terek cossacks were soon joined by the Greben' cossacks (cossacks of the 'mountain ridge'). Their numbers were not large by the time under consideration here. By the end of the seventeenth century, the Yaik cossacks could raise some 3,000 fighting men while the remaining Volga cossacks and Greben' cossacks together could field only some 2,500 men.[64]

Tatar and Tribal Troops

There were several Tatar enclaves in Muscovy, including, most importantly, in Kasimov and Temnikov. They fought within the Muscovite army, since they belonged to the Muscovite state. Most were nominally Muslims. They were led by their tribal leader, generally a prince or *murza* (noble), organised into units based on the decimal system, which was traditional on the steppe, and, as has been demonstrated, also greatly influenced Muscovite military organisation. There were non-Tatar tribal forces too. Among them were the Meshchory, a Finno-Ugrian population linked to the Kasimov Tatars who fought as irregular tribal cavalry. So did large numbers of Bashkirs, Chuvash, and Mordvins, who entered Muscovite military service in tribal groups.

Following the conquest of Kazan' and Astrakhan', significant contingents of yet more Tatar cavalry entered Muscovite military service, as did often groups of Noghai Tatars from the steppes north of the Caucasus. It seems likely that up to some 10,000 Tatars may have served in the armies of Muscovy at any given time, together with up to some 8,000 Chuvash, Mordvins, and others.[65] While still independent, Kazan' had mustered at least 5,000 cavalry and 10,000 infantry, and it is likely that many of them were later available for Muscovite service.[66] Tatars and other tribal troops served in cavalry units under their own leaders well into the seventeenth century. When mentioned in the sources, they appear under the leader's name, typically recognisable by his choice of title, most commonly that of *murza*.[67] They often operated in conjunction with cossack cavalry, since their style of fighting was very similar.

The main difference between the tribal troops and other Muscovite forces was that the tribals less frequently carried firearms and accordingly were limited to the light cavalry role. Fletcher described the Tatar way of war:

---

63 I.E. Porfiriev, *Peter I: Grundläggare av den ryska reguljära arméns och flottans krigskonst* (Stockholm: Hörsta, 1958), p.41.

64 *Ibid.*

65 Chernov, *Vooruzhennye sily*, ch. 4, based on the estimate for 1630.

66 Fennell, *Kurbsky's History*, 37. Elsewhere Kurbskiy gives much higher numbers, which seem exaggerated. *Ibid.*, 41.

67 For an example from 1614, see Oleg A. Kurbatov, *Tikhvinskoye osadnoye sidenie 1613* (Moscow: Zeughaus, 2006), pp.35–6.

Their manner of fight or ordering of their forces is much after the Russe manner (spoken of before), save that they are all horsemen and carry nothing else but a bow, a sheaf of arrows, and a falcon sword [sabre] after the Turkish fashion. They are very expert horsemen and use to shoot as readily backward as forward. Some will have a horseman's staff like to a boar spear besides their other weapons. The common soldier hath no other armour than his ordinary apparel, viz., a black sheepskin with the wool side outward in the day time and inward in the night time, with a cap of the same. But their *mirza* or noblemen imitate the Turk both in apparel and armour.[68]

The sheepskin clothes of the Tatar rank and file, the appearance of whom was quite different from that of the often splendidly dressed Tatar nobility, can be confirmed by a seventeenth-century illustration by Adam Olearius (1603–1671), a member of a Holstein embassy.

Prominent Muslim Tatars, such as the Khan of the Kasimov Tatars, did not form part of the *mestnichestvo* system of order of precedence and served as commanders as the tsar saw fit. However, most Tatars in Muscovite service converted to Christianity, married into the Muscovite nobility, and in time were assimilated. As noted, a considerable number of Muscovite noble families claimed Tatar descent. However, this pattern began to change in the early seventeenth century.[69] The explanation may be as simple as most Tatars by then already having been assimilated into Muscovite society. But it is equally possible that the xenophobia encouraged by the Church, which labeled all foreigners as heathens and, moreover, wanted to forget Muscovy's old links to the Chinggisid Khans, had produced an environment in which Tatar descent was no longer regarded as desirable. Certainly the Church by then had formulated an ideology according to which Mongols were evil, had contributed nothing to Orthodox Muscovy, and had to be resisted at all costs. By the late sixteenth century, the church had already begun to spread the myth of the 'Tatar yoke' which supposedly had held the Christians back.[70] This ideology did not only affect the Tatars and other easterners; the church continuously encouraged the population to regard all non-Orthodox as heathens worthy of nothing but hostile contempt. By the seventeenth century, foreigners, including foreign embassies, were almost daily faced with obscene gestures and verbal abuse inspired by the Church as the appropriate treatment of heathens, which

14. Noghai Tatar family, illustrating the sheepskin dress of the Tatar rank-and-file. (Adam Olearius, 1656).

---

68 Giles Fletcher, *Of the Russian Commonwealth* (1591), in Berry and Crummey, *Rude & Barbarous Kingdom*, p.193. Spelling slightly amended.

69 Halperin, *Russia and the Golden Horde*, p,113.

70 Ostrowski, *Muscovy and the Mongols*, pp.244–5.

included all but the Orthodox.[71] In the plain words of the Swedish intelligence officer Erik Palmquist: "They despise all foreigners."[72]

Foreign Mercenaries

The attitude of the Church towards foreigners clashed with the state's need for foreign expertise. Foreign mercenaries had been employed already by Ivan III, in particular as military engineers, artillerymen, and gunsmiths, and during the reign of Ivan IV the number of foreign soldiers increased further. Some Italians still served with the Muscovite army, and the number of Germans and Lithuanians rose. It was a German who led the siege works that led to the conquest of Kazan' in 1552. English, Scots, Dutch, French, Danes, and Swedes also appeared in Muscovite service. In most Russian-language sources, all West Europeans were labelled Germans (*nemtsy*), since this term, which originally meant 'mute', implied anybody who could not speak the Russian language.

According to the (almost certainly incomplete) service registers, there were in 1578 a total of 400 'Germans' in Muscovite service.[73] About a decade later, an English merchant and diplomatic agent, Jerome Horsey (d. 1626), noted that Ivan had about 1,200 foreign mercenaries in his army. Horsey, who was in Muscovy from 1572 to 1591, presumably thought primarily of the West Europeans in Muscovite service, mentioning French, Scots, Dutch, Poles, and a few English.[74] There were others as well. In addition to Tatars who for one reason or another had been incorporated into the Muscovite army, another contemporary Englishman, Giles Fletcher, added: "Of mercenary soldiers that are strangers (of whom they call *nemtsy*) they have at this time 4,300 of Poles; of Circassian that are under the Poles about 4,000 whereof 3,500 are abroad in his garrisons; of Dutch and Scots about 150; of Greeks, Turks, Danes and Swedes, all in one band, an 100 or thereabouts."[75] At the time of Fletcher's writing, his description "Circassian that are under the Poles" most likely referred to the Petyhortsy Circassians who began to migrate to Poland in 1562 (more on which below) but then, nonetheless, often took service with Muscovy.

The Conquests of Kazan' and Astrakhan'

In northern Europe, winter was a major campaign season. Russia contained extensive uninhabited, or only sparsely inhabited, territories. There was a shortage of roads. As a result, it was often easier to move by sledge over frozen ground than to attempt to traverse the same terrain in summer. Frozen

71 Birgegård, *Sparwenfeld's Diary*, pp.83, 265 n.170.

72 Palmquist, *Några observationer*, p.98.

73 V.I. Buganov (ed.), *Razryadnaya kniga 1475–1598 gg.* (Moscow, 1966), pp.300–301; Poe, 'Muscovite Personnel Records', pp.361–78; citing Buganov.

74 Jerome Horsey, *Travels* (concluded in 1621), in Berry and Crummey, *Rude & Barbarous Kingdom*, pp.287, 288–9.

75 Giles Fletcher, *Of the Russian Commonwealth* (1591), in Berry and Crummey, *Rude & Barbarous Kingdom*, p.180.

rivers, too, were easier to cross than would have been the case in warmer weather. But there were risks, too. A spell of warm weather might weaken the ice. Indeed, the first campaign in which Ivan IV took part, when he was 17 years old, was an attempt to conquer Kazan'. The Muscovite army set out in November 1547. However, when after a long journey the army attempted to cross the Volga, it had already begun to thaw. A common problem was that since the long rivers stretched in a north-south direction, thaw began in the south much earlier than in the north. As a result, the flowing waters frequently caused flooding over the still frozen northern channels of the rivers. This is what happened to Ivan's army as it reached the Volga. A layer of water covered the ice, which made it difficult to see the weak spots in the ice coverage. As a result, many men and several cannons were lost. Tsar Ivan, an intellectual who by all accounts was not physically brave, decided to return to Moscow with the main army. Instead he dispatched Prince Dmitriy Bel'skiy and a Tatar Prince, Shah Ali, with a smaller force towards Kazan'. Bel'skiy and Shah Ali defeated the Tatars in the battle of Arsk, located some 60 km from Kazan', laid siege to Kazan' for a week, but then had to withdraw in March 1548, when the thaw prevented further overland travel while the rivers were not yet sufficiently free of ice to enable river transport.

In November 1549, another attempt was made to march against Kazan'. However, this time, too, a period of thaw caused the ice to melt to the extent that the Muscovite army failed to reach Kazan' altogether. The expeditionary force had to return in February 1550. It was obvious that Kazan' was so far from Moscow that the campaign pushed the Muscovite logistics system to its limits, and that Muscovy's capacity to get an army there and back in a single campaign season was doubtful, unless the enemy surrendered almost at once.

Another means of campaigning was by river transportation, which certainly was faster and easier than travel overland. Having failed to bring substantial forces to Kazan' twice, Ivan and his advisors decided to make another attempt in summer. In spring 1551, the necessary materials for the construction of a wooden fortress, many of them already prefabricated, were prepared for movement by raft to the vicinity of Kazan'. In April, these were shipped downriver to the mouth of the Sviyaga river, 20 km from Kazan'. Heinrich von Staden, a German in Muscovite service, described the undertaking as follows:

> The Grand Prince commanded that a city be erected with wooden walls, towers and gates, like a real city, and that the beams and timbers be numbered, all of them, from top to bottom. Then the city was dismantled and the timber was placed on rafts and floated down the Volga, together with the soldiers and the heavy artillery. When he arrived near Kazan' he commanded that this city be erected and all [the fortifications] be filled with earth.[76]

---

76 Cited in Wipper, *Ivan Grozny*, p.64. See also Fritz T. Epstein (ed.), *Heinrich von Staden: Aufzeichnungen über den Moskauer Staat* (Hamburg: Cram, de Gruyter & Co., 1964), p.82.

The construction materials having arrived in May, they were rapidly assembled into a fortress, henceforth known as Sviyazhsk. Setting out from this forward operating base, Muscovite units began to attack and harass Tatar territory. Prince Peter Serebryanyy raided the outskirts of Kazan', liberating some of the Russian captives held as slaves there. Muscovite riverine craft also took control of the rivers Volga, Kama, and Vyatka. As a result of these successes, several nearby tribes (the Cheremis, Mordvins, Chuvash, and some Tatars) switched allegiance to Muscovy. In June, the tribes joined the Muscovites in the attack on Kazan'. Although the tribal contingents, reportedly consisting of some 4,000 men, failed to take Kazan', which was well fortified and defended by artillery, the siege continued.[77] The ongoing siege exacerbated existing tensions within Kazan', in particular between the Kazan' Tatars and the local representatives of their overlords, the Crimean Tatars. As a result, a coup took place within the Tatar leadership, and in August 1551 the throne was offered to Prince Shah Ali, who would rule as an ally of Muscovy.

However, having received the throne, Shah Ali could not appease all factions in Kazan', especially since he also was expected to return all Russian slaves to Muscovy – a severe blow to the Tatar economy. In February 1552, Ivan ordered Shah Ali to be replaced, but in March, before this order could be carried out, Shah Ali was deposed and eventually succeeded by a Noghai Prince, Yadegar, who unlike Shah Ali was not friendly to Moscow.

In June 1552, Ivan again led the Muscovite army out of Moscow to conquer Kazan'. On 13 August, the army arrived in Sviyazhsk, and 10 days later, the Muscovites began preparations for a formal siege of Kazan', building earthworks and siege towers. A Tatar sortie was easily repulsed by the streltsy, the Tatars learning the hard way that the matchlock muskets had a greater range than their bows. The Muscovites had brought significant numbers of artillery, ranging from siege guns to smaller field guns, and their fire easily suppressed the Tatar artillery, which was fewer in numbers.[78] Meanwhile, a siege engineer of German origin known as Erasmus prepared a mine which when it was exploded, on 4 September, brought down a part of the city wall and started several fires. Yet more mines were prepared and exploded on 30 September and, again, on 2 October, which brought down another portion of the city wall. The Muscovites then stormed the city, after which Kazan' surrendered. Tsar Ivan reluctantly took part in the final assault, joining his troops at the last moment, according to one contemporary (but admittedly hostile) witness after being physically dragged out of the chapel erected in the camp, where he had spent the early morning in prayer, by his chief men "taking his horse by the bridle, they placed the tsar himself, whether he liked it or not, near the banner."[79] Yet, Ivan's physical presence was unneeded; his men had already taken most of the city. The territory of the Kazan' Khanate was subsequently incorporated into Muscovy.

River transport was also used for the conquest of the Astrakhan' Khanate. In the summer of 1554, a Muscovite army consisting of cavalry and streltsy

---

77 Fennell, *Kurbsky's History*, p.33.
78 *Ibid.*, p.41.
79 *Ibid.*, p.61.

under Yuriy Shemyakin, Mikhail Golovin, and Ignatiy Veshnyakov went by river to Perevolok or thereabouts, the place where the Volga and the Don came most close, which was on the northern border of the Astrakhan' Khanate. The Tatars were defeated in a riverine clash. Meanwhile, another riverine navy under Prince Yuriy Pronskiy blockaded Astrakhan' itself. Astrakhan' surrendered, and by July 1554 its territory too was annexed. Muscovy appointed a new Khan as ruler of Astrakhan'.

South-east of Astrakhan' was the steppe territory of the Noghai Tatars. Ivan did not neglect to use diplomacy as a means to gain allies and clients in Inner Asia and the Caucasus that could assist in neutralising the Tatar threat. In November 1555, the Noghai Prince, Ismail, swore allegiance to Ivan. This was fortunate for Moscow when, in early 1556, the newly appointed Khan of Astrakhan', who supposedly ruled in the name of Muscovy, rebelled. As a result, a joint Muscovite-Noghai expedition was launched to restore order in Astrakhan'. In late winter 1556, Ivan sent 550 town cossacks on a ski march towards Astrakhan'.

It is unclear when skis, at this time employed with one long pole only for locomotion, were first

15. Muscovite skiers and sledges. (Sigismund von Herberstein, 1549)

used by Muscovites for military purposes. Although certainly known to some Finno-Ugrian peoples in the north, there is no evidence that skis were commonly used by Muscovite troops. It is, accordingly, possible that Ivan had been inspired by an event in the previous year. This was the first significant Muscovite battle in which skis were used, although they then were employed by the other side. In the battle of Joutselkä in 1555, a small Swedish-Finnish ski-equipped army under Jöns Månsson ambushed and defeated a significantly stronger Muscovite cavalry army under Ivan Bibikov, primarily because the cavalry had difficulty moving through the deep snow. It was the ski-equipped Finnish arquebusiers who had been particularly hard-hitting, and as a result, all able Finnish men were told henceforth to serve "with skis, arquebuses, crossbows, bows, short spears, and shields."[80] The winter snow accordingly caused both difficulties and advantages, which was one reason why winter campaigns persisted in the region.

In 1556, Ivan may have argued that since the Tatar army, too, depended on its cavalry, it might face similar problems in snowy terrain as the Muscovites. However, nothing came out of the ski march, and in May, additional forces,

---

80 Arvo Viljanti, *Gustav Vasas ryska krig 1554–1557* (Stockholm: Kungl. Vitterhets Historie och Antikvitets Akademiens Handlingar, Historiska serien 2:2, 1957), pp.391–402, 405, 518.

streltsy and cossacks, were sent down the River Volga by boat. During the summer, Astrakhan' was retaken.

The Livonian War

The campaigns against Kazan' and Astrakhan' showed that with regard to artillery, firearms, field fortifications, and siege works, Muscovy enjoyed an obvious technological advantage over the Tatars. The Muscovite army took full advantage of this superiority in the south and east. However, against European enemies in the west, the Muscovite army, paradoxically, operated more in the Tatar manner. When in January 1558, an 8,000-strong Muscovite army invaded Livonia, the launching point of the Livonian War, its objective was no more than a grand raid, Tatar-style, so as to show the Livonian Order, which still ruled Livonia, that it would have to pay tribute, or else. That the Muscovite army was commanded by Prince Shah Ali, the recent ruler of Kazan', and that his vanguard division was led by Prince Tokhtamysh, a Crimean Tatar, and his right wing division by Prince Kaibulla (or Abdullah) from Astrakhan', certainly did not make the strategy any less eastern.[81] During two weeks, the Muscovites burned large numbers of villages and estates, while the knights of the Order and their troops stayed in their castles, refusing to engage. Although the Muscovites later in the year also took several castles, most of which lacked sufficient supplies and troops, there was otherwise little to distinguish this operation from those traditionally carried out by Tatars against Muscovy and other Russian principalities, before these were unified under Moscow. The objective of the campaign was to force the Livonians to pay tribute, and the means employed primarily consisted of raiding and looting.

When in January 1559, Ivan's second invasion of Livonia took place, there were far more Muscovite troops, according to some (not fully credible) sources up to 50,000 in seven separate divisions.[82] However, again the objective was a grand raid, not siege warfare. Muscovy did not aim for long-term conquest but the enforcement of the payment of tribute.

Yet another winter raid took place in January 1560. Its objective was no different from those in previous years, and the Muscovites returned with captives, cattle, and other loot.

The situation changed only with the demise of the Livonian Order in 1562 and the passing of most of Livonia under the rule of the Grand Duchy of Lithuania and Poland. Fighting had already occurred in Livonia between Lithuanian and Muscovite units. In response, Ivan in November 1562 began to plan for the conquest of the Lithuanian border town of Polotsk. On 30 November, Ivan led a large Muscovite army bound for Polotsk. It was one of the largest Muscovite armies in the sixteenth century. Its total number of fighting men was more than 34,600, including 12,044 hereditary servicemen, some 12,000 streltsy and artillerymen, 6,114 cossacks, and 4,468 Kasimov Tatars, Astrakhan' Tatars, Noghai Tatars, and Mordvins (Table 1). When

---

81 See, e.g., Keep, *Soldiers of the Tsar*, pp.77–78.
82 Filjushkin, *Ivan the Terrible*, p.163.

reviewing the numbers, it should be remembered that key elements of the army, such as the serving men brought by the hereditary servicemen, were not included in the figures. Ivan also brought heavy siege artillery and a supply train consisting of thousands of levied commoners who served in the host. On 31 January 1563, Muscovite troops took up positions around Polotsk. The original plan was to take advantage of winter conditions, attacking across the frozen Polota river since riverside fortifications were weaker. However, the ice being too thin, this plan was abandoned and the Muscovite army settled down for a conventional siege. The town held out until 15 February, then surrendered.

Great Division		Rearguard Division	
Hereditary Servicemen	2,929	Hereditary Servicemen	1,855
Tatars	1,629	Tatars, Mordvins, and Meshchory	1,111
Cossacks	1,295		
Right Arm Division		Left Arm Division	
Hereditary Servicemen	2,027	Hereditary Servicemen	1,900
Service Tatars and Mordvins	966	Tatars	933
Cossacks	1,009	Cossacks	605
Vanguard Division		Artillery	
Hereditary Servicemen	1,900	Hereditary Servicemen	1,433
Service Tatars	940	Cossacks	1,048
Cossacks	1,046		

Table 1. The army that in 1562 set out towards Polotsk, excluding the unknown number of armed serving men brought by many hereditary servicemen, the 12,000 streltsy and artillerymen, and the large number of levied labourers. (Source: A.I. Filyushkin, *Russko-litovskaya voyna 1561–1570 i datsko-shvedskaya voyna 1563–1570 gg.* (St. Petersburg: Milhist.info, 2015), p.245).

Following this success, the Muscovites returned to the previous strategy of grand raids. In January 1564, another grand raid began, consisting of at least some 20,000 men commanded by Prince Peter Shuyskiy. However, this time the Lithuanian forces were prepared. On 26 January, a possibly 10,000-strong Lithuanian army under Mikalojus Radvila Rudasis (better known in Polish as Mikolaj Radzivill Rudy, 'the Red'; 1512–1584) and Grigorijus Chodkevičius (better known in Polish as Hrehory (Grzegorz) Chodkiewicz; c.1513–1572) attacked the Muscovites on the Ula River, a tributary of the Daugava north of Chashniki in the present-day Vitebsk region, in a late afternoon attack. There are conflicting reports on what really happened during the battle. So much is certain, however, that the overconfident Muscovites, who were superior in numbers, due to lax discipline were caught unprepared and defeated. They may not even have donned their armour, instead still carrying most armaments on sledges. Prince Shuyskiy, too, fell in the battle, together with many of his men.

The Southern Border Defences

Ivan devoted considerable resources to reinforcing Muscovy's southern border, which was particularly weak. By tradition, Tatars raided for people, livestock, and goods the sale of which produced substantial revenue. The captives were sold in the slave markets in the Tatar-held cities in the south. Moscow itself was vulnerable to Tatar grand raids, so the threat was real.

The fortification of the southern border defences was a gradual process. In the south-east, border defences had been maintained along strategically important rivers already since the mid-fourteenth century. As noted, the Oka River constituted the main defensive line. This line was known, in Muscovite military parlance, as the Oka border (*Okskiy rubezh*) or river-bank (*bereg*). Traditionally, field divisions and garrisons secured the towns of Kaluga, Aleksin, Tarusa, Serpukhov, Kashira, and Kolomna. However, Ivan in 1551 advanced the Muscovite border southwards into the *Dikoye Polye*, the largely uninhabited steppe between Muscovy and the Crimean Khanate, through the foundation of new fortresses. A more remote defensive line through Tula existed as early as the fifteenth century, with a wooden fortress built there in 1507–1509.[83] Ivan strengthened and extended the Tula line, creating a proper defensive line of timber obstacles (*zasyechnaya cherta* or *liniya*), along which he organised, and constantly maintained, men on guard duty.[84] He also had fortresses that grew into towns built on, or south of, the line, such as Mikhailov (1551), Shatsk (1553), Dedilovo (1554), Bolkhov (1555), Oryol and Yepifan' (1566), and Dankov (1568). The new fortresses each had permanent garrisons and each was responsible for reconnaissance in its surrounding area.

A timber obstacle (abatis, *zasyeka* in Russian) consisted of barricades of felled trees. This was a traditional feature of northern warfare, which was used in Sweden and Finland, too, against cavalry incursions.[85] Reinhold Heidenstein described it in the following way:

> [They] hacked trees under one side, felled them on the other side, entangled the tree trunks and felled more trees on top and so surrounded themselves by timber obstacles thousands of paces long and more secure than any wall; the sunlight barely penetrated into the forest and even during the day it aroused in those who entered it fear like during the night.

The bands of felled tree obstacles were from some 20 to 120 metres wide, the forests were allowed to grow dense around the obstacles, and peasants were strictly forbidden to cut passes through the line. Where there were few or no trees, they erected log palisades on earth ramparts instead, and in many locations, dug dykes. In addition, the Muscovites built small wooden forts and block houses at regular intervals to supply the garrison manning the defensive line. Despite Heidenstein's words, the defensive line was less

---

83 Nossov, *Russian Fortresses*, p.33.
84 Krylov, et al., *Military-Historical Museum*, p.229.
85 Viljanti, *Gustav Vasas ryska krig*, pp.468, 476, 723, 768.

a physical obstacle than a defensive base that was used for patrolling and, when an enemy had been located, for signalling his location. Moreover, the Muscovites would burn the grass on the steppe side of the defensive line after the frost in October or November, so that there would be no fodder for Tatar horses and to deny the Tatars the opportunity to start fires with the intention to burn through the timber obstacles.

The defensive line was never intended as a continuous system of fortifications. The fortifications merely aimed to slow down any Tatar invaders, while the garrisons acted as bases for patrols that aimed to find any raiding party before they penetrated too deep into the settled territories. Prince Mikhail Vorotynskiy (d. 1573), who earlier had taken part in the conquest of Kazan', set up a system for frontier military service on 16 February 1571. The field commanders and their personal forces were rotated every six months. A garrison was usually divided into two halves, one of which served at any one time. In spring, one half was called up, serving until mid summer. Then it was replaced by the second half, which served until late autumn. Beginning in April, patrolmen would go into the steppe at semi-monthly intervals. There were eight patrol shifts, the first one beginning patrol on 1 April, the second following two weeks later, and so on until the first shift set out again on 1 August. The eighth patrol shift set out last, on 15 November, and patrols continued if there was no snow and weather permitted. The patrol service consisted of multiple layers. On the strategic level, the frontier service consisted of units of 70 mounted steppe patrolmen (*stanichniki*) who would leave their fortified station (*stanitsa*) at six-day intervals, following a special patrol route to watch for signs of Tatars. Such men would also relay messages and goods, provide escorts, and stand guard over distant fields. Each patrol shift, which consisted of hereditary servicemen, cossacks, and local Tatars, Chuvash, and Mordvins, was ordered to appear at headquarters two weeks before its scheduled patrol, so that it could be deployed immediately if the preceding patrol had been lost. On the tactical level, individual patrols (*storozh*, pl. *storozha*), consisting of two men each, set out at one-and-a-half-day intervals, so that nearly every day a patrol inspected each segment of the border. If they noticed any Tatars, one man would return to headquarters to report, while the other would stay and observe.[86] When news arrived about a Tatar raid, the field divisions set out against the invaders while messengers were sent to warn residents of outlying villages to move themselves and their livestock into fortified towns or forests. When needed, units were mobilised from Moscow as well.

In 1585, the border was moved further southwards. Eight new fortresses were established, the first two at Livny and Voronezh in 1586. By 1600 new defensive outposts were added including around the fortress towns of Voronezh, Yelets, Belgorod, Kursk, and Staryy Oskol.[87]

---

86 Chernov, *Vooruzhennye sily*, ch. 2; Hellie, *Enserfment and Military Change*, pp.176–7; Stevens, *Soldiers on the Steppe*, p.131.

87 Stevens, *Soldiers on the Steppe*, p.123.

The Battle of Molodi

In 1571, the Crimean Khan, Davlat Ghirai (1512–1577), led an army of reportedly 40,000 men (consisting of Crimean Tatars, Tatars of the Great and Small Noghai Hordes, and several contingents from the North Caucasus) which broke through both the new defensive line and the Oka border. The Tatars continued to the outskirts of Moscow and on 24 May burned them. Heinrich von Staden, a German mercenary in Muscovite service, relates how this was only the most visible aspect of the campaign; the Kazan' and Astrakhan' Tatars too "rose and went to the land of the Grand Prince, set fire to many undefended towns and took away with them an immense number of Russian captives, not counting those who were put to death."[88]

In 1572, Davlat Ghirai led a possibly even larger Crimean army in a new grand raid towards Moscow. Again it consisted of Crimean Tatars, Tatars of the Great and Small Noghai Hordes, and several contingents from the North Caucasus (Circassians and Adyghes), but also an Ottoman artillery contingent. This time, the Crimean Khan had plans not only to raid but also to take control over all Muscovy and restore it, and its possessions Kazan' and Astrakhan', to Tatar rule.

However, Moscow had learnt a number of lessons from the previous year's disaster. In late autumn 1571, Moscow had ordered the burning of large areas of the steppe between the towns of Novosil', Dankov, Oryol, and Putivl', which constituted the main access route for Tatar invasions. As the Crimean army approached, this caused difficulties for the Tatars, since fodder no longer was available for the tens of thousands of horses brought with them. In addition, the Muscovites had built two lines of stockade, 1–1.2 metres high, along the Oka river between the fortresses of Serpukhov and Kolomna. The two defensive lines were manned by streltsy. Yet more Muscovite troops including artillery were defending the fords of the Oka.

The Muscovite commander, Prince Mikhail Vorotynskiy, commanded an army consisting of possibly some 32,000 men, including 12,000 hereditary servicemen cavalry plus an unknown number of other fighting men brought by the hereditary servicemen, 2,035 streltsy, 1,800 town cossacks, and at least 2,000 mercenary cossacks, presumably on horseback. Although detailed lists of the number of men still exist, the total force will still have to be estimated since the personal retainers brought by the hereditary servicemen were never listed.

Prince Vorotynskiy's army was divided as follows:[89]

---

88 Cited in Wipper, *Ivan Grozny*, p.154.

89 Original documents are published in Buganov, *Dokumenty o srazhenii pri Molodyakh*; Aleksandr R. Andreyev, *Neizvestnoye Borodino: Molodinskaya bitva 1572 goda* (Moscow: Mezhregional'nyy tsentr otraslevoy informatiki Gosatomnadzora Rossii, 1997; available from the website <www.e-reading.by/bookreader.php/1003521/Andreev_Aleksandr_-_Neizvestnoe_Borodino._ Molodinskaya_bitva_1572_goda.html>, accessed on 25 January 2018). See also V.V. Penskoy, *Srazheniye pri Molodyakh 28 iyulya – 3 avgusta 1572 g.* (Milhist.info, 2012; available at <www. milhist.info/2012/08/23/penskoy_1>, accessed on 25 January 2018).

- The great division, commanded by Prince Mikhail Vorotynskiy with Ivan Sheremetyev as his deputy, consisting of a total of 8,255 men plus an unknown number of servicemen's retainers, the total including some 4,000 hereditary servicemen, 1,000 streltsy divided into two contingents, and some 2,000 mercenary cossacks.
- The right arm division, commanded by Prince Nikita Odoyevskiy with Fyodor Sheremetyev as his deputy, consisting of a total of 3,590 men plus an unknown number of servicemen's retainers, the total including some 2,590 hereditary servicemen, 500 streltsy in a number of distinct towns contingents, and some 500 mounted cossack arquebusiers.
- The vanguard division, commanded by Prince Andrey Khovanskiy with Prince Dmitriy Khvorostinin (c.1535–1590) as his deputy, consisting of a total of 4,475 men plus an unknown number of servicemen's retainers, the total including some 2,390 hereditary servicemen, 535 streltsy divided into one major and two smaller contingents, and some 650 cossack arquebusiers on foot.
- The rearguard division, commanded by Prince Ivan Shuyskiy with Vasiliy Umnyy-Kolychov as his deputy, consisting of a total of 2,063 men plus an unknown number of servicemen's retainers, the total including some 1,713 hereditary servicemen, and some 350 cossack arquebusiers on foot.
- The left arm division, commanded by Prince Andrey Repnin with Prince Peter Khvorostinin as his deputy consisting of a total of 1,651 men plus an unknown number of servicemen's retainers, the total including some 1,351 hereditary servicemen, and some 300 cossack arquebusiers on foot from Smolensk.

Vorotynskiy had at first deployed his army, including the great division which contained most of the artillery and the *gulyaygorod*, several kilometres long, in Kolomna. However, as the Tatar army approached, Vorotynskiy moved his forces westwards, to intercept the Tatar army. He moved his own, great division to Serpukhov, where he and his staff, which was a component of the Muscovite army that recently had been formalised through one of Tsar Ivan's reforms, deployed. The great division's objective was to hold the Tatars if they succeeded in crossing the Oka.

To his right was positioned Prince Nikita Odoyevskiy with the right arm division, deployed in the town of Tarusa.

To his left was Prince Andrey Repnin with the left arm division, deployed on the Lopasnya River and held in reserve.

Further to his left was Prince Ivan Shuyskiy with the rearguard division, deployed in the town of Kashira.

The vanguard division under Prince Andrey Khovanskiy was deployed on the extreme right flank between Tarusa and Kaluga, where it was based.

The Crimean Tatar army bypassed the Muscovite fortified town of Tula and on 26 July attempted to cross the Oka at the Sen'kin ford near Serpukhov. Heinrich von Staden, who guarded the river with 300 men who were swept away by the Tatars, noted the fundamental difficulty in attempting to prevent Tatar raiding through the use of fixed positions: "The Crimean Tsar stood opposite us on the other bank of the Oka. Divai-Mirza, the Crimean Tsar's Commander-in-Chief, crossed the river with a large force, at a great distance from us, so that all the fortifications proved useless."[90] Nonetheless, Shuyskiy's rearguard division slowed down their crossing through artillery and musket fire, then counter-attacked those Tatars who in fact managed to cross, driving them back.[91]

On 27 July, the Ottoman artillery opened fire against the positions held by the great division and the right arm division in order to suppress the Muscovite artillery. The Muscovite divisions had by then left their extended positions and drawn closer to Serpukhov, but they remained based vis-à-vis each other as they had been previously, in effect holding a front between the River Lopasnya in the east and the town of Tarusa in the west. But the front was still long, and Tatar units succeeded in crossing the Oka River. First, a Noghai unit under Tereberdey-murza successfully captured the Sen'kin ford and crossed the river by night, the ford having only been defended by 200 servicemen and their retainers. However, the Noghai then continued deep into Muscovite territory, where they found themselves trapped behind the Muscovite lines and out of the action. The Noghai unit was too small to make an impact, yet it was unable to loot since the Tatars had no means to remove either captives or cattle as long as the road back home was blocked.

Then more substantial Tatar units crossed the Oka in two places. The left arm division failed to hold them, being too few in numbers. The right arm division, too, was too small to hold the Tatars. By the end of the day, major elements of the Tatar army were on the road from Serpukhov to Moscow.

However, the remaining Muscovite forces regrouped around Vorotynskiy at the village of Molodi. By the end of the day, the main Tatar army found itself hemmed in between Moscow to the north and Vorotynskiy's army to the south.

On 29 July, Tereberdey-murza and his Noghai cavalry reunited with the main Crimean army. They attacked the Muscovite cavalry; however, the latter feigned a retreat, drawing the Tatars into the line of fire of the *gulyaygorod*, which had moved near Molodi. This repulsed the Tatars.

On 30 July, the Crimean army attacked the *gulyaygorod*, in the hope of breaking through. However, the *gulyaygorod* withstood the attack, as Muscovite units carried out repeated counterattacks from the flanks. Staden acknowledged the vital importance of the *gulyaygorod* in this kind of warfare: "If the Russians had not had their moving town the Crimean Tsar would have defeated us, would have captured us all, and would have led us bound to the Crimea, and the land of Russia would have become his."[92]

However, the Muscovites, too, had suffered serious losses. Not only had the left and right arm divisions lost men when they were previously overrun by the Tatars, the supply train had been lost, too. Moreover, the Muscovites were being besieged within their *gulyaygorod*. The Tatars had cut them off

---

90   Cited in Wipper, *Ivan Grozny*, p.155.
91   On the campaign, see Penskoy, *Srazheniye pri Molodyakh*; Andreyev, *Neizvestnoye Borodino*.
92   Cited in Wipper, *Ivan Grozny*, p.155.

from the nearby river, and the Muscovites were out of water. Their horses in particular were suffering, and many had to be killed.

If the siege had continued, it is likely that the Crimean Tatars would have prevailed. However, Prince Yuriy Tokmakov, away from the area of operations, sent a letter to Vorotynskiy with the forged news that the Tsar's vassal Prince Magnus, the Danish King of Livonia, was on his way with 40,000 troops from Novgorod as reinforcements. The messenger with the letter was intercepted by Tatar scouts. Alarmed by the news, the veracity of which he had no means to verify, the Crimean Khan ordered a general attack on 2 August, to conquer before the arrival of what he believed would be fresh Muscovite reinforcements.

However, the Tatar attack failed. As the main Tatar army assaulted the *gulyaygorod* from one side, Prince Vorotynskiy led the cavalry out of the *gulyaygorod* on the other, hidden by terrain out of sight of the Tatars. Vorotynskiy himself led the cavalry into an attack on the Tatar rear, while Dmitriy Khvorostinin made a sortie with his hereditary servicemen and the German mercenary reiter cavalry, 100 pistoleers in the great division commanded by a Livonian soldier of fortune named Jürgen Farensbach (1551–1602), russified as as Yuriy Franzbek. Despite his youth, Farensbach had previously been in Swedish, French, Dutch, and Imperial military service and, following a short imprisonment in Muscovy, had gone into Muscovite service.[93] This broke the Tatar army, which dispersed in defeat, suffering huge losses. Among those lost were the son and grandson of Davlat Ghirai, Tereberdey-murza and three princes from the Caucasus, and Divai-murza, the senior commander of the Tatar army, who was captured.

The Navy

Being a Mongol successor state, Muscovy had no blue-water navy. There were river craft, and even a few merchant ships, but no dedicated war fleet as such. This caused particular problems during the Livonian War. Muscovite forces found themselves unable to blockade those port cities which they laid siege to. Tsar Ivan realised that a maritime lever was needed, so on 30 March 1570, he signed a letter of marque to a well-known Danish privateer, Carsten Rode. The Dane was commissioned to form a private navy which would operate in the Baltic on behalf of Muscovy. This resulted in the formation of a Muscovite privateering fleet in May 1570. A major facilitator of the arrangement was the Tsar's vassal Prince Magnus, who provided Danish sailors and bases in Livonia. Appointed admiral of the Muscovite fleet, Rode established a base on the Danish island of Bornholm, from which he launched attacks on Polish and Swedish shipping from June 1570 onwards. By July 1570, Rode and his men had already captured a fleet of 15 ships. However, Polish and Swedish privateers began to take action against Rode's fleet. In response, a Danish squadron moved in to support Rode, which in turn attracted a Swedish fleet to the area. As the Danes withdrew, the Swedish fleet defeated

---

93 *Svenskt biografiskt lexikon* (s.v. Farensbach (von), släkt).

and scattered Rode's ships. In September 1570, Denmark was forced by the Commonwealth and Sweden to withdraw its support to the Muscovite fleet. Rode himself was detained in Denmark. As a result, the remnants of the Muscovite fleet disbanded in November 1570.[94]

Information Warfare

Due to its isolation from Western Europe and close links to the steppe, West European observers commonly regarded Muscovy as an exotic and, indeed, oriental country. To some extent this was correct; as has been demonstrated, Muscovy emerged from the Golden Horde and derived many of its customs from those of the Eurasian steppe. However, this view of Muscovy also resulted from the depiction of the country presented in an influential book, *Notes on the Muscovites* by Sigismund von Herberstein (1486–1566), a Habsburg Imperial ambassador who was sent to Moscow in 1517 and 1526. His book, probably completed in 1527, was published in 1549.[95] Herberstein described many Muscovite customs in detail, but he also drew a number of conclusions, chief among them that Muscovy was ruled by an absolute despot and tyrant who possessed complete control over all institutions and all property in his realm, that all his subjects were slaves, and that they worshiped their ruler as they would God. Because of the very richness of detail in Herberstein's work, it became the seminal text on Muscovy in any West European language. Many later observers, including those who actually visited Muscovy, for this reason came to depend heavily on Herberstein well into the seventeenth century.[96]

There were also two other reasons for the persistence of Herberstein's conclusions. First, the emergence and growing influence of the printing press, in particular in the form of news pamphlets which during the first half of the sixteenth century grew increasingly prevalent in Europe as a source of information and greatly influenced the views of most readers. Second, the Livonian War, during which the printing of news pamphlets in German became an important element of warfare, in what rightly could be termed an early form of mass media-based information warfare.

Beginning in 1561, pamphlets that presented news from Livonia that were part propaganda, part fact, began to circulate widely in Europe. The pamphlets were strongly anti-Muscovite in character and informed the public of the shocking abuses committed against the Christians in Livonia by the tyrant of Muscovy and his cruel minions. The message was reinforced through the inclusion of graphic woodcuts that depicted the torture and killing of men, women, and children, and the abuse of Christian virgins by

---

94   Radosław Gaziński, 'Die Kaperflotte von Iwan IV. dem schrecklichen im Lichte von Akten des Herzoglich Stettiner Archivs', *Studia Maritima* 26 (2013), pp.29–38; Chernov, *Vooruzhennye sily*, ch. 2; Stevens, *Russia's Wars of Emergence*, p.90.

95   Sigismund von Herberstein, *Rerum moscoviticarum commentarii* (Vienna: Egydius Aquila, 1549).

96   Marshall Poe, 'Herberstein and Origin of the European Image of Muscovite Government', Frank Kämpfer (ed.), *450 Jahre Sigismund von Herbersteins Rerum Moscoviticarum Commentarii: 1549-1999* (Wiesbaden: Harrassowitz, 2002).

bestial Muscovites. The pamphlets warned that Muscovy aimed for nothing less than the total destruction of Livonia and all of Christendom, or so at least was the understanding of the news pamphlet writers.

The image of beastly Muscovites in blind obedience to their absolutist tyrant Ivan fit well into the interpretation of Muscovy presented in Herberstein's work, which henceforth was frequently reprinted and referenced by observers of Muscovite affairs. In short, the analysis presented by Herberstein, reinforced by gruesome details from the news pamphlets, henceforth was assimilated into the common knowledge among educated Europeans and thus greatly influenced the common view of Muscovy and its rulers and inhabitants. From the 1570s, Polish propaganda appeared too, following in the same pattern as the German news pamphlets.

In 1576, Stephen Báthory (1533–1586), a Hungarian noble, became the elected king of Poland and Grand Duke of Lithuania. When he took command of the Commonwealth forces, the character of the war changed. Báthory was energetic and brought innovations, including a field printing press, which he used to print propaganda pamphlets about his victories, or claimed victories. But the propaganda went further than this. Pamphlets were also produced that purported to prove that Muscovites were uncivilised barbarians who opposed good Catholics, and that they sold Christians into slavery among the Tatars. The propaganda emphasised that the Muscovites were far closer to Turks and other Asians than to good Christian Europeans. The propaganda pamphlets might also quote the Bible so as to prove how dangerous the Muscovites were, and what a considerable threat they presented to the Christian world. Tsar Ivan's excesses among his own people, which were real enough, provided plenty of inspiration for invented acts of cruelty, in particular against innocent women and children. The gruesome stories about barbarous Muscovites were added to by those with personal experiences from Muscovy but reasons to embellish reality. The latter included men such as Albert Schlichting, a German in Polish service who fell into Muscovite captivity; Heinrich von Staden, a mercenary who joined the *oprichnina* but later defected for service with Moscow's adversaries; Johann Taube and Elbert Kruse, two German Livonians who when captured joined the *oprichnina*, then escaped to Poland in 1571 where they wrote an angry indictment of Tsar Ivan; Jacob Ulfeldt (d. 1593), a Danish diplomat who visited Muscovy in 1575 and 1578; Paul Oderborn (d. 1604), a German priest who served in Riga after the death of Ivan; and Petrus Petreius (Peder Pedersson, c.1570–1622), a Swede who was in Muscovy during the years 1601–1605 and then returned, as a diplomat, in 1607–1608 and 1609–1614. The Livonian War was devastating and caused much suffering, but in comparison to wars elsewhere at the time, there is no reason to believe that the Livonians' situation was much worse than that of other lost causes. However, the image of Christian, defenceless Livonia being ravished by

Asiatic and heathen Muscovy was a powerful one, and this image came to persist in depictions of Russia in subsequent centuries.[97]

However, the image also came to play a political role. In 1570, Pope Pius V planned to send a representative to Moscow to bring about a reconciliation between Moscow and Poland. However, Polish King Sigismund II Augustus (1520–1572; r. 1548–1572) opposed the plan, since he did not want any further co-operation between Moscow and the Papal Curia. He accordingly instructed the aforementioned Albert Schlichting to write a treatise exposing the crimes of the Moscow tyrant, as Ivan was labeled. The King presented it to the Pope, who was greatly affected by its contents. Pope Pius accordingly dropped the plan to mediate, since he refused to enter into intercourse with those who displayed such savagery as, Schlichting had assured him, the Muscovites did.[98]

The conclusion that media was used as a form of information warfare should not be interpreted as a suggestion that all the gruesome stories were invented. As in all wars, everywhere, atrocities were common, and they were not limited to one side. The religious divide, too, served to dehumanise opponents and inflamed the passions that led to massacre and mutilation. It was a savage war, and large territories were depopulated during the conflict.

Muscovy eventually learnt the lessons on information warfare and propaganda imparted by Germans and Poles. In 1606, four pamphlets and a longer publication emerged in Narva, printed in German and Swedish. They presented Muscovy's views on current events during the Time of Troubles.[99] Henceforth, printed propaganda was a game that could be played by both sides.

The First Muscovite Military Revolution

It is often claimed, even by Russian scholars,[100] that Muscovy was late to take part in the European 'military revolution' of the fifteenth to seventeenth centuries, in which the European countries exchanged relatively small-scale, feudal, knightly military forces for much larger, professional, paid infantry-based armies that relied on gunpowder and artillery. The European states accomplished this process by finding the means to extract the resources needed to pay, train, and equip the new armies through new administrative and fiscal measures.[101] Muscovy, by implication, did not, or so it is said. However, this interpretation fails to take into account the dynamics that for centuries had ruled relations between steppe nomads and sedentary

---

97 See, e.g., Andreas Kappeler, *Ivan Groznyj im Spiegel der ausländischen Druckschriften seiner Zeit: Ein Beitrag zur Geschichte des westlichen Russlandbildes* (Bern: Herbert Lang, 1972); Filjushkin, *Ivan the Terrible*, pp.244–5.

98 Wipper, *Ivan Grozny*, p.135.

99 Margareta Attius Sohlman (ed.), *Stora oredans Ryssland: Petrus Petrejus ögonvittnesskildring från 1608* (Stockholm: Carlssons, 1997), p.51.

100 Filjushkin, *Ivan the Terrible*, p.17.

101 See, e.g., Michael Roberts, *The Military Revolution, 1560–1660* (Belfast: Queen's University of Belfast Inaugural Lecture, 1956); Michael Roberts, 'The Military Revolution, 1560–1660', Michael Roberts, *Essays in Swedish History* (London: Weidenfeld and Nicolson, 1967), pp.195–225; Geoffrey Parker, *The Military Revolution: Military Innovation and the Rise of the West, 1500–1800* (Cambridge: Cambridge University Press, 1988, 1996); David Eltis, *The Military Revolution in Sixteenth-Century Europe* (New York: Barnes & Noble, 1998).

states.[102] These were the dynamics that also ruled relations between Muscovy and Tatars, and a key achievement by the Muscovites was that they adopted modern technology, artillery and firearms, to change the steppe dynamics into their favour. For Muscovy, this was a military revolution no less important than the European one, subsequently carried out under Tsars Aleksey Mikhailovich and his son Peter. It could perhaps most properly be described as the first Muscovite military revolution.

But to see the significance of this military revolution, we must gain an understanding of what issues were important to a ruler of a steppe nomad empire, such as the Golden Horde and its successor states. Relying on his chief military advantage, the mobile horse archer, he was often militarily superior to any neighbouring sedentary state. Yet, such a ruler faced the same needs and demands as the leader of any other empire, whether sedentary and based on a bureaucracy or grown from an illiterate warrior society. The ruler needed daily supplies for his rank-and-file dependents, of everything in which they were not self-sufficient (equestrian nomads such as those on the Eurasian steppe were self-sufficient with regard to basic food products) and of luxury articles for distribution to favoured sub-chiefs and clan nobles.

The goods available to the nomad leader consisted of loot from raids as well as subsidies and trading rights received from agrarian states. The settled states in effect paid for protection, and these payments were the chief income of the nomad ruler and thereby his chief means to maintain control over his own peoples as well as, seldom mentioned in the sources from the settled states, the typically vast, often forested, hinterland of less powerful tribes that also had to serve the equestrian empire, for instance through the important fur tribute, *yasak*. The nomad imperial leader distributed the loot and the trading rights and subsidies to the local tribal leaders, who while they had lost their full autonomy, thereby received more material benefits than they could have amassed on their own. A nomad empire lasted as long as the imperial power was strong enough to retain central control. However, if the imperial system collapsed, for instance in a succession crisis, the local tribal leaders again became fully autonomous and the steppe reverted to the pre-unification situation, which is what eventually befell the Mongol Empire and the Golden Horde.[103]

Unlike a sedentary state, an equestrian nomad empire thrived not because of its ability to extract resources from the peoples that formed part of the empire (taxation), but because of the subsidies that the nomads extorted from neighbouring settled states. Fundamentally, this was the policy that the Mongol Empire and its successor, the Golden Horde, had employed against the Russian principalities. It was also the basis for the regular grand raids carried out by the Crimean Khanate against its neighbours, primarily

---

102 This issue is explored in greater detail in Michael Fredholm von Essen, *Nomad Empires and Nomad Grand Strategy: The Rise and Fall of Nomad Military Power, c.1000 BC–AD 1500* (Stockholm: Stockholm University, Asian Cultures and Modernity 9, 2005). See also Michael Fredholm von Essen, 'Gunpowder and the End of Nomad Military Power: The Military Revolution That Really Mattered', *Arquebusier* 28:5 (2005), pp.2–9.

103 Thomas J. Barfield, *The Perilous Frontier: Nomadic Empires and China, 221 BC to 1757 AD* (Oxford: Blackwell, 1992), p.8.

Muscovy and Lithuania. This strategy, sometimes referred to as the outer frontier strategy,[104] took full advantage of the nomad ability to live far beyond the borders of the sedentary state and thereby beyond its military range. The armies of the sedentary state were simply unable to reach the nomads in their core territory. It will be demonstrated that Muscovy's armies suffered from this particular difficulty as late as in 1687 and 1689, even though they then largely had been transformed into armed forces of the West European model. The strategy also took maximum advantage of the nomad mobility, that is, the ability of the nomads to make sudden raids and strikes deep into the settled state and then disappear before the soldiers of the agrarian state could react. The strategy consisted of three elements: violent raiding (what could be called a form of early state terrorism) to terrify the government of the sedentary state, a repeated alternation of war and peace to maximise the number of subsidies and trade privileges granted by the sedentaries, and a deliberate refusal to occupy the territory of the settled state even after major victories.

The outer frontier strategy relied on two assumptions: first, that the government of the sedentary state feared that disruptions along the border with the nomads might lead to the unraveling of the settled state and the overthrow of its ruling dynasty, second, that the central government would rebuild and resettle the devastated frontier areas so that they could be looted again. Another important factor was that warfare was far more expensive and disruptive for the agriculturalists than for the nomads.

Every raid was followed by nomad envoys who suggested that the raids could be stopped if the government of the sedentary state agreed to a new, and to the nomads more favourable, peace treaty. The nomads needed subsidies as well as trade in the form of border markets (where pastoral surpluses could be exchanged for manufactured goods such as cloth and metal or food products such as grain and wine). If the agrarian state agreed and subsidies and border markets were provided, relations between the two empires usually did stabilise, at least until the nomad empire needed increased subsidies, or until a new regime among the agriculturalists thought it could get away with not paying the nomads – a not unheard of phenomenon. With regard to the Crimean Khanate, there was an optional boon to be gained. Muscovy and Lithuania were rivals, so each had an interest in the Tatars raiding the other. The Crimean Khan could accordingly play the two off against each other, increasing his demands until he reached the level when either Muscovy or Lithuania chose to, or could not, pay any more. In effect the Crimean Khan auctioned off his ability to raid, by eventually going to war against the one who paid the least for protection in money, furs, and goods.[105]

This pattern of nomad-sedentary relations was intriguingly similar wherever such relations occurred, whether in the West, for instance, vis-à-vis the Roman and Byzantine empires, Lithuania, and Muscovy, or in the East, in relation to China.

---

104 *Ibid.*, pp.49–51, 63; Fredholm von Essen, *Nomad Empires and Nomad Grand Strategy*.
105 Cotossichin, *Beskrifning*, p.64.

The key to the relationship was the nomad military superiority over the sedentary state, due to its focus on highly mobile horse archers. If attacked by the armies of the settled state, the nomads typically retreated across the steppe. This made it difficult and expensive for the soldiers of the agriculturalists to follow them. It was not unusual for the nomads to attack and wipe out the exhausted enemy columns when they were on their way home and lacked supplies and water. The outer frontier strategy enabled the nomads to exploit the sedentary state despite the fact that they were considerably fewer than the soldiers of the latter and without losing their mobility, the chief weapon of the nomads.[106] Although nomads could mobilise a larger part of their population for military duty, nominally indeed the entire adult male population if the women and children managed the cattle and took over the work normally done by their menfolk,[107] nomad populations were because of their need for large areas for pasturage much smaller than the corresponding agrarian ones.

However, by the sixteenth century, powerful, sedentary states such as the Ottomans in the Middle East, the Safavids in Persia, the Moghuls in India, and Muscovy under Ivan IV found technology that enabled them to neutralise the common threat in the form of the nomad horse archer. By this time, mounted archers formed the main part of the military forces of the Crimean Tatars, the Uzbek Shaibanids, and the various Turco-Mongol nomad tribes. In addition, horse archers were ubiquitous throughout the region, and not only among nomads. To counter the threat from the mounted archer, the large sedentary powers for military purposes began to rely on the new gunpowder technology. For this reason, these states have become known as gunpowder empires.[108] Their chief weapons were firearms and artillery. The nomads could, and did, adopt the former in the shape of personal weapons but not the latter. They understood the importance of heavy firearms and artillery, but its adoption would have caused them to lose their traditional mobility.[109] They also did not have the manufacturing

---

106 Barfield, *Perilous Frontier*, pp.49–51.

107 A not uncommon situation in nomad society. A Mongol wife was even expected to perform her husband's duties in forced labour while he was on campaign. 'Ala-ad-Din' Ata-Malik Juvaini, *Genghis Khan: The History of the World Conqueror* (Seattle: University of Washington Press, 1997; tr. from the text of Mizra Muhammad Qazvini by John Andrew Boyle) 1.22, pp.30–31.

108 The term gunpowder empire was first used by the historians Marshall G.S. Hodgson and William H. McNeill, who applied it to the large 16th- and 17th-century Muslim states of the Ottomans, Safavids, and Moghuls. Marshall G.S. Hodgson, *The Venture of Islam-Conscience and History in a World Civilization 3: The Gunpowder Empires and Modern Times* (Chicago: University of Chicago Press, 1974 (published posthumously)). To the gunpowder empires are also usually counted the Muscovite empire as well as (to some extent) Ming China and (following the first Western contacts) Japan. The Portuguese and Spanish overseas empires are also typically included in this group – but not the European possessions of Portugal and Spain, or indeed any other European state. William H. McNeill, *The Pursuit of Power: Technology, Armed Force, and Society Since AD 1000* (Chicago: University of Chicago Press, 1984), pp.95–99.

109 See, e.g., Jeremy Black, *The Cambridge Illustrated Atlas of Warfare: Renaissance to Revolution 1492-1792* (Cambridge: Cambridge University Press, 1996), pp.10–11; Jeremy Black (ed.), *War in the Early Modern World: 1450-1815* (Boulder: Westview, 1999), pp.4–6; Jeremy Black, *War and the World: Military Power and the Fate of Continents* (New Haven: Yale University Press, 1998), pp.30–32.

facilities, or skills, to make firearms, nor was it possible permanently to set up such facilities within the fluid lifestyle of the nomad world.

The use of gunpowder and cannon tended to centralise political and military power, since these weapons gave a strong advantage to a central power with large resources, as compared to smaller powers with less resources. The reason was that large resources and a certain level of technological proficiency were needed to produce the new weapons in sufficient number for them to make a decisive impact on the field of battle.

The early gunpowder empires have often been dealt with unkindly by modern historians. Some, especially those with a special interest in Islam, claim that they all emerged from the preceding Mongol world empire and "two centuries of decline and cultural turmoil" under pastoralist occupation and the "heavy adverse impact" of the influence of steppe institutions on the Islamic (and, incidentally, Russian-speaking) world. They, together with many Russian scholars, tend to see their favourite subjects as having been firmly under the 'Tatar yoke'.[110] Others have claimed that the Asian gunpowder empires, unlike the European countries, saw no advantage in developing fortifications and new weapons to counter the use of artillery, and that they on the contrary regarded any new inventions or devices that might make existing artillery pieces obsolete as potentially dangerous to those in power.[111] The failure of the Asian gunpowder empires to adopt European volley tactics as early as the European powers is often seen, by these historians, as an example of the lack of innovation displayed by them. The Muscovites, for sure, were slow in adopting volley tactics. However, it should be noted that even West European soldiers occasionally remained unconvinced of the supposedly great value of firing in volleys. The experienced soldier Maurice de Saxe, in his *Mes rêveries*, written in 1732, criticised a reliance on volley fire alone and instead advocated a combination of firepower and shock. "I have seen entire salvos fail to kill four men. And I have never seen, and neither has anyone else, I believe, a single discharge do enough violence to keep the troops from continuing forward and avenging themselves with bayonet and shot at close quarters. It is then that men are killed, and it is the victorious who do the killing." Saxe also made it clear that he preferred individually aimed fire to volleys: "The present practice is worthless because it is impossible for the soldier to aim while his attention is distracted awaiting the command. How can all these soldiers who have been commanded to get ready to fire continue to aim until they receive the word to fire?"[112]

The negative, and fundamentally Eurocentric, views on the capabilities of the Asian gunpowder empires are hard to reconcile with the available facts. By the second half of the sixteenth century, the European powers

---

110 Edmund Burke III, 'Introduction: Marshall G. S. Hodgson and World History', Marshall G.S. Hodgson, *Rethinking World History: Essays on Europe, Islam, and World History* (Cambridge: Cambridge University Press, 1993 (edited by Edmund Burke III)), pp.ix–xxi, on pp.xvii–xviii. On the alleged 'Tatar yoke', see, e.g., Halperin, *Russia and the Golden Horde*, p.7.

111 McNeill, *Pursuit of Power*, pp.95–99.

112 Maurice de Saxe, 'My Reveries upon the Art of War', Thomas R. Phillips, *Roots of Strategy* (Harrisburg, Pennsylvania: Stackpole, 1985), pp.177–300, on pp.206, 218.

gained oceanic predominance and made great advances in the Americas. Yet, the Europeans made only a limited and fundamentally coastal impact in Asia, and for that matter, Africa. While certain European powers expanded greatly in the seventeenth century, so did several non-European ones, such as the Manchus.[113] The reasons for decisions on armament taken in an Asian gunpowder empire accordingly must be sought there, not in Western Europe. The employment of volley tactics made excellent sense in Western Europe, where most armies consisted of fundamentally the same troop types, lined up one against another. European armies therefore gradually began to emphasise massed, close-range firepower through drill and discipline. By thus exposing their ranks to incoming fire, they ran the risk of suffering high casualties, but their concentrated firepower also enabled them to inflict casualties just as high. In much of the rest of the world, however, the tactical situation and the hostile troop types encountered by the early gunpowder empires were quite different. In Inner Eurasia, for instance, the key enemies of Ottomans, Muscovites, Safavids, Moghuls, and Chinese alike were equestrian nomads, not infantry armies. The nomads fielded dispersed groups of mounted archers, not dense masses of infantry. Even when most enemies were not nomads fresh out of the steppe, such as was the case for the Moghuls, they still had to deal with enemies who primarily fielded good quality cavalry of the type used by nomads.[114] Against such targets, individual muskets were important, but heavy firearms and artillery, as will be shown, even more so. The rapid introduction of gunpowder weapons among the sedentary, Asian empires (beside the obvious utility of the new weapons technology against other settled empires) are probably most easily explained by the fact that these weapons worked as intended – against nomad horse archers. In particular the Safavids and Muscovites, shortly afterwards followed by the Manchu Ch'ing dynasty, soon realised that in heavy firearms and cannon, they had finally found a tactical means to negate the traditional military advantages, mobility and firepower, enjoyed by the Inner Eurasian equestrian nomads. The fact that conditions were different from those in Europe also explains why the tactical solutions adopted by these empires were not necessarily identical to those in Europe, yet were tailored to the threats encountered by them. For instance, for reasons that will be explained, the Asian gunpowder empires – for good reason – emphasised the use of heavier firearms than what was preferred in Europe. For the same reason, the Muscovite army continued to rely on a wagenburg for protection and even upgraded it into the *gulyaygorod* which included cannons and arquebusiers. Such means proved effective against Tatar cavalry as late as in the aforementioned Muscovite victory at Molodi in 1572, in which Prince Mikhail Vorotynskiy defeated the Tatar army in a hard-fought battle.

The Asian gunpowder empires also diverged from the military-technological developments in Europe in that they did not introduce dense

---

113 See, e.g., Black, *War and the World*, pp.32–33, 60–61, 94–5; Michael Fredholm von Essen, *Eight Banners and Green Flag: The Army of the Manchu Empire and Qing China, 1600–1850* (Farnham, Surrey: Pike and Shot Society, 2009).

114 Jos Gommans, 'Warhorse and Gunpowder in India c.1000–1850', Jeremy Black (ed.), *War in the Early Modern World: 1450–1815* (Boulder: Westview, 1999), pp.105–27.

formations of infantry armed with long pikes. This did not happen even when European instructors trained their armies, such as under the Safavid ruler, Shah Abbas (1571–1629; r. 1588–1629).[115] Nor did Ivan IV deploy pike-armed infantry on the southern border. Yet, in Europe, it was arguably the pike, not the handgun, that was regarded as the decisive weapon when infantry had to face a cavalry charge.[116] Since heavy cavalry remained militarily very important in all Asian gunpowder empires, why did they not follow this development? Some might argue that there were social factors that made certain rulers of the gunpowder empires reluctant to introduce professional bodies of trained infantry (although such forces were in fact introduced, in particular by the Ottomans and Muscovites). However, the key reason would seem to be that a dense formation of infantry armed with pikes, however useful it might be in the face of a heavy cavalry charge, was the *least* viable formation when confronted by nomad horse archers. The nomad firepower would in time disrupt and annihilate any such force of enemy infantry, and the nomad mobility would ensure that the mounted archers could do this without suffering significant losses. This would be the key reason why such formations were never introduced in the military forces of the gunpowder empires. The only exception was Muscovy, which late in its development introduced a limited number of pike formations, but only for warfare against European enemies, as we have seen.

Before the introduction of firearms, most sedentary soldiers had nothing but ordinary bows or weak Chinese-style crossbows with which to confront nomad firepower. These weapons had not made a great impression on the nomads. What had scared the nomads, however, was the very occasional use of siege engines against them. Although the mobility of the nomads made them difficult to hit when they were aware of the danger, the use of long-range artillery was an efficient means to deny the nomads the use of their own capacity to inflict casualties, unless the nomads were prepared to accept heavy casualties of their own.

Even crude artillery had an effective range (in penetrative power if not accuracy) that far outranged the bow of the mounted archer. So did handheld gunpowder weapons. Ivan III took advantage of this characteristic of firearms when he confronted the Great Horde in 1480 on the River Ugra: "Our forces, using arrows and arquebuses, killed many Tatars; their arrows were falling among our forces but did not hurt anyone. They pushed the Tatars away from the river."[117] What Ivan experienced in 1480 corresponds to the very similar stories of two later eyewitnesses whose experiences may be helpful in answering the question of how the range and firepower of gunpowder weapons compared with those of the nomad bow.

In 1558, an English merchant named Anthony Jenkinson (d. 1611) on his way from Moscow to Bukhara, travelling with a caravan consisting of some 40 men, was attacked by a group of 37 Uzbek brigands, "well armed,

---

115 See, e.g., George Gush, *Renaissance Armies 1480–1650* (Cambridge: Patrick Stephens, 1975), p.92.
116 See, e.g., Eltis, *Military Revolution*, pp.45–7.
117 Dmytryshyn, *Medieval Russia*, 192. Spelling slightly amended.

and appointed with bows, arrows and swords." The brigands ordered the merchants to stand and deliver, but as Jenkinson related:

> we defied them, wherewith they shot at us all at once, and we at them very hotly, and so continued our fight from morning until two hours within night, divers men, horses and camels being wounded and slain on both parts: and had it not been for 4 hand guns which I and my company had and used, we had been overcome and destroyed: for the thieves were better armed, and were also better archers than we; but after we had slain divers of their men and horses with our guns, they durst not approach so nigh, which caused them to come to a truce with us[118]

In the early 1630s, the French traveller Guillaume Le Vasseur de Beauplan travelled across the Ukrainian steppe. There he was attacked by Crimean Tatars. Beauplan reported that the Tatars could shoot accurately to 60 or 100 paces (by which he most likely meant about 50 to 90 metres). He also made the following observation:

> I have encountered them many times in the country to the number of a good five hundred Tartars who wished to attack us in our tabor [wagenburg] and even though I was accompanied by only fifty or sixty Cossacks they could do nothing to us nor could we best them because they would not approach within the range of our weapons; but after making numerous feints to attack us and trouble us with clouds of arrows on the head because they shot in arcade easily at twice the range of our weapons, they retired[119]

Shooting in arcade is to shoot at a steep angle, of about 45 degrees, to extend the range as far as possible. The result is that the arrows drop almost vertically on the target, as indeed Beauplan makes clear. Such shooting is of course very inaccurate; however, a massed enemy of the type the horse archers often confronted was very vulnerable to such archery.

A sixteenth-century Arabic treatise on archery confirms the range of archery mentioned by Beauplan, pointing out that the extreme range for accurate fire is 45 bow lengths, or about 75 metres. However, the text continues, the range for effective (in penetrative power) although frequently inaccurate fire is more than twice this, or more than 150 metres.[120] This may explain why the Muscovites at River Ugra remarked that the Tatar arrows were falling among them but did not hurt anyone.

118 Richard Hakluyt (ed.), *Voyages and Discoveries: The Principal Navigations, Voyages, Traffiques and Discoveries of the English Nation* (Harmondsworth, Middlesex: Penguin, 1985), pp.83–4.

119 Cited and partly translated in Erik Hildinger, *Warriors of the Steppe: A Military History of Central Asia, 500 B.C. to 1700 A.D.* (New York: Sarpedon, 1997). French original: Guillaume Le Vasseur, sieur de Beauplan, *La description d'Ukranie de Guillaume Le Vasseur de Beauplan* (Ottawa: Les Presses de l'Université d'Ottawa, 1990). Edited by Dennis F. Essar and Andrew B. Pernal.

120 *Arab Archery: An Arabic Manuscript of About A.D. 1500: A Book on the Excellence of the Bow and Arrow and the Description Thereof* (Princeton: Princeton University Press, 1945). Translated and edited by N.A. Faris and R.P. Elmer.

The bows used by nomads and soldiers of settled states in Inner Eurasia were not that different from one another. In other words, it was not the missile power of the nomad bow that led to the many centuries of nomad victories, but the nomad mobility. This characteristic of the Muscovite cavalry was one key reason why the knights of the Livonian Order stayed in their castles when Muscovite troops carried out their grand raids in the early years of the Livonian War. The nomads were able to harass the infantry of the settled states until it lost morale, cohesion, and thus became vulnerable to a traditional cavalry charge. Yet more important, the nomads could do this to their enemy without suffering excessive losses themselves. On the strategic level, the mobility of the nomads was of course even more decisive, since they could then outmanoeuvre slower-moving enemies, hit them where they were weak, and avoid contact when the tactical situation was disadvantageous.

But with the introduction of heavy firearms and artillery, the nomads became vulnerable to the weapons of the settled states. The nomads no longer held a decisive edge in tactics. This was obvious to contemporary and near-contemporary observers. Edward Gibbon (1737–1794), writing in the 1770s, concluded: "The military art has been changed by the invention of gunpowder … Cannon and fortifications now form an impregnable barrier against the Tartar horse; and Europe is secure from any future irruption of Barbarians; since, before they can conquer, they must cease to be barbarous."[121] In other words, for a nomad ruler to make himself master of a settled state, the new strategic context demanded that he took the decision to cease being a nomad. The nomad military system had reached a dead end. The nomads retained superior mobility, but they had lost their offensive capability in the form of firepower that was at least no worse, and often far superior, to that of non-nomad pre-gunpowder armies. The new armament in the form of gunpowder weapons, and in particular heavy muskets and artillery, had a sufficiently long effective range that the nomad cavalry no longer could count on defeating the soldiers of the settled state without themselves suffering major casualties. However, the nomads could not absorb such losses, since their total manpower invariably was far below that of the agrarian states. The agriculture of a settled state supported a larger population and thus possessed the resources for armed forces far more numerous than the nomads could hope to raise. It was thus not the mere introduction of new weaponry that changed the strategic situation. The prowess of the individual horse archer remained as high as in the past, and the rate of fire, accuracy, and penetration of the nomad bow did not compare badly with the early firearms. However, the aggregate firepower of close-order formations armed with sufficient numbers of heavy firearms did make a difference. The individual nomad remained as good, if not better, a fighter than the individual non-nomad soldier, but in time even the personal musket acquired the range of heavier firearms and developed into a far more powerful weapon than the nomad bow. That the individual nomad remained as able as his settled adversary

---

121 Edward Gibbon, *The History of the Decline and Fall of the Roman Empire* 4 (London: Methuen & Co., 1898), pp.166, 167. Edited by J.B. Bury.

was then simply not good enough, even if the nomad traded in his bow for a new weapon. The old nomad strategies thus gradually lost their former utility, as the military and technological development relegated the nomads to the place of have-beens.

In the west, the Muscovites, Safavids, and their successors were finally able to defeat and, in Muscovy's case, even conquer the nomads, although this shift in the balance of power depended more on demography than weapons technology. Colonisation in time caused the settlers to greatly outnumber the nomads even in the latter's traditional steppe habitats.[122] The new gunpowder technology meant that henceforth, the nomads could only – without excessive risk – attack and loot mere caravans, such as the ones in which Jenkinson and Beauplan travelled. That the introduction of firearms was a decisive military-technological factor is also indicated by the fact that the steppe nomads were able to unite even then, under for instance Altan Khan who raided beneath the walls of Peking in 1550, in fact raided China almost every year for decades, and ambushed and defeated a Chinese army in 1552, but even so failed to achieve their old military and political superiority vis-à-vis their settled neighbours.[123] Meanwhile, also in 1552, the Muscovite Tsar, as noted, conquered the Mongol successor state of Kazan', reportedly with the help of 150 heavy cannon and mortars as well as many field guns.[124] Soon Muscovite settlers moved east to consolidate the conquest and incorporate it into the Muscovite empire by the construction of a series of forts to impede nomad mobility.[125] The age of nomad empires had passed, never to return. But Muscovy, the successor state to the Golden Horde that had combined the traditional equestrian military system of the horde with the new technical innovations of a gunpowder empire, rose in their stead.

Dress and Appearance

What did the Muscovite soldiers look like? For this we have to consult contemporary descriptions. Turberville gave his impression of the Muscovites in a letter in verse, written in 1568 or 1569. Turberville's not very positive descriptions nonetheless give a fair picture of the Muscovites of his time:

> The Russian men are round of bodies, fully fac'd,
> The greatest part with bellies big that overhang the waist,
> Flat-headed for the most, with faces nothing fair,
> But brown, by reason of the stove, and closeness of the air.
> It is their common use to shave or else to shear
> Their heads. For none in all the land long lolling locks doth wear

---

122 See, e.g., Ira M. Lapidus, *A History of Islamic Societies* (Cambridge: Cambridge University Press, 1988), pp. 420–23.

123 Frederick W. Mote and Denis Twitchett (eds.), *The Cambridge History of China* 7, Part 1: *The Ming Dynasty, 1368–1644* (Cambridge: Cambridge University Press, 1988), pp.476–9.

124 According to Prince Andrei Kurbskiy, who was there, but writing some 20 years after the event. Fennell, *Kurbsky's History*, p.41.

125 See, e.g., Forsyth, *History of the Peoples of Siberia*, pp.29–30.

...

Their garments be not gay nor handsome to the eye:
A cap aloft their heads they have that standeth very high,
Which *kolpak* [high pointed hat] they do term. They wear no ruffs at all.
The best have collars set with pearl, *rubashka* [shirt] they do call
Their shirts in Russia long, they work them down before,
And on the sleeves with coloured silks, two inches good or more.
Aloft their shirts they wear a garment jacketwise
Hight *odnoryadka* [long tunic without collar]; and about his burly waist he ties
His *portki* [pants], which instead of better breeches be;
Of linen cloth that garment is, no codpiece is to see.
A pair of yarnen socks, to keep the cold away,
Within his boots the Russian wears, the heels they underlay
With clouting clamps of steel, sharp pointed at the toes.
And over all a *shuba* [fur coat] furred, and thus the Russian goes.
Well button'd is the *shuba*, according to his state;
Some silk, of silver other some, but those of poorest rate
Do wear no shuba at all, but grosser gowns to sight
That reacheth down beneath the calf, and that *armyak* [cloth tunic] hight—[126]

The Muscovite state awarded valuable objects (furs, cloth, precious metals, and so on) in recognition of success, in particular to commanders. But Moscow also awarded medals. Fletcher describes them as "a piece of gold stamped with the image of St. George on horseback, which they hang on their sleeves and set in their caps."[127] In reality, this was a golden kopek coin, which the recipient commonly would display fastened to his hat.

---

126 George Turberville, *Letter* (1589), in Berry and Crummey, *Rude & Barbarous Kingdom*, p.81. Spelling slightly amended.
127 Giles Fletcher, *Of the Russian Commonwealth* (1591), in Berry and Crummey, *Rude & Barbarous Kingdom*, p.186.

Plates by Maksim Borisov
Plate 1

The Southern Front: Voivode; Tatar Cavalryman

(Illustration by Maksim Borisov, © Helion & Company)

See Colour Plate Commentaries for further information.

Plate 2

Expansion to the East: Cossack; Noble Officer; Infantryman

(Illustration by Maksim Borisov, © Helion & Company)

See Colour Plate Commentaries for further information.

Plate 3

**Garrison Duty, Mid to Late Seventeenth Century:
Artilleryman; Dragoon; Strelets**

(Illustration by Maksim Borisov, © Helion & Company)

See Colour Plate Commentaries for further information.

Plate 4

**The Western Front, Mid to Late Seventeenth Century:
New Formation Musketeer; Reiter; New Formation Pikeman**

(Illustration by Maksim Borisov, © Helion & Company)

See Colour Plate Commentaries for further information.

Plate 5

The Eastern Front: Kalmyk Cavalryman; Ostyak or Vogul Auxiliary

(Illustration by Maksim Borisov, © Helion & Company)

See Colour Plate Commentaries for further information.

Plate 6

Eastern and Western Influences: Circassian Noble Cavalryman; Hussar

(Illustration by Maksim Borisov, © Helion & Company)

See Colour Plate Commentaries for further information.

Flags – Graphic Reconstructions by Lesley Prince

Infantry company flag, 1679. This flag belonged to the fourth company of Colonel Yakov Gavrilov syn Lovzyn's new formation regiment, raised near the border with Swedish Estonia. The flag, of a type and design common for infantry company flags, was made of red cloth of taffeta with sewn-on or painted ornaments, on black Chinese silk, and measured 153 cm in breadth and length. The four stars on the field corresponded to the company's number.

Infantry company flag, 1679. This flag belonged to the first company of Colonel Yakov Gavrilov syn Lovzyn's new formation regiment. Like many Muscovite banners, its chief component was the six-armed Orthodox cross. However, since this was the Colonel's own company, it did not include any star to signify a company number and also had a different base colour. The Colonel's company flag should not be mistaken for the regimental colour, which typically was larger and yet more elaborate, with biblical scenes, the image of Christ, the Virgin and the Holy Child, a saint such as the Archangel Michael, or even a multitude of saints with their hands extended in prayer.

Reiter company standard, 1665. This standard belonged to the fourth company of one of the two reiter regiments raised for service in the Belgorod division, which formed the main military force of the Belgorod regional military command on the southern frontier. Reiter standards were square but, unlike dragoon guidons, had no swallow-tails. Reiter standards were the smallest of the Muscovite banners, up to no more than about a metre in breadth and length. The number of stars again signified the company number.

Streltsy infantry regimental colour, based on Colonel Peter Abramovich Lopukhin's Moscow streltsy regiment, 1674. A traditional streltsy regimental colour fundamentally consisted of a simple cross, set within a frame consisting of one, two, or at most, three colours. In 1680, however, the streltsy were reorganised into Western-style regiments, during which they also received a new type of banner, with religious motifs and similar to those used by new formation regiments. Note that when Palmquist depicted this regimental colour, he painted the cross not white but pink, which is more likely to be correct. The frame, too, was slightly different in Palmquist's depiction, although the chosen colours were the same.

Streltsy infantry regimental colour of Colonel Davyd Grigor'yevich Vorontsov's Moscow streltsy regiment, 1674. As depicted by Palmquist, this colour too reflects the traditional, quite simple pattern of streltsy regimental colours.

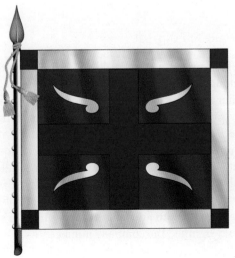

Streltsy infantry regimental colour based on Colonel Lagovskin's Moscow streltsy regiment, 1674. Even the traditional, simple cross pattern of traditional streltsy regimental colours might include minor embellishments of which this a typical example. Note that when Palmquist depicted this regimental colour, he depicted the corners of the frame a dark shade of green, not blue.

3

The New Formation Army of the Romanovs

The Romanov Dynasty

Ivan IV was succeeded by a number of weak tsars, during whose rule cossacks and others challenged Muscovite supremacy while Poles and Swedes took advantage of the situation to further their own interests. This was the Time of Troubles (*Smutnoye vremya*, or *Smuta*), the difficult period of Russian history between the death in 1598 of the last tsar of the Rurik Dynasty, Fyodor Ivanovich, and the establishment of the Romanov Dynasty in 1613. During this time, Muscovy suffered from uprisings, usurpers, anarchy, famine, the suppression of a revolt in Moscow by an invited Swedish intervention army in 1610, and the occupation of Moscow by the Polish-Lithuanian Commonwealth later in the same year. In desperation, Muscovite representatives offered the crown to Polish and Swedish princes. Indeed, Novgorod land grants from 1612 show that Swedish King Gustavus II Adolphus by then, briefly, had assumed the title of Tsar, with the support of Moscow.[1] The difficult times persisted until the young noble Michael Romanov (1596–1645, r. 1613–1645), related with Ivan IV through marriage through his paternal grandfather's sister, in 1613 became the first tsar of the Romanov dynasty as the result of a palace coup. At first too young to have an immediate and personal impact on the political situation, he and his advisors nonetheless gradually succeeded in restoring order.

By then, Muscovy's armed forces faced two organisational challenges. First, there was a need for a new, and preferably standing, military structure along West European lines, which was difficult to achieve since the old Muscovite social system was incompatible with what was needed. Second, there was a need to fund and supply the new army, despite the fact that cash taxation was insufficient (the existing system to a large extent depended

---

1   Elisabeth Löfstrand and Laila Nordquist, *Accounts of an Occupied City: Catalogue of the Novgorod Occupation Archives 1611–1617*, Vol. 2 (Stockholm: Riksarkivet, 2 vols., 2005 and 2009), p.41.

on the collection of grain in kind instead of monetary taxation) and most existing soldiers still had to make a living from land grants.

As a result, Muscovy carried out what most properly could be termed the second Muscovite military revolution, the raising, funding, and building of an army structured along West European lines but still capable of projecting power on the steppes on Muscovy's eastern and southern frontiers. This was a challenge that most other European powers did not have to meet.

Yet it was done. Work began in 1630. The result was a new military structure consisting of what was referred to as 'new formation regiments' (*polki novogo stroya*) based on West European lines. Both infantry and cavalry were raised.

The immediate reason for raising the new formation regiments was the attempt to retake Smolensk, This important town had been conquered, after a long siege, by the Polish-Lithuanian Commonwealth in 1611 during the Time of Troubles. This attempt to regain Smolensk was made during the ultimately unsuccessful Smolensk War (1632–1634), during which the old boyar Mikhail Borisovich Shein led an army which combined old-style cavalry and streltsy with the new formation regiments, in total some 35,000 men (and an unknown number of soldier bondsmen in the traditional cavalry).[2] The siege was conducted entirely along European lines; however, Moscow failed to arrange the transportation of heavy siege artillery to Smolensk until March 1633, when it was already too late. The delay was the effect of weather conditions, the lack of good roads, but also logistical and administrative mistakes. Muscovy therefore remained unable to regain Smolensk. Unlike previous campaigns, Shein's army contained plenty of European-style infantry but insufficient reliable cavalry. Surrounded by a relief force, Shein lacked the cavalry to regain freedom of manoeuvre and was unable to extricate his men. As a result, he surrendered in early 1634, an act for which he was subsequently executed.[3] The new formation regiments were disbanded after the war, when funding no longer was available to sustain them.

Religious considerations also began to play an increasingly important role in Muscovite politics. Religious feelings had always been strong, and apparently grew stronger still in the seventeenth century. Reasons were several. First, the ignominies suffered during the Time of Troubles had caused an increase in religiosity. Second, the attempts of former tsars such as Ivan IV to take control of the Church, in his case through the *oprichnina*, had failed. Ivan's activities had not prevented the high mark of Church influence, the establishment of the Moscow patriarchate in 1589, not long after Ivan's death.[4] The Orthodox Church pleaded hard for the superiority of the Orthodox faith, which translated into a high degree of xenophobia, against Catholics, Protestants, and other faiths as well. Henceforth, land grants were no longer to be given to warriors of Tatar, Mordvin, or other non-Russian background

---

2   Chernov, *Vooruzhennye sily*, ch. 5; Hellie, *Enserfment and Military Change*, pp.172, 226, 271.

3   Robert I. Frost, *The Northern Wars: War, State and Society in Northeastern Europe, 1558–1721* (Harlow, Essex: Pearson Education, 2000), pp.146–7.

4   Ostrowski, *Muscovy and the Mongols*, p.246.

who went into Muscovite service, unless they also adopted the Orthodox faith. As a result, nobles of non-Russian origin henceforth often found it convenient to downplay their family origin. Likewise, there was a reaction against foreign mercenary officers. West Europeans, too, henceforth only received land grants if they converted to the Orthodox faith.[5]

Fresh attempts to create a modern, standing army were made under Tsar Aleksey Mikhailovich (1629–1676; r. 1645–1676). Like so many other tsars, Aleksey was a young man at the time of his ascension. Although not an autocrat like many others, Tsar Aleksey quietly and carefully presided over a military and administrative overhaul of the Muscovite military system. Aleksey appointed his tutor Boris Morozov, a perceptive noble open to West European ideas, his chief advisor. This receptiveness to foreign ideas, together with personal corruption, eventually caused Morozov's downfall, due to the religious xenophobia that then characterised the Muscovite population.

16. Tsar Aleksey Mikhailovich.

Then came the devastating Thirteen Years War (1654–1667) against the Polish-Lithuanian Commonwealth. A war with Sweden took place in 1656–1661 as part of the greater conflict. A major cause for the war was the cossack uprising in the territory on the steppes north of the Black Sea known as the Ukraine, meaning 'borderland'. The territory had come under the control of first the Grand Duchy of Lithuania, then the Kingdom of Poland. In a process similar to the one that took place in the southern territories of Muscovy, a number of cossack communities emerged on the border with the Ottoman Empire and the Crimean Khanate. The Zaporozhian cossacks lived beyond the rapids of the Dnieper River, from which they took their name (*za porogi*, 'beyond the river rapids'). In the sixteenth century, the Zaporozhian cossacks established a settlement that can only be called a proto-state, known as the Sech'. However, they gradually fell under Polish rule, which they resented, in particular for religious reasons since the cossacks were Orthodox Christians and the Poles were not. As a result, in 1648 an uprising took place among the cossacks subject to the Polish-Lithuanian Commonwealth. The cossack leader, Bogdan Khmel'nitskiy (1595–1657), first sought support from the Ottoman Empire, but none came. When the uprising failed, he in 1650 instead approached Moscow for assistance. In 1654, Khmel'nitskiy signed the Treaty of Pereyaslav, in which he acknowledged the Muscovite Tsar as his suzerain. In return, Moscow recognised Khmel'nitskiy's territory, which included Kiev, Bratslav, and Chernigov, as independent but under Moscow's suzerainty.

---

5   Hellie, *Enserfment and Military Change*, p.55–6.

In 1655, a Muscovite field army consisting of both traditional forces and new formation infantry and dragoon regiments was sent in support of Khmel'nitskiy, as well as Muscovite interests in the Ukraine. The war exposed the old-style cavalry army's inability to arm, feed, and supply itself during prolonged war. The need for new formation regiments increased rapidly, and the significant losses suffered in the 1660s accelerated this process.[6] In a break with prevailing tradition, Tsar Aleksey in 1658 initiated mass conscription into the army on the basis of census rolls. Muscovy entered the war with a field army of some 40,000 troops but finished it with more than 100,000.[7] Unlike the Smolensk War, Muscovy won the Thirteen Years War, but the victory was costly. Muscovy gained the eastern parts of the Ukraine, but lost much of its best old-style cavalry through the attrition of war.[8] A significant share of the population was militarised. In the south, where military duties were heavy and population sparse, an estimated five percent of the population was enlisted in military service in one way or another.[9] Military service also required a significant share of manpower on the Western border, including in key towns such as Novgorod and Smolensk. However, the war also resulted in significant migration into Muscovy from the Ukraine. Many were settled in distinct communities as cossacks with duties to serve in the Muscovite army.

By the 1667 Truce of Andrusovo, Muscovy and the Polish-Lithuanian Commonwealth divided the Ukraine along the Dnieper River. Muscovy received left-bank Ukraine, with Smolensk and, for a period of two years, Kiev, while right-bank Ukraine remained with the Commonwealth. When the 1676–1681 Muscovite-Ottoman War ended with the Treaty of Bakhchisarai, the Ottoman Empire, too, recognised Muscovite possession of left-bank Ukraine and Kiev.

Innovations did not only take place in conscription practices. There were technological innovations as well. In 1632, a modern arms manufacturing facility was built in Tula, together with an arsenal. Until then, Moscow had produced most of its weapons. By then, or soon thereafter, the Muscovite army began to adopt the flintlock, which was a major technological improvement and previously only had been used in one-of-a-kind luxury guns for the most wealthy nobles (for instance, the flintlock revolver from about 1625 since held in the Kremlin armoury). Already in 1634, Adam Olearius noted that the streltsy assigned to guard the embassy from Holstein, to which he belonged, was armed with flintlocks.[10] Flintlocks were used on a large scale by 1637, and a large distribution of flintlock muskets was made in 1651. By the second half of the seventeenth century, only some of the streltsy retained the traditional matchlocks, and even they did so only until the 1670s. Even provincial hereditary servicemen and cossacks re-armed with flintlock

---

6   Stevens, *Soldiers on the Steppe*, pp.28–9.
7   Hellie, *Enserfment and Military Change*, pp.271–2.
8   Stevens, *Soldiers on the Steppe*, p.103.
9   *Ibid.*, p.29.
10   Adam Olearius, *The Travels of Olearius in Seventeenth-Century Russia* (Stanford: Stanford University Press, 1967; tr. by Samuel H. Baron), pp.46, 47.

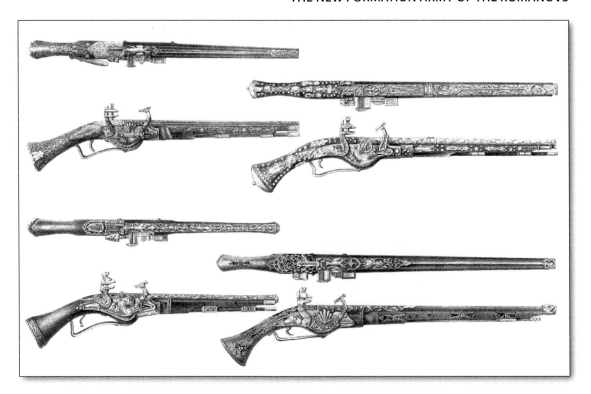

17. Muscovite pistols.
(Viskovatov, 1841)

muskets.[11] By the early 1650s, large numbers of modern firearms were also imported from Sweden, the Netherlands, England, France, and the Ottoman Empire.[12] Although chiefly used by infantry, the introduction of the flintlock also facilitated the introduction of firearms to the cavalry, in the form of flintlock carbines. The flintlock was easier for cavalrymen to use than the old matchlock and far cheaper to manufacture than the complicated wheellock.

While Muscovy succeeded in creating a new military structure along West European lines, its rulers were less successful in addressing the challenge to fund and supply the new army. Moscow continued to rely on non-cash payment of its troops through the traditional means of distribution of land grants and continued extraction and redistribution in kind. Moreover, Moscow failed to extend its provisioning system for food and supplies to its cavalry, which still was expected to provide for itself. Moscow also largely failed to create a supply system that could supply an army across the largely unpopulated territories beyond its southern border. This became clear during the failed campaigns against the Crimean Khanate in 1687 and 1689 (and the provision of supplies across unpopulated territories, incidentally, remained a significant problem for centuries after, during the subsequent expansion into the desolate wastelands of Inner Asia).

Despite these difficulties, there were significant and substantial territorial gains. Eastern Ukraine has already been mentioned. In 1681, after the death

---

11   Hellie, *Enserfment and Military Change*, pp.181, 204.
12   *Ibid.*, p.183.

of its last ruler, the Kasimov Khanate was finally, and expectedly, annexed by Muscovy, having played out its role long ago. Meanwhile, most of Siberia became Muscovite lands, including territory all the way to the Pacific and to the border of Manchu-held China.

Streltsy

In 1630, the number of Moscow streltsy had dropped to 4,000.[13] Most were used for police duties. Others were used as jail guards, or even as firemen.[14] However, the number of provincial streltsy kept growing. In 1625, there were a total of 20,539 streltsy.[15] In 1632, this number had risen to 33,775. In 1663, they were 65,000. In 1681, their total number had declined to 55,000, due to reforms and reorganisation.[16] During the construction of the Belgorod defensive line (see below), increasing numbers of streltsy were transferred south, including some Moscow-ranked units. Streltsy remained as garrison troops in several towns, including in the Ukraine, the Caucasus, and Siberia, and former streltsy were also recruited into several of the new formation infantry regiments. By the 1660s, there were 20 Moscow-ranked streltsy regiments, each of from 800 to 1,000 men.[17] Not all were based in Moscow, but they were armed and equipped much as in the past. By 1674, 14 Moscow-ranked streltsy regiments remained in Moscow, consisting of an estimated total of 14,000 men.[18] In 1681, there were 22,500 Moscow-ranked streltsy, divided into 28 regiments, but many of them were no longer stationed in Moscow.[19] Uniforms came in several colours, which can be identified from the depictions made by the Swedish intelligence officer Erik Palmquist in 1673–1674 (fig. 18) and from eyewitness reports from foreign diplomats.[20] However, as late as in the 1660s some, in particular standard bearers, continued to wear armour, often a cuirass imported from western Europe.[21]

The streltsy formed the solid backbone of the Muscovite army from the time of Ivan IV well into the seventeenth century. As noted, some of them even retained their old matchlock muskets into the 1670s. However, with the introduction of the new formation regiments in the mid-seventeenth century, the streltsy began to lose their earlier importance. In 1680, all remaining streltsy were reorganised into Western-style regiments, each led by a colonel (*polkovnik*), and companies, each led by a captain (*kapitan*), following the style of the new formation regiments.[22] The streltsy regiments also received

---

13 Chernov, *Vooruzhennye sily*, ch. 4.
14 Cotossichin, *Beskrifning*, p.96.
15 Chernov, *Vooruzhennye sily*, ch. 4.
16 Chernov, *Vooruzhennye sily*, ch. 6; Hellie, *Enserfment and Military Change*, p.202; Stevens, *Soldiers on the Steppe*, p.45 with note. The figures provided by Chernov, Hellie, and Stevens do not always exactly correspond, but the trend is clear.
17 Cotossichin, *Beskrifning*, p.95.
18 Palmquist, *Några observationer*, p.229.
19 Chernov, *Vooruzhennye sily*, ch. 6.
20 See, e.g., Birgegård, *Sparwenfeld's Diary*, pp.147, 149, 151.
21 Roberto Palacios-Fernandez, 'Moskovskiye strel'tsy', *Zeughaus* 1 (1992), pp.8–15, on p.15.
22 Hellie, *Enserfment and Military Change*, p.207; Keep, *Soldiers of the Tsar*, p.67.

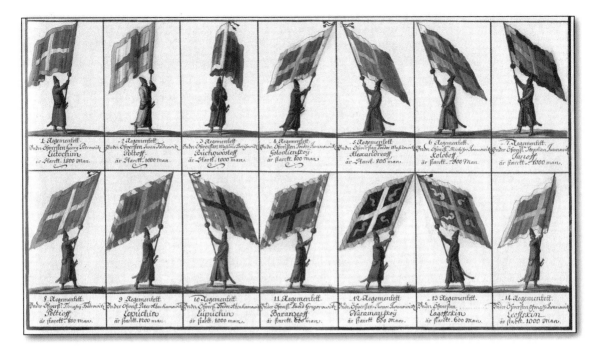

a new type of banner, with religious motifs and similar to those used by new formation regiments. These colours were 2.2–3 metres in breadth and length, and made of silk or cloth of taffeta, with sewn-on or painted ornaments. In comparison, the streltsy regimental colours from the time before the 1680s were even larger, up to 2.8–3.5 metres in breadth and length. They were generally simpler in style and with ornaments based on a cross. The colours were mounted on staves with a wooden apple immediately below the flag.[23] In addition to the unit flags, many high-ranking streltsy officers followed the tradition of sixteenth-century boyars and fielded a personal pennon (*prapor* or *praporets*). These flags were smaller than the unit colours and swallow-tailed when fielded by colonels, single-tailed when fielded by lieutenant colonels.[24]

During the 1680s' reorganisation of the streltsy into Western-style regiments, the first company of every streltsy regiment was re-armed with pikes. This weapon, still known as 'spear' (*kop'yo*) among the Muscovites, was up to three or four metres long and used on the western front only.

As the importance of the streltsy as fighting soldiers diminished, they in a manner not unlike their spiritual ancestors, the Ottoman janissaries, gradually began to meddle in dynastic power struggles in Moscow. In the last quarter of the seventeenth century, streltsy took part in a number of

18. The Moscow streltsy and their colours.
(Erik Palmquist, 1674)

23 Several streltsy colours have been preserved in the Army Museum, Stockholm. Arne Danielsson, 'Utländska fälttecken utställda i Trofékammaren', *Meddelande från Kungl. Armémuseum* XXV (Stockholm: Kungl. Armémuseum, 1964); Arne Danielsson, *Catalogue of Foreign Colours, Standards, Guidons Exhibited in the Trophy Room of the Royal Army Museum, Stockholm*. n.d.; Vladimir Velikanov, 'Salatskiye trofei': Polkovoye imushchestvo streletskikh polkov Nechayeva i Protopopova, poteryannoye v srazhenii pri Salatakh, 1703', *Zeughaus* 52 (2013): pp.3–13, on p.8.

24 Lars-Eric Höglund, Åke Sallnäs, and Alexander Bespalow, *Stora Nordiska Kriget 1700–1721* Vol. 3: *Ryssland, Sachsen, Preussen och Hannover – Fanor och uniformer* (Karlstad: Acedia Press, 2004), p.46. Several have been preserved in the Army Museum, Stockholm.

uprisings against the government. Most serious were the Moscow mutiny in 1682 and the streltsy revolt in 1698.

The streltsy mutiny of 1682 was an uprising in Moscow, at least partly caused by decreased wages. The participants in the mutiny were the Moscow streltsy, Matvey Krovkov's second selected new formation infantry regiment, and some artillery units. At first successful, the government paid the mutinying streltsy large amounts of cash, and the mutineers called off their opposition in exchange for an amnesty. Nine of the 28 Moscow streltsy regiments were disbanded, its men becoming eligible for other branches of service. As a result, the Moscow streltsy were reduced to 14,000 men in 19 regiments.

Problems were not over, however. Tsar Peter I accordingly transferred the Moscow streltsy to border guard service. Even this measure did not quieten the streltsy. Several campaigns followed, among them one against the Ottomans at Azov (formerly Tana) near the mouth of Don on the Sea of Azov, adjoined to the Black Sea. But the hardship suffered by the troops in these campaigns merely added to other reasons for discontent. In early 1698, four Moscow streltsy regiments (about 4,000 men) mutinied. The government suppressed the mutiny with much bloodshed, and disbanded the mutinying regiments. The remaining Moscow streltsy regiments were reformed, the soldiers and their families exiled from Moscow. Because of these disturbances and although streltsy also served in the subsequent Great Northern War, Tsar Peter reformed the remaining regiments of the streltsy corps in the 1720s. By this act, the last remaining vestiges of the traditional Muscovite army disappeared.

New Formation Regiments

Already during the sixteenth-century Livonian War, it had became clear that to oppose modern Polish troops, a new type of military formation was needed. What worked well against the horsemen of the khanates did not necessarily serve as well against Western troops.

The introduction in the 1630s of 'new formation regiments' (*polki novogo stroya*) or, as they were also called, 'foreign formation regiments' (*polki inozemnogo stroya*) marked the beginnings of the modern Muscovite army, organised in the West European style. The old term *polk* was retained, but for the new formation regments, it was no longer used with the old meaning of cavalry division. The new formation regiments were under the administration of a special foreign formation chancellery (*Inozemskiy prikaz*). As compared to the old land-grant system of supplying military forces, the new formations were better organised, better trained, and equipped with more modern as well as unified armament. Many contained German, Dutch, Scots, and English mercenaries, some 200 of whom were hired, and a few were accordingly called 'German' regiments. Soon, however, most men except a few officers were Muscovites, trained and armed on European lines.[25] Still, for many

---

25 Hellie, *Enserfment and Military Change*, pp.170–72.

years the old nobility scorned the new formation regiments and refused to serve in them even as officers.[26]

The introduction of new formation regiments can be divided into three phases. First, the introduction of new formation regiments in the early 1630s. Second, the introduction of what essentially was a system of nationwide conscription which began in the 1640s and can be said to have reached its completed form by 1658. Although conscription was not universal, it was then sufficiently prevalent to be regarded as general conscription. Third, and finally, the thorough reform of the Muscovite military system that took place in the period 1678–1682 and essentially completed the groundwork for subsequent military reforms along West European lines.

The 'new formation regiments' consisted of three fundamental categories of troops:

1. Infantry regiments (*soldatskiye polki*, so named after the word *soldat*, pl. *soldaty*, meaning soldier).
2. Cavalry regiments of two types:
   a. Reiter regiments (*reytarskiye polki*), styled on the German reiters and armed with pistols and carbines.
   a. Hussar regiments (*gusarskiye polki*), styled on the Polish winged hussars and armed with lances.
3. Dragoon regiments (*dragunskiye polki*), of mounted soldiers who were cheap to raise and primarily fought as mounted infantry, although a limited few were lancers inspired by the Polish winged hussars.

Infantry

The first new formation regiments consisted of infantry. By late 1631, two new formation infantry regiments had been recruited from primarily cossacks, converted Tatars, and others from the southern frontier. Each regiment consisted of 1,600 men in eight companies (*rota*, pl. *roty*) under 176 officers. There were also musicians, drummers, and so on. Based on such recruits, and the fact that the regiments were led by foreign officers, it was obvious that the new formations would not attract members of the elite. Most companies consisted only of musketeers. However, there were also mixed companies, each of which included 120 musketeers and 80 pikemen (in Russian known as 'spearmen'; *kopeyshchiki*).[27] Some companies were armed only with pikes, about 3.5 metres long. The pike companies were regarded as the best of the regiment.[28] There was also an attached regimental artillery unit of 2–7 light cannon.[29]

By 1632, the new formation corps had grown to six new formation infantry regiments, as well as two new formation cavalry regiments (see

---

26 *Ibid.*, p.192.
27 Chernov, *Vooruzhennye sily*, ch. 5.
28 Belyayev, *O russkom voyske*, p.61.
29 Chernov, *Vooruzhennye sily*, ch. 6.

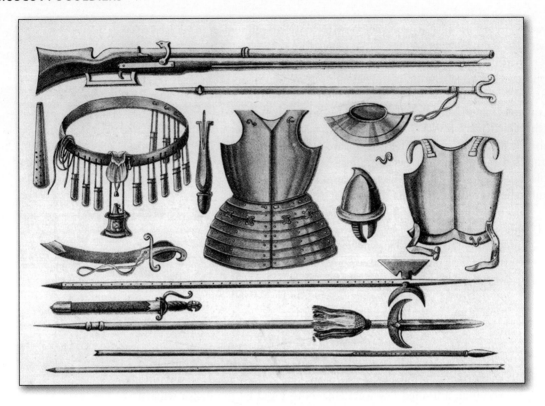

19. Above: Weapons and accoutrements used by new formation infantry, 1647 (Viskovatov, 1841, based on older print). Below: Muscovite officers' partizans and halberds. (Viskovatov, 1841).

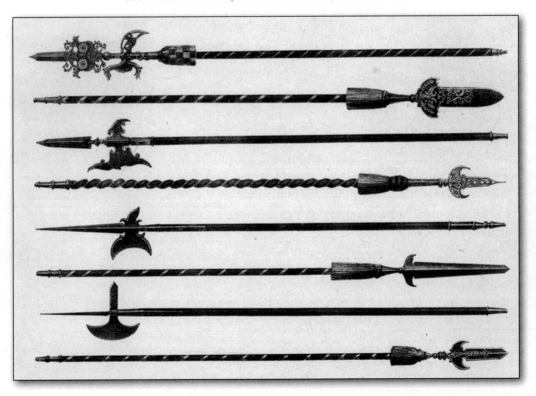

below).[30] Two additional new formation infantry regiments were formed during the Smolensk War, but they did not participate in the siege itself.[31]

The regiments also included dedicated blacksmiths, carpenters, physicians, and apothecaries.[32]

Reiters

The first new formation cavalry regiment was a reiter regiment raised by mid 1632. Originally a German troop type, reiters were pistoleers protected by an iron helmet (*shishak*) and half-armour (*laty*; plate armour covering the upper body and, possibly, arms). The reiter regiment consisted of 2,000 pistoleers divided into 14 companies (*roty*), with 400 dragoons added to the regiment for support.[33]

Each soldier of the new formation cavalry was expected to equip himself, at his own expense, in the same way as the old-style cavalry. Each reiter was required to muster with a horse, musket (later carbine), a pair of pistols, rapier or sabre, half-armour, and helmet.[34]

There is little remaining information on how the Muscovite reiter cavalry actually fought. However, considering that even these Muscovite units in most cases were not standing forces, and that there was little unit training except when called up for duty, it is unlikely that they relied on complicated unit tactics such as the caracole, that is, shooting by ranks, which was common in Western Europe.

Dragoons

Soon after mid-1632, a dragoon regiment of 1,440 men, divided into 12 companies each of 120 men, and 136 officers was raised, too.[35] Later on, additional dragoon regiments were raised. The dragoon regiments effectively functioned as mounted infantry; they were not intended to fight as cavalry.

Hussars

The hussars (*gusary*) were the last type of new formation cavalry to be formed in Muscovy. Styled on the famous Polish winged hussars, who on several occasions had been used with devastating effect against Muscovite units, the Muscovite hussars, too, were armed with long lances and pistols.

All hussars were well-off hereditary servicemen or boyars. Only raised in the north-western towns, hussars were never used on the southern border, where their function was carried out by similarly armed but less distinguished troops merely known as lancers. The first hussar regiment was raised in 1662, consisting of 350 hereditary servicemen and 20 officers under Lieutenant Colonel Nikifor Karaulov. Since there never were many hussars,

---

30   *Ibid.*, ch. 5.

31   *Ibid.*, ch. 5; Keep, *Soldiers of the Tsar*, p.81; Brian L. Davies, *Warfare, State and Society on the Black Sea Steppe, 1500–1700* (London: Routledge, 2007), p.71.

32   Stevens, *Soldiers on the Steppe*, p.117.

33   Chernov, *Vooruzhennye sily*, ch. 5.

34   Belyayev, *O russkom voyske*, p.38, Chernov, *Vooruzhennye sily*, ch. 5; Hellie, *Enserfment and Military Change*, p.199.

35   Chernov, *Vooruzhennye sily*, ch. 5; Davies, *Warfare, State and Society*, pp.71–2.

some uncertainty remains with regard to their arms and equipment. Their lances were known as 'hussar lances' (*gusarskiye kopeytsy*), which implies that they were slightly different from other cavalry lances. It would seem likely that hussar lances were longer than those used by other cavalrymen; however, the actual term employed was a diminutive form of the word for spear, which implies that the hussar lance instead was of smaller dimension than others, which presumably meant light in weight. Likewise, their armour was reportedly lighter than those used by the reiters. On the other hand, a hussar wore lower arm defences (vambraces, *naruchi*), which many reiters lacked. In 1673, the hussar regiment consisted of five companies of hussars with a total of 417 men, a number that in 1679 had risen to 465 men.[36]

Since the hussars were so few, similarly armed but less elite units were formed elsewhere. Reiter and dragoon regiments included special lancer companies made up of cavalrymen known as 'spearmen' (*kopeyshchiki*) or, in foreign terminology, lancers. Armed with lance and pistol, the first such company was formed no later than 1657 when it was referred to as a 'company armed with spear, in hussar formation' (*kopeynaya rota gusarskogo stroya*).[37] Since no Muscovite hussar regiment had yet been formed, it follows that the lancers, too, were clearly inspired by the Polish winged hussars. Some reiter companies appear to have counted two thirds reiters and one third lancers. There were also independent lancer-reiter regiments, consisting of several lancer companies and a single reiter company. In 1662, two regiments of lancers existed within the Belgorod division (more on which below).[38] By the winter of 1679/1680, six new formation cavalry regiments were raised each with 1,000 reiters and 250 lancers.[39]

Service Conditions

At first, the new formation regiments formed only a part of the Muscovite army. In the period from 1630 to 1634, Moscow formed 10 'foreign formation regiments' with a total of 17,400 men. The new formation regiments and foreign mercenaries formed a significant part of the army of some 35,000 men sent to lay siege to Smolensk (as usual, the old-style cavalry also included an unknown number of military bondsman soldiers; see Table 2). However, the new formation regiments were disbanded in 1634.[40]

The new formation troops were not quite standing troops, but many of them came as close to this ideal as any soldiers did in Muscovy. Despite being disbanded after the end of the campaign season, it was common to recall the soldiers for duty the following spring. At times, the men were indeed recalled every spring, in particular on the southern border.

---

36 Chernov, *Vooruzhennye sily*, ch. 5; Hellie, *Enserfment and Military Change*, pp.199–200.
37 Viskovatov, *Istoricheskoye opisaniye* 1, p.100; Chernov, *Vooruzhennye sily*, ch. 5; Hellie, *Enserfment and Military Change*, p.199.
38 Chernov, *Vooruzhennye sily*, ch. 5.
39 Davies, Warfare, *State and Society*, p.172.
40 Hellie, *Enserfment and Military Change*, pp.172, 226, 271.

In 1638, several regiments of dragoons and new formation infantry were formed in the south as part of preparations for war against the Tatars. However, they were all disbanded by the end of the year. In 1639, they were recalled for service.[41]

The new formation cavalry (excluding dragoons) was essentially treated like the old-style cavalry. Reiters, lancers, and hussars were generally of hereditary service origin, so could aspire to receiving land grants and were expected to provide for themselves while on campaign duty, including arranging for a horse, weapons, armour, food, and fodder. The focus was on new organisation and armaments, not re-training, so the difference between a reiter and an old-style cavalryman might, at first, not have been that great.[42] However, as time passed, fewer hereditary servicemen were initiated. This prevented them from claiming land grants in the traditional manner. By 1675, nearly half the men in one province served without having been initiated.[43]

The new formation infantry and dragoons were treated as contract servicemen. Many held land, but this was in most cases a parcel (*nadel*, pl. *nadely*) of land held as the collective property of all personnel serving in a particular unit, for peacetime income. They became soldier-service landholders (*soldaty-pomeshchiki*). They were not permitted to lay claim to hereditary status, nor were they initiated. As for supplies while on campaign, contract servicemen, unlike hereditary servicemen, received money for food purchases. On campaign, supply wagons followed the army so that the men with cash allowances could purchase food.

The infantry in some ways had it easier than the cavalry. Unlike the hereditary servicemen, who had to provide for themselves, the contracted servicemen and infantry received both arms and money for food while on campaign.

In the new formation regiments, organisation, arms, equipment, and tactics aimed to follow European standards. This, however, did not necessarily apply to uniforms. Most Muscovite infantry, unlike the foreign officers, seems to have been

20. Regimental officers. (Erik Palmquist, 1674)

---

41 Chernov, *Vooruzhennye sily*, ch. 5.
42 Stevens, *Russia's Wars of Emergence*, p.132.
43 Stevens, *Soldiers on the Steppe*, p.143.

Hereditary Servicemen (plus an unknown number of bondsman soldiers)	11,688
Streltsy	1,612
Cossacks	2,215
Tatars	1,667
New formation cavalry	2,400
New formation infantry	10,962
Dragoons	400
Foreign Mercenaries	3,744
Total:	34,688

Table 2. The army sent to lay siege to Smolensk, 1632. (Source: Hellie, *Enserfment and Military Change*, pp.172, 271)

dressed similarly to the streltsy, in caftans and boots.[44] Cavalry, too, including reiters, wore Muscovite dress – caftan and boots – under their Western-style cuirass.[45] Soldiers were armed with muskets, rapiers or sabres, berdyshes, long and short pikes, hand grenades, and, in some cases (the pikemen in particular), West European half-armour. In winter they received fur coats.[46] Regimental colonels only carried a sabre and, perhaps, a pistol or two. Other high-level officers often carried a partizan (*protazan*), which was a broad ornamental spear, decorated with a tassel. When not in use, the partizan's head was protected by an elaborate cloth cover (*kutasa*, pl. *kutasy*) of the type that also was used as a cover for the officer's personal pennon (*prapor*).[47] The cloth cover, when mounted on a partizan or pennon, may have been used as a sign for the commander's quarters while in camp.[48] Lower-level officers instead carried an ornamental halberd.[49]

In winter, Muscovite infantry at times were issued skis, just like in the days of Ivan IV and possibly earlier. During the Thirteen Years War, ski troops were particularly effective against the Polish cavalry, since the latter had difficulty moving when the ground was covered in deep snow, with the uppermost layer frozen into ice, a phenomenon which frequently occurred on sunny winter days when the uppermost layer of snow first melted, then refroze at sunset.[50]

During the period 1642–1648, some lands were confiscated and peasants already settled there were freed and enlisted in new formation dragoon regiments for garrison service, retaining the land they worked as a means of support. They were supposed to be used for frontier defence only, and not for campaign service. However, by the 1670s such units were nonetheless

---

44 Aleksandr Malov, 'Russkaya pekhota XVII veka: Gosudarevo zhalovan'ye-sluzhiloye plat'ye', *Zeughaus* 17 (2002), pp.10–16; Aleksandr Malov, 'Gosudarev vybornyy polk Aggeya Shepeleva: Pervoye soldatskoye sluzhiloye plat'ye', *Zeughaus* 20 (2002), pp.10–13; Aleksandr Malov, 'Garnizon Borisoglebskoy kreposti: Gosudarevo sluzhiloye plat'ye, 1666', *Zeughaus* 21 (2003), pp.3–7.

45 Igor' B. Babulin, *Bitva pod Konotopom, 28 iyunya 1659 goda* (Moscow: Zeughaus, 2009), p.14.

46 Belyayev, *O russkom voyske*, pp.59–60, 61, 62; Hellie, *Enserfment and Military Change*, 196; Malov, 'Russkaya pekhota XVII veka: Gosudarevo zhalovan'ye-sluzhiloye plat'ye', pp.10–16.

47 Several have been preserved in the Army Museum, Stockholm. For illustrations, see Velikanov, 'Salatskiye trofei', p.13.

48 This was the traditional interpretation of their function in Sweden, which appears to have been based on the Muscovite use of drum cloth covers for the same purpose (see below).

49 Hellie, *Enserfment and Military Change*, p.191.

50 *Ibid.*, p.197.

committed to campaign service far from home, which made them little different from other units.[51]

Selected Regiments

On the outbreak of the Thirteen Years War in 1654, there were still no permanent new formation regiments. This problem was to some extent overcome in 1656–1657, when two new formation infantry regiments were raised that became known as the 'selected regiments' (*vybornyye polki*). The men selected for the first of these regiments were already trained soldiers and sergeants who had combat experience from at least two campaigns. The regiment was envisioned as being larger then others, with a planned strength of 2,000 men, divided into 20 companies. As colonel of the first selected regiment was appointed Aggey Alekseyev syn Shepelyov, who went on to command the regiment from 1656 to 1687, after which he retired, having then already received the rank of general. Shepelyov's regiment was fully raised in late 1657. Yet, even in this regiment, the majority of the rank and file demobilised during winter.[52] As usual, Muscovy lacked the means to fund the army it wanted.

The second selected regiment was recruited in the same period, only slightly later, and was headed by colonel Yakov Maksimov syn Kolyubakin (d. 1661). Unlike the first selected regiment, it was manned with fresh recruits, many of them peasants. It was for this reason not referred to as a selected regiment from the outset; however, it was called a 'court' (*dvortsovyy*) regiment and received its supplies through the Tsar's privy chancellery (more on which below) so clearly enjoyed a particular status as a Moscow regiment. It became known as a selected regiment in 1659. The second selected regiment was settled in Butyrki, a Moscow suburb, after which it eventually was named, becoming known as the Butyrsk regiment. Following Kolyubakin's death in battle in 1661, he was replaced as colonel by Matvey Osipovich Krovkov in the same year. Krovkov remained its commander until he was removed in 1682, in the aftermath of the streltsy uprising. He was then replaced by Rodion Zhdanov, and eventually, from 1687, the well-known Scots general in Muscovite service, Patrick Gordon (1635–1699).[53]

In the early 1660s, both the first and second selected regiments grew in size, first to 3,000, then to 5,000. In 1674, Palmquist noted the number of the men in the first selected regiment, which he described as the Tsar's guard, as 6,000.[54] This may have been its establishment strength, since Palmquist elsewhere noted information from an informant that the regiment's then current strength, while on campaign duty, was only 4,000. Or perhaps he conflated the two selected regiments into what he termed the Tsar's guard,

---

51   Chernov, *Vooruzhennye sily*, ch. 5.

52   Aleksandr Malov, 'Gosudarevy vybornyye Moskovskiye polki soldatskogo stroya: Kratkiy ocherk istorii i organizatsii', *Zeughaus* 13 (2001), pp.2–7, on pp.3–5; Aleksandr Malov, 'Gosudarevy vybornyye Moskovskiye polki soldatskogo stroya: Komandiry vybornykh polkov', *Zeughaus* 14 (2001), pp.2–7, on pp.4, 5, 6.

53   Malov, 'Gosudarevy vybornyye Moskovskiye polki soldatskogo stroya: Kratkiy ocherk', pp.3–5; Malov, 'Gosudarevy vybornyye Moskovskiye polki soldatskogo stroya: Komandiry', pp.4, 5, 6.

54   Palmquist, *Några observationer*, p.229.

since the second regiment by then apparently comprised 2,500 men.[55] Whatever explained this fluctuation, by 1677–78 the size of the first selected regiment had apparently reached 7,000 men.[56] This, it should be remembered, was at a time when other military units were reduced in strength.

By 1658–1660, the various companies within the two regiments wore differently coloured caftans: red, green, blue, and yellow, respectively.[57] From 1658, the men of the second selected regiment appear to have been issued green, red, and pink hats, while raspberry red and brown caftans followed in 1660. It is possible that the rank and file within the first 'thousand' of the second selected regiment wore brown caftans while sergeants wore raspberry red caftans, while in the second 'thousand' of the same regiment, the rank and file wore raspberry red and sergeants brown.[58] At least this corresponds to the known practice within the first selected regiment, in which within each given company, the sergeants wore caftans of a different colour from those of the rank and file. For instance, in 1661 the rank and file within the first 'thousand' of the first selected regiment wore green caftans while sergeants wore blue caftans, while in the second 'thousand' of the same regiment, the rank and file wore blue and sergeants green.[59]

Armament followed what was customary for the new formation regiments. The men were armed with muskets and pikes. However, they were also issued helmets, rapiers or sabres, and even the old berdysh, the latter indeed as late as for the 1687 Crimean expedition.[60]

Nationwide Conscription

Most new formation regiments were formed under Tsar Aleksey Mikhailovich. The number of recruited troops grew too. In August 1653, the reiter cavalry was revived, with 2,000 being recruited.[61] Yet more were raised during the Thirteen Years War.

In 1658, and again in 1659, 1660, 1661, and 1663, what were to all extents mass nationwide conscription efforts took place. Throughout much of Muscovy, one man was drafted from every 25 taxable households.[62] Moreover, in 1659-1660, sons of hereditary servicemen who had not yet been initiated were, without their consent, drafted for permanent service into the new formation reiter cavalry. In total, 2,050 hereditary servicemen were thus removed from the old-style cavalry and reassigned into the new, since it was

55 *Ibid.*, p.246.

56 Malov, 'Gosudarevy vybornyye Moskovskiye polki soldatskogo stroya: Kratkiy ocherk', p.6.

57 Roberto Palacios-Fernandez, 'O proiskhozhdenii tsvetov petrovskoy leyb-gvardii', *Zeughaus* 5 (1996), pp.4–7; Malov, 'Gosudarev vybornyy polk Aggeya Shepeleva', pp.10–13.

58 Aleksandr Malov, 'Gosudarevo sluzhiloye plat'ye Vtorogo vybornogo polka v kontse 1650-kh – nachale 1660-kh gg.', *Zeughaus* 24 (2007): pp.5–7.

59 Aleksandr Malov, 'Gosudarevo sluzhiloye plat'ye Pervogo vybornogo polka 1661 g.', *Zeughaus* 22 (2006), pp.6–9.

60 Palacios-Fernandez, 'O proiskhozhdenii', pp.4–7; Malov, 'Gosudarev vybornyy polk Aggeya Shepeleva', pp.10–13.

61 Chernov, *Vooruzhennye sily*, ch. 5; Hellie, *Enserfment and Military Change*, p.198.

62 Stevens, *Russia's Wars of Emergence*, p.162.

considered more effective. Cossacks, experienced infantrymen, and even tax-paying, drafted peasants were put into the new formation cavalry. A decree of 1660 specified that a cavalry regiment should consist of 1,000 men, divided into 10 companies, with from 30 to 40 officers per regiment. The company was subdivided into three groups, with each group (*kapral'stvo*) led by a non-commissioned officer. Consequently, the number of new formation cavalrymen rose from 2,000 in 1653 to more than 19,300 in 1663.[63]

After the war, when the need for cavalry felt less pressing, the former infantrymen and peasants were dismissed and sent to the infantry or into garrison service.

The dragoons, too, were effectively revived during the war, even though some units had been formed previously in the south as a kind of frontier troops. At first armed with muskets like infantry, they were expected, indeed had to dismount to fire. By the time of the Thirteen Years War, many were re-armed with carbines. They were also armed with a rapier, an axe, or berdysh. They were considered the lowest priority new formation troops and were, as before, mainly raised in the south.[64]

The losses during the war, and the often harsh conditions during which troops were conscripted and assigned into units, often caused resentment. Desertions took place frequently, although perhaps no more frequently than in other armies. Punishments were harsh, although again possibly not more so than in other armies at the time. Moreover, they were not always carried out. Tsar Aleksey Mikhailovich once responded to a suggestion to execute deserters with the comment that "it is hard to do that, for God has not given courage to all men alike."[65]

The conscription efforts certainly resulted in increasing numbers of new formation troops. When Vasiliy Borisovich Sheremetyev in 1660 led an army of 40,000 (plus, as usual, thousands of serving bondsmen and servants, as well as men to handle the baggage train of at least 3,000 carts), many of them cossacks, into the Ukraine, more than 11,000 were new formation troops. In 1663, Muscovy claimed to have raised 98,000 men, including 31,000 infantry.[66] By then, no less than 50,000–60,000 men were available for service in 55 new formation infantry regiments. The number of reiter cavalry had risen to 18,000.[67] Muscovy indeed mustered more than 112,000 men for the campaigns in 1667–1669 against right-bank Ukraine Hetman Peter Doroshenko's cossacks who nominally remained subject to the Polish-Lithuanian Commonwealth.[68]

However, the new formation regiments did not yet constitute a standing army. Although command structure, armament, and tactics grew more alike, the troops were only paid when on active duty. After each campaign, many soldiers were regularly dismissed, with the serfs being returned to their fields.

---

63 Chernov, *Vooruzhennye sily*, ch. 5; Hellie, *Enserfment and Military Change*, pp.198, 216, 269.
64 Hellie, *Enserfment and Military Change*, p.200.
65 *Ibid.*, p.219; citing Samuel Collins, *The Present State of Russia* (London: John Winter, 1671), p.110.
66 Hellie, *Enserfment and Military Change*, p.271; Stevens, *Soldiers on the Steppe*, pp.57–8.
67 Chernov, *Vooruzhennye sily*, ch. 5; Hellie, *Enserfment and Military Change*, p.196.
68 Hellie, *Enserfment and Military Change*, p.271.

After the Thirteen Years War, the number of regiments was reduced to twenty to 25, and the number of troops to 25,000–30,000.[69] By 1673, Novgorod, which remained an important border town, had a garrison of an estimated 3,000 men, all infantry. Palmquist, who estimated their number, did not specify which type of force it was, but since he elsewhere noted non-familiar types of troops such as streltsy and cossacks, it can be assumed that the garrison consisted of new formation infantry units. The garrison also included 40 large-calibre cannons and the accompanying artillerymen. In addition to the garrison, a significant cavalry force had arrived to meet the Swedish embassy with which Palmquist travelled. This force consisted of 200 old-style cavalry, 200 cossacks, and 600 other cavalrymen, presumably from new formation units.[70] At the same time, Pskov, which the Muscovites regarded as "their foremost fortress on the border with Livonia," had a garrison of 2,000 men, whom Palmquist described as "among the best equipped there are."[71] In comparison, the garrison of Tver', which guarded the north-western approaches to Moscow, had an establishment strength of 1,000 men, but Palmquist counted barely 500 when the embassy passed through the town. These, too, were presumably new formation infantry since he did not describe them further.[72]

But new wars soon followed. In 1676–1681, the Muscovite-Ottoman War took place. In 1677, Prince Grigoriy Grigor'yevich Romodanovskiy led an army of 48,866 men, consisting of both old-style and new formation troops, against the Ottomans, with orders to defend Kiev and other cities garrisoned by Muscovy, as well as the fortresss of Chigirin. A quarter of the army was infantry. Two thirds of the men came from the south.[73]

The 1678–1682 Reforms

In 1678–1682, Moscow introduced ambitious military and administrative reforms. Some were designed to provide for the funding of campaigns better than in the past and for supplying the armies. Others aimed to eliminate remaining differences between old-style and new formation troops, including increasing the share of infantry within the armed forces.

The social and economic conditions of hereditary military service were standardised through a decree in December 1678. The decree defined the conditions of military service for all hereditary servicemen while on campaign, whether in the old-style or new formation units. The idea was to conflate the old styles of military service into the new formations. However, the decree also limited access to the old-style cavalry units as well as the new formation cavalry, establishing minimum standards of wealth, lineage, and status. Service in the old-style cavalry was limited to hereditary servicemen of Moscow rank who owned at least 24 serf households. Everybody else would have to serve in the new formations. Even so, service in the reiter

---

69 *Ibid.*, p.196.
70 Palmquist, *Några observationer*, p.167.
71 *Ibid.*, p.284.
72 *Ibid.*, p.218.
73 Stevens, *Soldiers on the Steppe*, p.76.

THE NEW FORMATION ARMY OF THE ROMANOVS

cavalry regiments was limited, too, to those hereditary servicemen who met a lower but still significant standard of wealth. The rest would have to serve in the new formation infantry units, together with the commoners.[74] Previous rules had in reality allowed a certain level of social mobility, based on need and ability. The new rules were explicit, rigid, and inflexible. Additional legislational changes limited mobility among the services, and thereby social mobility as well. Any provincial hereditary serviceman, regardless of previous family history, who failed to achieve Moscow rank, would have to see his son serve in the new formations. The purpose of the reforms clearly included the streamlining of the armed forces without regard for the old types and conditions of service. As a result, the number of new formation infantry regiments grew in number rapidly, while cavalry units remained defined by hereditary service status.[75]

In 1680, weaponry was standardised within the army. Each reiter was required to bring a carbine and a pair of pistols, while each lancer had to bring a lance and pair of pistols. Each infantryman was required to carry a musket or arquebus and a poleaxe.[76]

In November 1681, Prince Vasiliy Vasil'yevich Golitsyn (1643–1714) chaired a commission of key officers of new formation regiments that met to reform the army further. On 12 January 1682, the precedence system (*mestnichestvo*) was abolished, the system according to which the nobility had only assumed posts according to tables of ancestry.[77] All elite service registers (*razryadnyye knigi*) were ordered to be burned.[78] The reason for this decision was that when the documents that had been used to prove precedence no longer existed, any arguments over it could no longer be sustained. Hitherto, the precedence system had governed all relationships except for foreign-born new formation officers and men, linking family history, military service, social status, and economic conditions. Henceforth, the sons of even court-ranked Muscovites had to enter military service as junior officers in the new formations.[79] This, incidentally, also eliminated the traditional service in the old-style cavalry within the sovereign's division which hitherto had survived for ceremonial functions, if no more. Henceforth, such members of the elite that still served would do so in cavalry regiments consisting of six companies, each of 60 men under a *rittmeister* (cavalry captain; Russian: *rotmistr*).[80] Moreover, many provincial hereditary servicemen of limited means were forced into the infantry regiments.[81] The same fate overtook numerous cossacks and artillerymen. The provincial streltsy were affected too, although in a different way. In 1679, the streltsy stationed in Ukrainian garrisons were mixed with conscipted serfs (*datochnyye lyudi*). In 1680, many provincial streltsy regiments were reorganised as new formation infantry. The officers' titles were

---

74 Stevens, *Russia's Wars of Emergence*, p.197.
75 Stevens, *Soldiers on the Steppe*, p.81.
76 *Ibid.*, p.113.
77 Chernov, *Vooruzhennye sily*, ch. 7.
78 Filjushkin, *Ivan the Terrible*, p.30.
79 Stevens, *Soldiers on the Steppe* (1995), pp.77–8.
80 Chernov, *Vooruzhennye sily*, ch. 7; Hellie, *Enserfment and Military Change*, p.221.
81 Stevens, *Soldiers on the Steppe*, p.80.

changed into the new titles, that is, a regimental headman (*golova*) became a colonel (*polkovnik*), and so on.[82] When provincial regiments were mobilised and departed for campaign service, they were replaced by newly raised units of dragoons, who henceforth served as garrison troops in exchange for parcels of land granted as collective property.[83]

With the introduction of new formation units and new officers' titles, the old term military voivode eventually disappeared, too, although the title lingered on until it eventually was abolished by Tsar Peter. (The old term military voivode should not be confused with the new class of administrative officers with the title of military governor or 'town voivode' (*gorodovoy voyevoda*) which was introduced in the mid-sixteenth century, each heading and combining the civil and military leadership of a town and its district (*vyyezd*). This type of governor became particularly prominent during the seventeenth century. As a civil post, voivodes remained until 1775.)

The abolishment of the precedence system did much to allow individuals of merit to gain command, as long as these individuals adhered to the minimum standards of wealth, lineage, and status already introduced, or were foreign officers. The situation remained uncodified and fundamentally unchanged until Tsar Peter in 1722 introduced his Table of Ranks which from this time onwards came to govern the lives and careers of both civilian and military officers.[84]

By 1681, Muscovy had 55 new formation infantry regiments, 20 reiter regiments, and six lancer regiments, totalling more than 90,000 men. The new formation units then constituted close to half the total of the Muscovite armed forces. Their proportion continued to grow. By 1689, the share of new formation troops constituted two thirds of the army,[85] even though the dragoon regiments had been abolished at the beginning of the 1680s (and were only reconstituted under Tsar Peter).[86]

Over time, service in the new formation regiments changed the traditional social distinctions between different categories of fighting men. By the end of the seventeenth century, there was little real distinction between many who were the descendants of hereditary servicemen and those who were recruited for service. Only those who remained in the old-style cavalry retained some of their traditional stature. Others found their hereditary status disregarded and were forced into infantry service regardless of their personal desires. There was simply too great a need for new formation infantry regiments. This process was particularly noticeable in the south. Many of the southern servicemen were forbidden access to the Moscow ranks in 1685, and in 1686 southern hereditary servicemen then in the infantry were forbidden to join the cavalry.[87] Many of these changes in both military and social system came to be further accentuated under Tsar Peter; however, the process began already before his time.

---

82 *Ibid.*, p.81.
83 *Ibid.*, p.131.
84 Keep, *Soldiers of the Tsar*, pp.123–9.
85 Hellie, *Enserfment and Military Change*, pp.200, 269, 272.
86 Chernov, *Vooruzhennye sily*, ch. 5; Hellie, *Enserfment and Military Change*, p.200.
87 Stevens, *Soldiers on the Steppe*, p.151.

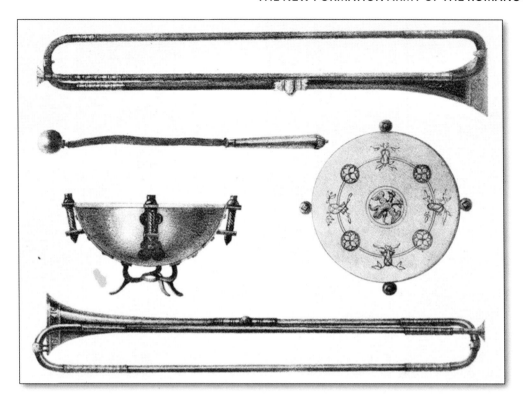

21. Above: Muscovite trumpets and kettledrum; below: Trumpets and kettledrums used by new formation regiments.
(Both Viskovatov, 1841)

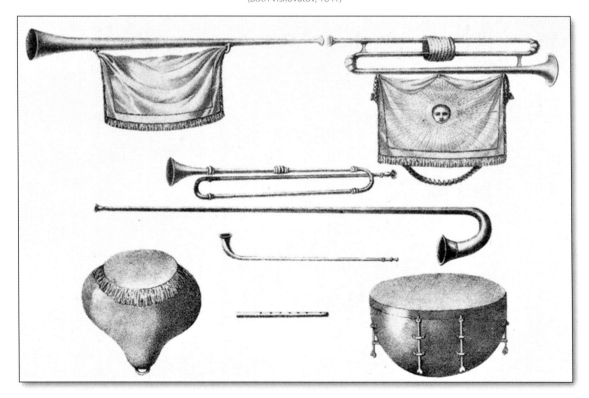

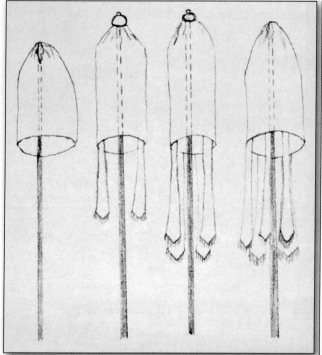

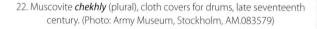
22. Muscovite *chekhly* (plural), cloth covers for drums, late seventeenth century. (Photo: Army Museum, Stockholm, AM.083579)

Field Artillery

Major changes took place within the field artillery attached to new formation regiments. By the early 1680s, the number of cannons in the field artillery had increased from 2–7 to 5–21 cannons per regiment. The calibre of the field artillery had been reduced too, to make the regimental artillery more mobile. Henceforth, two-, three-, and six-pounders were most common. By 1686, regiments of 1,000 men were to have 11 cannon, smaller regiments from six to eight cannon, and the selected (*vybornyye*) regiments 20 cannon each (two-pounders), with sufficient gunpowder and shot for 100 to 150 firings per gun. For major campaigns, such as the one against the Crimean Khanate in 1687, that much shot was not always available.[88]

Regimental Music

Attached to the regiments were musicians of various kinds. Kettledrummers and trumpeters had existed at least since Mongol times, but with the new

---

88 Chernov, V*ooruzhennye sily*, ch. 6; Stevens, *Soldiers on the Steppe*, p.116; Davies, *Warfare, State and Society*, p.135.

formation regiments also came European music. Musicians in new formation regiments might be boys aged 13 to 16 who played the drum, flute, or shawm. They would typically wear West European dress, decorated with silver or gold lace.[89] In 1674, Palmquist noted about the shawm players, who marched before the colonel and lieutenant colonel: "They play all kinds of tunes with a full sound, but mostly hymns, and the music is quite pleasant." However, the companies had only flute players and drummers, and they played "in the ordinary way" (that is, like military musicians in other armies).[90] By the second half of the seventeenth century, the drums seem to have come in fundamentally two sizes (approximately 38 and 50 cm in diameter and height, respectively), depending on its purpose. When the drums were not in use, they were protected by elaborate cylindrical cloth covers (*chekhol*, pl. *chekhly*) with a diameter of 38–50 cm and a height of 65–85 cm, each painted with religious and other motives, or occasionally decorated in appliqué in the same style.[91] The cloth covers may also have been used as signs for the commander's quarters while in camp, if so hung from a spear.[92] While on this topic, it should be mentioned that officers used dedicated cloth gunlock covers of similar patterns, chiefly consisting of stylised flowers. Their dimensions were about 25 x 37 cm and they were made of fulled woollen fabric.[93]

Banners

Each regiment had its own banner, made of silk damask, unpatterned silk, or cloth of taffeta, with sewn-on or painted ornaments. Most common ornaments were the six-armed Orthodox cross and biblical scenes, the image of Christ, the Virgin and the Holy Child, a saint such as the Archangel Michael, or even a multitude of saints with their hands extended in prayer. These images often appeared in combination. The sun, moon, stars, and other ornaments were common, too. Infantry regimental colours were large, 1.5– 2.5 metres in breadth, and highly decorated.[94] Many Muscovite colours bore the toothed saltire or Burgundian cross, which presumably was introduced by West European officers. Flags used by companies and lesser units were normally of single-colour fabric with an Orthodox cross of differently coloured fabric on the upper left corner, with one or more stars elsewhere on the field corresponding to the company's number.[95]

89 Roberto Palacios-Fernandez, 'Muzykanty vybornykh moskovskikh soldatskikh polkov', *Zeughaus* 7 (1998), pp.7–9.

90 Palmquist, *Några observationer*, p.245.

91 Several drums and drum covers have been preserved in the Army Museum, Stockholm. For illustrations, see Velikanov, 'Salatskiye trofei', pp.7, 13.

92 This was the contemporary interpretation of their function in Sweden, which may have been based on eyewitnesses. See, e.g., official battle reports from the Swedish victory at Saladen, 1703; reprinted in Höglund, Sallnäs, and Bespalow, *Stora Nordiska Kriget*, pp.47–8, 71–2.

93 Several were taken as trophies, together with the drum covers, and have been preserved in the Army Museum, Stockholm.

94 Many have been preserved in the Army Museum, Stockholm. Danielsson, 'Utländska fälttecken'; Danielsson, *Catalogue of Foreign Colours*.

95 Aleksandr Malov, 'Znamena polkov novogo stroya', *Zeughaus* 15 (2001), pp.6–10; Aleksandr Malov, 'Znamena polkov novogo stroya: Simvolika kresta', *Zeughaus* 16 (2001), pp.2–7.

23. Clockwise from top left (all Army Museum, Stockholm): Muscovite dragoon guidon, mid-seventeenth century (AM.083826); Muscovite infantry colour, seventeenth century (AM.082187); Muscovite infantry colour, seventeenth century (AM.082190); Muscovite dragoon guidon, mid-seventeenth century (AM.083824); Muscovite dragoon guidon, Colonel Grigoriy Andreyevich Sukhotin's dragoon regiment, second half of the seventeenth century (AM.082448).

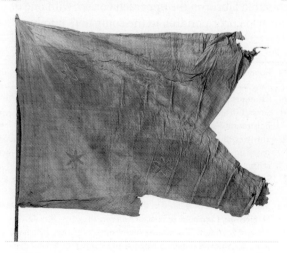

Dragoon guidons were square in shape with swallow-tails and half the size of the colours used by infantry regiments. Reiter standards were square but had no swallow-tails and were even smaller than those used by dragoons.[96] The old-style cavalry, too, carried smaller standards, approximately 1.3 metres in breadth and length.[97]

Many standards were mounted on staves with a finial on top and a wooden apple immediately below the standard.[98]

Foreign Officers

Until the 1680s, Muscovy continued to rely heavily on foreign mercenary officers. Based on data from the 1660s, of 277 known staff officers (colonels, lieutenant colonels, and majors), all but 18 were foreigners. Of 1,922 company officers (captains, lieutenants, and ensigns), about two thirds were foreigners, with only 648 Muscovites among them. The high share of foreign officers had a significant impact on the units under their command, since Muscovy aimed to maintain a high proportion of officers to men (1:20 on average in the infantry and dragoon regiments).[99] Few groups within the Muscovite population had as frequent contact with foreigners as soldiers, and most conscripted soldiers would never have even have seen a foreigner, unless they had been recruited into the army. For this reason, it can be assumed that army service made Muscovites somewhat less parochial, and despite the strong influence of the Church, may have contributed to moving Muscovite daily life more in line with developments elsewhere in Europe.

The introduction of the new formation regiments did much to enhance the capability of the Muscovite army. However, again the reform fundamentally failed to address the need for standing forces that upheld their skills through continuous training. There were no tactical exercises and manoeuvres. The Muscovite economy in the seventeenth century was no more able to sustain a large, standing army than it had been in the sixteenth century. As a result, the men had to be effectively demobilised when no longer needed because of a lack of funding, and like the streltsy before them, they then switched to individual trades or farming to support themselves. Again most standing units were standing on paper only. They could be mobilised, but to prepare them for campaign duties, training often would have to start all over again. The high proportion of officers to men was essential for retaining some level of continuity in organisation and military skills.

The Southern Border

The population movement towards the south, consisting of people who escaped war, poverty, and enserfment, continued into the seventeenth century. While

---

96   Malov, 'Znamena polkov novogo stroya', pp.6–10; Malov, 'Znamena polkov novogo stroya: Simvolika', pp.2–7.
97   Several have been preserved in the Army Museum, Stockholm.
98   Palmquist, *Några observationer*, pl. 19.
99   Davies, *Warfare, State and Society*, p.135.

Map 1. Muscovy and the Southern Frontier

some continued all the way to the cossack settlements, many settled near the southern fortress towns. Southern farmland was far more fertile than farmland in the north, and there was plenty of it, so for those who sought better prospects, the south seemed a better choice, despite the threat of Tatar raids.

The southern defensive line failed again in 1632, when a Tatar invasion force moved against Moscow at the time when the Muscovite army had withdrawn from the Oka River line because of the Smolensk War on the western front.

As a result, between 1635 and 1653 a new defensive line was built far to the south of Tula, near the edge of the forest-steppe. French Huguenot and Dutch military engineers may have assisted with the fortifications, even though the line still relied on abatis, as had the previous one. Survey work began in 1635, immediately after the Smolensk War, but actual construction commenced only in 1638, probably in direct response to worries over the possible repercussions of the Don cossacks' latest foreign adventure. In 1637, Don cossack forces and boats had unexpectedly attacked and captured the Ottoman fortress of Azov. This had not been too difficult; Azov was mostly of commercial importance due to its location on the communications line to the eastern Caucasus, at this time did not even rate a military commandant, and its Ottoman garrison had consisted only of some 4,000 men.[100] Being unable to hold the fortress, the Don cossacks offered it to Muscovy, which, however, declined. Nonetheless, Moscow feared that an Ottoman and Crimean reaction to the cossack conquest might be forthcoming, and that it might be aimed at Muscovy.

Named the Belgorod defensive line (*Belgorodskaya cherta*), the new defensive line was completed in 1653 and proved an effective means to stop Tatar intrusions.[101] The Belgorod defensive line reached about 800 kilometres from Tambov, through Voronezh on the middle River Don, Staryy Oskol, and Belgorod, before moving westwards to Akhtyrka.[102] Soon additional settlement took place north of the Belgorod line, which gradually lost its frontier character. From 1646, the old-style cavalry no longer met annually on the Oka defensive line but instead did so on the Belgorod line.[103] In the 1640s and 1650s, a new defensive line was built, extending eastwards to Simbirsk.[104]

The threat from Tatar raids persisted, however, and increasing number of men were needed to defend the southern towns. In 1626, eight towns alone had garrisons encompassing a total of 7,500 troops. By 1635, 11 towns for which information is available had nearly 14,000 garrison troops. In 1651, about 17,000 men were enrolled in garrison service.[105]

There was also an attempt to form regional military commands. In 1653, during the Thirteen Years War, the concentration of forces in the south became known as the Belgorod division (*Belgorodskiy polk*). In 1658, this term became official with the introduction of a Belgorod regional military command (*Belgorodskiy razryad*) as part of the general reform of government

---

100 Stevens, *Soldiers on the Steppe*, p.20; Davies, *Warfare, State and Society*, pp.80, 89.
101 Stevens, *Soldiers on the Steppe*, p.123.
102 Stevens, *Russia's Wars of Emergence*, p.134.
103 *Ibid.*, p.137.
104 *Ibid.*, p.134.
105 Stevens, *Soldiers on the Steppe*, p.21.

along the borders. The Belgorod division, in modern works often referred to as the Belgorod Army Group, included about 17,000 garrison troops and nearly 20,000 on campaign service, the latter including two new formation cavalry units, four dragoon regiments, six new formation infantry regiments, and only 2,000 old-style cavalrymen (that is, less than 10 percent of the total), in addition to a regiment (*prikaz*) of 600 streltsy. In total, there were then 16,600 new formation servicemen in the Belgorod division.[106]

In 1664 or 1665, the western provinces of the Belgorod division were detached to form a new Sevsk regional military command.[107] Soon, by 1680 at the latest, several new regional military commands had been created, including in Smolensk and Novgorod. As a result, a system of nine regional commands (Belgorod, Sevsk, Novgorod, Smolensk, Moscow, Vladimir, Ryazan', Kazan', and Tambov) covered all Muscovite territories, except Siberia which, still being a frontier, remained outside the new system (Tambov was subsumed into the Belgorod command in 1681–1682).[108] The regional military command structure remained until abolished by Tsar Peter in 1711.

In 1679–1681, by the end of the Muscovite-Ottoman War (1678–1681), a new defensive line of abatis, the Izyum defensive line, was constructed to the south of the Belgorod defensive line. The Izyum line was mostly complete by 1682. More than 30,000 servicemen, on campaign and garrison duty, were involved in building and defending the new line.[109] The new defensive line was needed; in 1680 Tatar raiders again succeeded in penetrating the Muscovite defences. Yet, henceforth they no longer constituted as great a threat as in the past.

Old-Style Cavalry

The old-style cavalry remained much as it had been in the past.[110] A thousand selected men continued to serve in the old-style cavalry in the sovereign's regiment (*sotennaya sluzhba*), a formation still organised in the traditional 'hundreds' (*sotni*).[111] They changed little, even though Tsar Aleksey Mikhailovich raised the age of initiation for service to 18.[112] As before, they were not uniformed but turned out in civilian dress.[113] In 1643, requirements for their armament was slightly updated, but not very much. The new regulations said that henceforth, all were required to have a pair of pistols (typically wheellocks) and a musket. However, those who still considered the bow their primary weapon could choose to have either a pistol or a carbine as an auxiliary firearm. The bondsman

---

106 *Ibid.*, p.34; Davies, *Warfare, State and Society*, p.92. The figures do not quite add up and likely result from incomplete surviving records.

107 Stevens, *Russia's Wars of Emergence*, p.166; Davies, *Warfare, State and Society*, p.93.

108 Chernov, *Vooruzhennye sily*, ch. 7; Paul Bushkovitch, 'The Romanov Transformation, 1613–1725', Fredrick W. Kagan and Robin Higham (eds.), *The Military History of Tsarst Russia* (New York: Palgrave, 2002), pp.31–45, on p.35; Stevens, *Russia's Wars of Emergence*, p.202.

109 Stevens, *Soldiers on the Steppe*, p.123.

110 See, e.g., Aleksandr Malov, ' 'Konnost', lyudnost' i oruzhnost'' sluzhilogo 'goroda' pered Smolenskoy voynoy: Na materiale Velikikh Luk', *Zeughaus* 18 (2002), pp.12–15.

111 Cotossichin, *Beskrifning*, p.134.

112 Belyayev, *O russkom voyske*, p.26.

113 See, e.g., Aleksey Abramov, 'Reforma sluzhilogo plat'ya, 1680', *Zeughaus* 45 (2012): pp.2–11.

soldiers could be armed with bows only, but only as long as they were trained archers. If not, they had to serve with muskets or carbines. Those who carried muskets in most cases had to dismount to fire, which in effect made them no more militarily useful than levied infantry. Even less militarily useful were the very poor hereditary servicemen who, according to lenient exceptions in the new regulations, were allowed to serve with a spear and axe instead of firearms. There were regional differences in armament, which may have been caused by local conditions or differences in wealth. On the western front, as many as 87 percent carried firearms, 10 percent carried a bow as their main weapon, and no more than three percent carried only a sabre, an axe, or a bear spear. But on the southern frontier facing the Tatars, in 1649 no more than 38 percent carried firearms while the rest relied on bows. Later in the century, the old-style cavalry grew even less effective. During a muster in 1663, many of the hereditary servicemen even lacked horses.[114] In the 1670s, from 75 to 90 percent of the old-style cavalrymen were armed with only pistols and sabres.[115]

The hereditary servicemen suffered enormous losses during the Thirteen Years War (1654–1667). On 28 June 1659, a Muscovite army under Prince Aleksey Nikitich Trubetskoy (1600–1680) and his lieutenant, the aforementioned Prince Grigoriy Grigor'yevich Romodanovskiy (d. 1682), was wiped out in the battle of Konotop by Ukrainian cossacks and Crimean Tatars under Hetman Ivan Vygovskiy (d. 1664), Bogdan Khmel'nitskiy's successor.[116] Of 4,769 Muscovite soldiers known to have been lost in the battle and its aftermath, almost half (2,276 men, including 243 of Moscow rank) were hereditary servicemen.[117] This meant that almost a tenth of the men available to the sovereign's division were lost, with a similar percentage lost of the old-style cavalry in general. This was the largest loss suffered by the Moscow elite in any battle during the war. Yet, the attrition continued, on both sides in the conflict, and multiplied as the war went on. As a result, the old-style cavalry lost much of its earlier significance.

The old-style cavalry was sidelined further through the reform decrees of 1678. However, the decrees failed to mention the hereditary servicemen who served as garrison troops. One major reason for this was that by this time, such men remained on active duty only in the south and in Siberia, that is, on the frontier where they were still needed. In the borderlands, garrison troops continued to exist for a considerable time. Elsewhere garrison troops, if they existed at all, primarily consisted of retired servicemen or those who were too poor to serve in any other role.

In 1681, there were about 6,385 members of the nobility in Muscovy as a whole. Of these, 3,761 were officers in the provincial hereditary servicemen cavalry, while the remaining 2,624 were earmarked for the sovereign's division, each bringing on the average nine bondsmen soldiers, which would produce a total of over 26,000 old-style cavalry available to the Tsar.[118] However, the

---

114 Hellie, *Enserfment and Military Change*, pp.211–12.
115 *Ibid.*, p.219.
116 *Ibid.*, p.217.
117 Igor' B. Babulin, *Bitva pod Konotopom, 28 iyunya 1659 goda* (Moscow: Zeughaus, 2009), p.37.
118 Hellie, *Enserfment and Military Change*, pp.24, 269.

reforms and the subsequent reorganisation of the old-style cavalry reduced this number sharply, and the Muscovite army, when called up, henceforth included no more than, at most, 10,000 old-style cavalry.[119]

The military importance of the old-style cavalry and the other Mongol-inspired organisational components of the Muscovite army diminished from the middle of the seventeenth century with the introduction of the new formation regiments. This was hardly surprising, since an increasing number of the latter were led by foreign officers, who did not form part of the old Muscovite military tradition. By the 1680s there were 47 foreign colonels in the cavalry and 77 in infantry.[120] The last reference to a great division occurred in a muster roll from 1687. Finally, the old-style cavalry was abolished by Tsar Peter in 1701.

Cossacks

Relations with the free cossacks can be said to have been formalised in 1623, when Muscovy transferred official relations with the Don cossacks to the ambassadors' chancellery (*Posol'skiy prikaz*), in effect the foreign ministry, which signified that they were not subjects of Muscovy. However, Don cossacks continued to play an important role for Muscovy, which paid money, weapons, cloth, and grain to them in return for their support in protecting the border against incursions by Crimean and Ottoman invaders.

In 1670, the Don cossacks rebelled. Led by Stepan 'Sten'ka' Razin (c.1630–1671), the rebellion acquired great momentum and Razin eventually led the rebels up the Volga towards Moscow. Defeated at Simbirsk, Razin was brought to Moscow where he was executed. The Razin rebellion spelled the end of Don cossack independence. From 1671 onwards, the Don cossacks had to swear allegiance to the Tsar which concluded their formal existence as free cossacks.

As noted, the Thirteen Years War resulted in significant migration into Muscovy from the Ukraine. Many were settled in distinct cossack communities with duties to serve in the Muscovite army. A system of registering cossack soldiers emerged, with those who succeeded in being listed in the cossack register (*reyestr*) becoming exempt of taxes and only had to serve in times of war. In effect, they became contract servicemen. By the end of the seventeenth century, the Ukrainian cossacks settled in Muscovy could field some 5,000 fighting men.[121] The cossack register became a pattern for how to handle cossacks within the Muscovite army and can be said to have formalised the transformation of free cossacks into service cossacks.

Logistics

The logistics system of the Muscovite army developed considerably during the seventeenth century. This was the effect of both more efficient administrative and fiscal means, introduced over time, and the very real

---

119 Stevens, *Soldiers on the Steppe*, p.78.
120 Stevens, *Russia's Wars of Emergence*, p.234.
121 Porfiriev, *Peter I*, p.41.

need for keeping the increasingly large armies supplied, both in peacetime and while on campaign. Provisioning necessarily changed in character. The smaller, predominantly cavalry armies consisting of hereditary servicemen of the sixteenth century were largely self-supporting. Not only was each serviceman supposed to handle his own supplies, such an army was more mobile and hence more able to live off the land, Tatar-style, if required.

However, the massed new formation infantry and cavalry regiments of the seventeenth century lacked these means. First, most of the men were no longer expected to handle their own supplies but depended on the state for all their needs. Second, they carried muskets issued by the state, which meant that ammunition and replacement arms had to be supplied, too. Finally, the armies at the time were simply too large to live off the land. Yet, by the end of the seventeenth century, Muscovy was able to send expeditionary forces of more than 100,000 troops each on extended campaigns. The logistics system then developed relied on both carts and river barges. In the late 1670s, a system for collecting carts and escort troops for logistical purposes was put in place.[122] Although mistakes took place, it is fair to say that a system had been created that served Muscovy well, and without which the major campaigns of later centuries would have been impossible.

A key change concerned the collection and distribution of grain. Previously, this had been a regional effort that only was intended for emergency supplies. There had been several collection systems, which fundamentally were collection of taxes but in kind. However, in the early years of the seventeenth century these various systems were streamlined. They were also applied to most of Muscovy, so that grain collection became a nationwide effort.

It was again the streltsy which provided the pattern for the rest of the Muscovite army. The *Streletskiy prikaz* set up a nationwide organisation that would provide a year-round supply of grain to the streltsy. Based on taxation, this system collected and paid out actual grain, alternatively collected money for which the state bought grain. Since market conditions were poorly developed in Muscovy, there was no guarantee that food would be available on the market, at least for a reasonable price, under wartime conditions. It was accordingly more effective to distribute actual grain than cash allowances for the purchase of food.[123] Yet, the streltsy, especially the provincial streltsy, retained their small plots of land and their trading privileges, which which they supported themselves in times of peace.

The *gulyaygorod*, too, remained in use in the seventeenth century, although over time, it was employed less often. It was used, successfully, in 1609 against the Polish cavalry. In 1648–1653, Ukrainian cossacks, too, employed it against the Poles. This was unsurprising, since the Poles, like the Tatars, relied on cavalry as the main arm. When no dedicated *gulyaygorod* was available, a Muscovite army might instead revert to former practices, drawing up its large number of supply carts into a rough circle, which was

---

122 Stevens, *Soldiers on the Steppe*, p.113.
123 *Ibid.*, pp.45–6.

then used as a fortification (*oboz*).[124] In the sixteenth century, Fletcher had noted that *oboz* and *gulyaygorod* were indeed interchangeable terms.[125]

The Navy

Tsar Aleksey Mikhailovich made an attempt to build a Muscovite navy. He had a warship, the *Oryol*, built for service on the Caspian Sea, together with four smaller ships. However, all were taken and destroyed in 1670 by Razin's cossacks. Yet, plenty of reasonably seaworthy but fairly small merchant ships were, in fact, built throughout the seventeenth century, in ports such as Arkhangel'sk, Ledinovo near Moscow, Nizhniy Novgorod, Kazan', Astrakhan', and along the Don, particularly in Voronezh.[126]

The Crimean Campaigns

By late 1685 and early 1686, surveyors were sent to the south to determine what provisions and other resources might be available there. There was already a system in place for grain shipments to the Don cossacks. However, more was needed since by late April 1686, Muscovy had committed to an alliance, the Holy League, with the Holy Roman Empire, the Polish-Lithuanian Commonwealth, and the Venetian Republic against the Ottoman Empire. Together they would strike a blow against the Ottomans. Moscow would fulfil its commitment to the Holy League by attacking the Crimean Khanate, which served the Ottoman empire as a client state. This would tie up the Crimean forces so that they could not support the Ottomans elsewhere. In return, the Commonwealth agreed to recognise Moscow's annexation of Kiev and left-bank Ukraine. In August 1686, a decree ordered a special levy of grain. Together with regular taxation and purchased grain, a total of nearly 22,283 tonnes were collected for the campaign. The grain was collected and carted to the applicable forward depots by February 1687. In addition, the grain provided by the cavalrymen from their own means were received, carted, and put in storage as well, to become part of the baggage train. This was a nationwide effort, unlike preparations for previous campaigns. The depots worked around the clock, and in at least one fortress, the only available scribe was too overworked to keep up with the necessary book-keeping, which made his commander complain to Moscow.[127] In mid May, Muscovy's largest army ever, more than 112,000 troops under Prince Vasiliy Golitsyn, crossed the southern border in order to join up with some 50,000 cossacks under left-bank Ukraine Hetman Ivan Samoylovich (c.1630–1690) who would join the campaign.[128] The army included some 75,000 men in new formation regiments (Table 3).[129]

124 Hellie, *Enserfment and Military Change*, p.164.
125 Giles Fletcher, *Of the Russian Commonwealth* (1591), in Berry and Crummey, *Rude & Barbarous Kingdom*, p.185.
126 Porfiriev, *Peter I*, p.43.
127 Stevens, *Soldiers on the Steppe*, pp.114–16.
128 *Ibid.*, pp.111–12, 119.
129 Hellie, *Enserfment and Military Change*, p.272.

From a logistics point of view, Moscow owed cash or food to at least half the army, and yet others relied on Moscow for firearms, ammunition, and equipment. Moreover, there were no established river transport routes or garrison towns with forward magazines in the area of operations, since the entire campaign took place south of the border and there was no means to provide easy river transport south and east of the Dnieper raids. Some supplies were shipped down the Desna and Vorskla Rivers towards the rapids. The steppe offered fodder but little else, the lands being relatively unpopulated. While the Tatar cavalry was, rightly, assessed as inferior to the modern Muscovite forces, Moscow underestimated the logistical demands for the campaign.[130] At least 20,000 carts were mobilised for the effort. Each needed a carter. Other men, beside the troops, were required too, including workers of various kinds. This meant that far more than 20,000 additional men accompanied the army. It has been estimated that the total requirement for grain alone amounted to some 18,000 to 23,000 tonnes.[131] Even though all cavalrymen were required to collect their own provisions, it still had to be transported. A Muscovite army by tradition carried one or two months' food while on campaign.[132]

Muscovites	
Old-style cavalry soldiers (presumably including bondsman soldiers)	8,712
Moscow-rated streltsy	11,262
Cossacks	15,505
New formation cavalry	26,096
New formation infantry	49,363
Others	1,964
Total:	112,902
Ukrainian cossacks	50,000

Table 3. Golitsyn's army during his first Crimean campaign, 1687
(except logistics personnel).
(Source: Hellie, *Enserfment and Military Change*, p.272; Stevens, *Soldiers on the Steppe*, pp.94, 111–12, 119).

When moving across the steppe, Prince Golitsyn's army was formed into an advance guard of 10 regiments, followed by a slow-moving rectangular formation of an estimated 100 regiments surrounding the supply train which consisted of 14,000 horse-drawn carts arranged in 10 rows and flanked on the sides by 6,000 more carts in 17 parallel rows. The fronts and flanks of this rough rectangle, which was almost two kilometres across and close to four kilometres in length, was protected by cavalry. It was followed by the artillery, which brought up the rear. Every fourth or fifth day of march, the

---

130 Stevens, *Soldiers on the Steppe*, p.112.
131 *Ibid.*, p.113.
132 *Ibid.*, p.114.

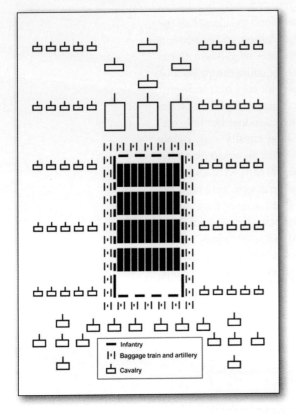

Old-style cavalry soldiers (presumably including bondsman soldiers)	7,936
Moscow-rated streltsy (in 11 regiments)	9,270
Ukrainian Cossacks (Cherkassy, i.e. recently settled migrants from the Ukraine who served in separate formations)	14,471
New formation cavalry (247 new formation lancers, 29,216 new formation cavalry in 28 regiments)	29,463
New formation infantry (in 35 regiments)	49,189
Others	1,737
Total:	112,066

Table 4. Golitsyn's army during his second Crimean campaign, 1689 (except the significant contingent of left-bank Ukrainian Cossacks and logistics personnel)
(Source: Hellie, *Enserfment and Military Change*, pp.230, 272)

24. Order of march for a contingent during Golitsyn's Crimean campaign, 1689.

army needed to disperse to gather fodder.[133] This was a major endeavour, since the army counted more than 100,000 horses.[134]

In addition to carts, no less than 660 riverboats were built at three river ports, the boats then being moved to the area of operations. Yet, because of a lack of qualified workmen, many of the riverboats were in bad condition and hardly seaworthy.[135]

None of the logistics efforts turned out to be sufficient. The almost 200,000-strong army had to turn back because of problems in logistics and supply. Most seriously, the Tatars burned the steppe grass, which deprived the army of fodder.

In 1689, Prince Golitsyn made a new attempt. In this second campaign, his large army (which included more than 78,000 men in new formation regiments; see Table 4) again ran out of food and water.[136] The key logistical problem was, again, the organisation of grain transport. A cart carried some 200 kg only, and the post service could not supply a sufficient number of carts. Technically, it was the grain suppliers themselves who should have moved the grain, but for these campaigns, distances were too long as the armies operated far beyond the frontier. There were also difficulties in supplying enough riverboats for transportation. However, the army had

133 *Ibid.*, p.119.
134 *Ibid.*, p.120.
135 *Ibid.*, pp.117–18.
136 *Ibid.*, p.102.

learnt from previous mistakes, and the order of march and logistics system were duly improved. Moreover, Golitsyn arranged to burn the steppe grass himself, under controlled circumstances, so as to deny the Tatars the use of this stratagem. There was also a rudimentary system for the evacuation and treatment of the wounded, with 65 carts assigned for this purpose.[137]

The 1689 campaign did result in enemy contact, however. Crimean cavalry made several attempts to engage Golitsyn's army. Their attacks failed, and the Muscovite army reached the isthmus of Perekop, the fortress that guarded the entry point to the Crimean peninsula and the Tatar heartland. However, there the Muscovites found that there was no access to fresh water, nor was sufficient grazing available. Under these conditions, Golitsyn's army lacked the means to carry out a protracted siege, so had to turn back without achieving its objective. To add to its difficulties, the Tatars had again burned the steppe, so grazing was largely unavailable on the return journey as well. Although the army reached its planned destination, it failed to reach its objective.

Artillery and Rocketry

Artillery continued to develop in the seventeenth century. Bronze cannons were, as noted, not a new innovation, but their share of the total number of cannons increased significantly. By the first half of the century, two thirds of all cannon were cast of bronze. Artillery ordnance was also being standardised. By the second quarter of the century, the number of calibres being manufactured for artillery usage was reduced to only 13. By then, bombs and hand grenades of various types were being manufactured, too.[138] Explosive ordnance became increasingly common during and after the Thirteen Years War. Ordnance factories then existed in several town, with those in Moscow, Tula, and Kashira being the most prominent. In the period 1668–1673, in Tula alone more than 25,000 explosive grenades were produced. In the same period, more than 154,000 hand grenades were produced, too, and more than 42,000 cannon balls.[139] Some have argued that this suggests that hand grenades were introduced in the Muscovite army only in 1668.[140] As before, foreign expertise was used to enhance Muscovite military technology. The Tula factories, for instance, were by then directed by a Dane, Peter Marselius.[141] Gun carriages were commonly painted red.[142] The exception was during ceremonies in Moscow, when both cannons and carriages instead might be gilded.[143]

---

137 Keep, *Soldiers of the Tsar*, p.39.
138 *Hellie, Enserfment and Military Change*, p.184.
139 Chernov, *Vooruzhennye sily*, ch. 6.
140 V.V. Zvegintsov, Russkaya armiya 1: 1700–1763gg. (typescript, 1967; translated into German by Oscar Urbonas, Army Museum archive, Stockholm, F 18 BI, Vol. 1).
141 Palmquist, *Några observationer*, p.263.
142 *Ibid.*, pl. 29; Roberto Palacios-Fernandez, 'Moskovskiye pushkari', *Zeughaus* 6 (1997), pp.5–11.
143 Palmquist, *Några observationer*, pp.262–3.

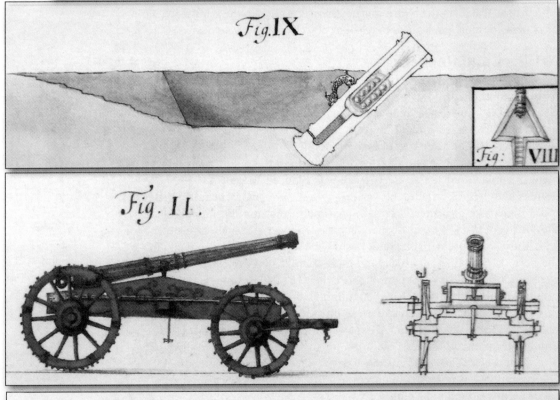

25. Left, from top: positioning of bronze mortar dug into the ground, as seen from the side (main) and from above (detail); bronze mortar, firing, dug into the ground; artillery carriage that enables fire in any direction; a similar gun on the move, with crew mounted. All Erik Palmquist, 1674

By the early 1680s, the number of cannons in the field artillery had, as noted, increased from 2–7 to 5–21 cannons per regiment. The calibre of the field artillery had been reduced, too, to make the regimental artillery more mobile.[144]

Palmquist noted that Muscovy had all the usual types of artillery, which were used by other European armies. However, Muscovy also carried out innovations in artillery. One type of cannon and associated gun carriage, which greatly impressed Palmquist, was a type of cannon with a calibre from 1 to 6 pounds that rested in a carriage that enabled the gun not only to move in a vertical direction but to be turned, and fired, horizontally. The ability to fire rapidly in any direction, without moving the carriage itself, was the chief advantage of this type of artillery. According to Palmquist, at the time this type of carriage was indeed generally used for all kinds of field artillery. The carriage contained room to store cannon balls, quoins, wadding, and other required equipment.[145] As far as is known, Palmquist had no opportunity to see this kind of cannon being fired. It accordingly remains unknown how well the carriage handled the recoil, when fired in a non-standard direction. Yet, it remains certain that artillery of this type was being produced, and that Palmquist managed to acquire technical details. It is accordingly likely that this type of gun and carriage proved helpful in particular during the subsequent Crimean campaigns, during which the entire army at times travelled in the formation of a wagenburg. Artillery which could be moved forwards, yet at any moment stop to fire towards the flank, was no doubt of great utility in a wagenburg.

Another Muscovite innovation in artillery was a very large bronze mortar, with a diameter of up to 1.2 metres. Because of its size, it could only be used dug into the ground. Its chief advantage was that it could fire a large quantity of stones together with casks filled with smaller shells, incendiary fire-balls, and gas bombs.[146] Fire-balls were incendiary weapons that by then had a long tradition of use in northern warfare. The gas bombs were probably similar to chemical bombs known to have been used in Scandinavia in the early eighteenth century, if not before. By adding certain ingredients to the bomb, including sulphur and quicksilver, it would generate poison gas after reaching its target.[147] The result was that each shot fired from such a mortar would saturate an area covering a distance of "a few hundred paces" in which the effect would be great damage and the ignition of fires in many places. Being, most likely, regarded as a kind of siege artillery, this type of mortar was only brought on campaign when transport was available by ship or barge.[148]

---

144 Chernov, *Vooruzhennye sily*, ch. 6.

145 Palmquist, *Några observationer*, pp.262–3.

146 *Ibid.*, 263. Palmquist's words for the incendiary and gas bombs were, in seventeenth-century Swedish, *Fÿr= och dunstKuhlor*.

147 Michael Fredholm von Essen, 'On the Trail of Rocketry 2: Early Eighteenth-Century Gas Warfare and Other Norwegian Innovations in Naval Pyrotechnics', *Arquebusier* 32: 1 (2010), pp.2–5.

148 Palmquist, *Några observationer*, p.263.

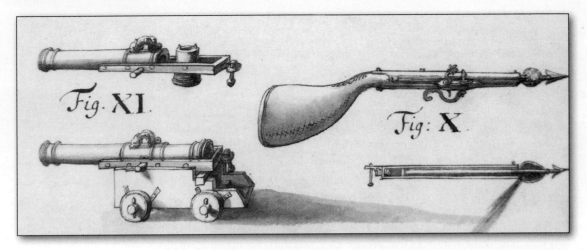

26. Breech-loaded naval gun with ready-made cartridges (left) and musket for shooting fire-arrows (right). (Erik Palmquist, 1674)

Muscovy also developed a specialised musket for shooting iron fire-arrows, which were used to set fire to timber.[149] The Muscovites used the weapon in siege warfare. Fire-arrows, too, had a long tradition in northern warfare, but the specialised musket was apparently another Muscovite invention. In Scandinavia, for instance, fire-arrows were by then primarily launched from light cannon and were regarded as anti-ship weapons.[150]

Despite having no real navy, Muscovy's artillerymen were innovative in naval artillery as well. By 1674, they experimented with breech-loaded naval guns with ready-made cartridges.[151] Although stated to have been produced to avoid risk to the gunners, it can be assumed that a breech-loaded naval gun was an asset onboard the generally quite small river craft used by the Muscovites.

Muscovy entered the field of military rocketry early, as did the rest of northern Europe.[152] The first recorded use of rockets within the Russian cultural sphere reportedly took place already in 1516 near Belgorod, while the first known employment of rockets in Ustyug dates from around 1675.[153]

Grenades, incendiaries, and rockets were no later than by the 1660s subordinated the new office instituted by Tsar Aleksey Mikhailovich in 1656 and referred to as the privy chancellery (*Prikaz taynykh del*). This institution, which was taken out of the ambassadors' chancellery (*Posol'skiy prikaz*) and consisted of 10 officials led by a *d'yak* (a court rank), functioned as the Tsar's personal secretariat, directing troop movements and deployments, and controlling envoys and embassies to foreign countries. However, it also carried out the

---

149 *Ibid.*, p.263. Palmquist's word for fire-arrow was, in seventeenth-century Swedish, *Fÿrpijhl*.

150 Fredholm von Essen, 'On the Trail of Rocketry 2', pp.2–5.

151 Palmquist, *Några observationer*, p.264.

152 Michael Fredholm von Essen, 'On the Trail of Rocketry: The Enigma of Scandinavian Naval Pyrotechnics in the Sixteenth to Eighteenth Century', *Arquebusier* 30:6 (2008), pp.24–39; Michael Fredholm von Essen, 'On the Trail of Rocketry 2', pp.2–5; Michael Fredholm von Essen, 'Early Eighteenth Century Naval Chemical Warfare in Scandinavia: A Study in the Introduction of New Weapon Technologies in Early Modern Navies', *Baltic Security and Defence Review* 13: 1 (2011), pp.122–151.

153 V. Glushko (ed.), *Entsiklopediya kosmonavtika* (Moscow: Sovetskaya entsiklopediya, 1985), s. v. 'Raketnoye oruzhiye'; Krylov, et al., *Military-Historical Museum*, p.207; website, <www.russianspaceweb.com/rockets_pre20th_cent.html>, accessed on 25 January 2018.

27. Above, left: artillerymen, Moscow, wearing the *alam* (Erik Palmquist, 1674); right: an *alam*. (Author's photo)

Tsar's most secret business. It was responsible for the production and use of grenades, incendiaries, and rockets, no doubt because of the common use of these materials for recreational fireworks in the vicinity of the Tsar but possibly also in an attempt to retain related technical knowledge as state secrets.[154]

In or around 1680, during the childhood of Tsar Peter, the first Muscovite rocket factory (*raketnoye zavedeniye*, 'rocket establishment') was established. It manufactured both recreational (civilian) and incendiary (military) rockets (*feyerverochnyye i zazhigatel'nyye rakety*). First located in Moscow, this factory provided the Muscovite army with rockets designed for battlefield illumination and for signalling purposes.[155] Whether incendiary rockets as well were adopted for military use remains unclear. Tsar Peter had a great interest in rocketry. When he was young, he personally experimented with rockets together with the Scots general in Muscovite service, Patrick Gordon, letting off fireworks and rockets during drunken, all-night revelries.[156]

Muscovy, like other northern countries such as the Scandinavian ones, did not distinguish between the function of rockets and other pyrotechnics on the one hand, and gun-barrel artillery on the other. They were regarded as related categories of weapons. This became particularly obvious immediately after the period under consideration here. In 1711, Tsar Peter founded the Arsenal artillery factory (*pushechnyye liteynyye masterskiye*, 'cannon foundries') in Russia's new capital, St. Petersburg.[157] A signal rocket with a parachute flare developed there in 1717 could reportedly reach an altitude of

154 Cotossichin, *Beskrifning*, p.90.

155 *Sovetskaya voyennaya entsikoplediya* (8 vols.; Moscow: Voyennoye izdatel'stvo, 1976–1980), s. v. 'Raketnoye oruzhiye'.

156 See, e.g., Ian Grey, *Peter the Great: Emperor of All Russia* (Philadelphia: J. B. Lippincott, 1960); Stephen Graham, *Peter the Great: A Life of Peter I of Russia* (New York: Simon and Schuster, 1929).

157 A.V. Karpenko, S.M. Ganin, and P.P. Buzayev, *50 let 'KB Arsenal' imeni M. V. Frunze* (St. Petersburg: Nevskiy Bastion, 1999); website, <www.russianspaceweb.com/rockets_pre20th_cent.html>, accessed on 25 January 2018.

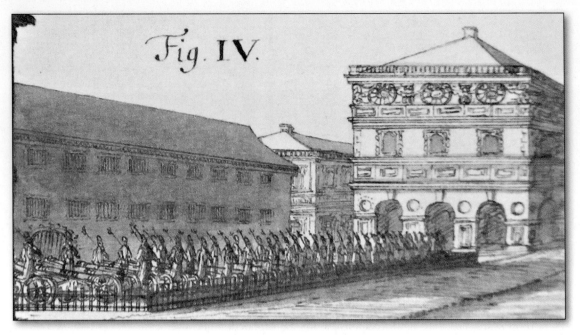

28. Artillerymen in parade uniforms at a Moscow reception. (Erik Palmquist, 1674)

several hundred metres, and similar rockets were used by the Russian army in the early eighteenth century.[158] In 1732, the Arsenal factory produced 20 rocket-launching devices for the Russian border fortress of Brest.[159]

Artillerymen dressed similarly to the infantry, although their caftans and headgear were commonly red or reddish brown. In addition, the artillery had a parade uniform, the primary item of which was referred to as an *alam*. For artillerymen in Moscow, this consisted of a pair of discs of steel or copper hung on chest and back. The disc could be engraved or embossed with the mask of a lion with a gun barrel between its teeth, or with a doubleheaded eagle with a sword in its right claw and a cannon in its left. Alternatively, the discs might lack the engraved or embossed decoration, being instead brightly burnished. Foreign observers thought that the discs were made of tin-plate. At times, red, blue, or green cloth for caftans was handed out in reward of good marksmanship.[160]

Erik Palmquist's Treatise on the Muscovite Army

Erik Palmquist (c.1650–1676?) was, as noted, a Swedish fortification officer (military engineer) who in 1673–1674 participated in an embassy to Moscow. His task was to prepare a military intelligence report on the Muscovite army and military geography. His work resulted in a manuscript that detailed Muscovite fortresses, artillery, garrisons, foreign officers in Muscovite service,

---

158 S.P. Umanskiy, *Rakety, nositeli, kosmodromy* (Moscow: Restart+, 2001); website, <www.russianspaceweb.com/rockets_pre20th_cent.html>, accessed on 25 January 2018; *Sovetskaya voyennaya entsikoplediya*, s. v. 'Raketnoye oruzhiye'.

159 Karpenko et al., *50 let 'KB Arsenal'*; website, <www.russianspaceweb.com/rockets_pre20th_cent.html>, accessed on 25 January 2018.

160 Palacios-Fernandez, 'Moskovskiye pushkari', pp.5–11; Birgegård, *Sparwenfeld's Diary*, p.161.

regiments, and armament, with particulars on the colonels, uniforms, and standards of the various regiments. Palmquist also described the roads and waterways to Moscow. He worked through personal observation as well as by bribing Muscovite informants.[161] It is believed that the manuscript was the appendix to a large map of Muscovy that was the main result of his work but did not survive into the present. The uses to which the Swedish army put Palmquist's reports are no longer known; however, it has been suggested that Palmquist's map of Pskov was studied in preparation of a contemplated Swedish attack on the city by King Charles XII in 1706.[162] Palmquist was less successful in a subsequent mission; he appears to have been captured by Danish troops in 1676 and apparently died soon afterwards.

Palmquist noted that his Muscovite informants, likely those whom he bribed, estimated the total number of men, foot and horse, who were available for military purposes in Muscovy to be 300,000. Most were intended to serve as a defence against the Ottoman empire and the Crimean Tatars. However, of this number only a third, somewhat more than 100,000 men, were on active duty. The troops in the north-west, facing Sweden, were no more than 6,000 recruited men (with which he presumably meant new formation troops). In addition, there were border fortresses in the Ukraine and on the Lithuanian border, such as Toropets and Velikiye Luki.[163] In the light of the subsequent Crimean campaigns, which in Palmquist's time had not yet taken place, and the strength of the Novgorod, Pskov, and Tver' garrisons, which he himself had seen, the information provided by his informants seems as correct as it could be.

Palmquist particularly interested himself in the standing military forces. He noted that there were 12 regiments that currently were on campaign duty. Since they were away from Moscow, he did not see them, nor could he record their uniforms, standards, and numbers of men. However, he listed them, and, since they were named after their colonels, also numbered them (the regimental numbers he provided were almost certainly arbitrary, yet modern scholars often cite them), in the following order:

161 Palmquist's manuscript was called *Någre widh Sidste Kongl: Ambassaden till Tzaren i Muskou giorde Observationer öfwer Ryßlandh, des Wägar, Paß medh Fästningar och Gräntzer. Sammandragne Aff Erich Palmquist. ANNO 1674*. It is retained in the Swedish National Archives (Riksarkivet, Kartor och ritningar utan känd proveniens, nr 636, Kartbok). A facsimile was, as noted, eventually published under the title *Några observationer angående Ryssland, sammanfattade av Erik Palmquist år 1674* (Moscow: Lomonosov, 2012).

162 Palmquist, *Några observationer*, p.81.

163 *Ibid.*, pp.242, 245. In this passage, Palmquist's original Swedish is more precise that the book's English translation. While Palmquist's estimate of Muscovy's total military strength would seem to echo the mid-sixteenth century English merchant Richard Chancellor, and may do so, Palmquist adds more detail based on his own observations. Moreover, by the time of Palmquist, unlike earlier, the total figure appears to be correct. It accordingly remains possible that Palmquist acquired the information from a Muscovite informant, not a dated literary source. Richard Chancellor, *Voyages* (1589), in Berry and Crummey, *Rude & Barbarous Kingdom*, p.27.

Regiment	Colonel
1st	Guibaiyedov[164]
2nd	Kaslaynov[165]
3rd	Yefimov
4th	G. Dokturov
5th	Peter Dokturov
6th	Sekerin
7th	Korsakov
8th	Vorob'yin
9th	Pishchov[166]
10th	Zhukov
11th	Zhemchuzhnikov
12th	Yelagin

Since the regiments were not commanded by foreign officers, most were presumably streltsy regiments. In addition to these regiments, Palmquist noted the first and second selected regiments of new formation troops, both of which were on campaign duty during Palmquist's stay in Moscow. According to his informants, the first selected regiment, under Colonel Aggey Shepelyov, comprised 4,000 men, while the second selected regiment, under Colonel Matvey Krovkov, comprised 2,500 men.[167] In addition, Palmquist noted the 14 regiments of Moscow streltsy, their colonels, and their strength (again likely with arbitrary regimental numbers), in the following order:[168]

Regiment	Colonel	Strength
1st	Georgiy Petrovich Lutokhin	1,500 men
2nd	Ivan Fyodorovich Poltyov	1,000 men
3rd	Vasiliy Borisovich Bukhvostov	1,000 men
4th	Fyodor Ivanovich Golovinskiy	800 men
5th	Fyodor Vasil'yevich Aleksandrov	800 men
6th	Nikifor Ivanovich Kolobov	900 men
7th	Stepan Fyodorovich Yanov	1,000 men
8th	Timofey Fyodorovich Poltyov	800 men
9th	Peter Abramovich Lopukhin	1,200 men
10th	Fyodor Abramovich Lopukhin	1,000 men
11th	Davyd Grigor'yevich Vorontsov	600 men
12th	Ivan Ivanovich Naramanskiy	600 men
13th	… … Lagovskin[169]	600 men
14th	Afanasiy Ivanovich Lyovshin	1,000 men

---

164 Spelling uncertain, name possibly of Tatar origin.
165 Spelling uncertain, name possibly of Tatar origin.
166 Spelling uncertain.
167 Palmquist, *Några observationer*, pp.245–6.
168 *Ibid.*, p.246.
169 Palmquist left blank space for personal name and patronymic, but he apparently never got the chance to fill them in.

Palmquist also made careful notes on the officers in the service of the Tsar who were either born in Moscow to foreign parents or were themselves foreigners. Their number in Moscow was significant: four major generals, 29 colonels, 25 lieutenant colonels, 25 majors, 15 captains of cavalry, and 53 captains. Most were Germans, but there were also Livonian and Prussian Germans, Scots, Englishmen, Dutchmen, a Norwegian, and a Pole. In many cases, the nationality was a moot point, since they were born in Muscovy.[170] Palmquist made notes on foreign officers who served elsewhere in Muscovy as well, in places such as Sevsk, Kursk, Kiev, Smolensk, Chernigov, Kozlov, Tsaritsyn, Pereslavl', Kazan', Astrakhan', Azov, and Siberia. They presented a similar picture, but also included an Italian and a Frenchman. Their number included 20 colonels, 12 lieutenant colonels, and one major.[171] Even though it can be assumed that Palmquist did not succeed in identifying all foreign officers, his information in any case shows the preponderance of foreign officers in the Muscovite army, and in particular in the new formation regiments. However, Palmquist also pointed out that most of the Moscow-based foreign officers in fact were in the reserve, since their regiments were not, at the time, called out for service. While in the reserve, they received a quarter of their active duty salary only.[172]

Having described the total number of troops, the Moscow regiments, and the foreign officers, Palmquist focused on the Muscovite artillery, which he described as "extremely beautiful and effective". Muscovy had all the usual types of artillery, which were also used by the Swedish army. However, as noted above, in addition Muscovy had its own innovations in artillery. In particular the artillery carriage that allowed fire in any direction was a clear improvement, and not only when a wagenburg formation was being used. The continued developments in incendiaries and chemical warfare, as described above, should also be noted, and were duly so noted by Palmquist.[173]

Palmquist's mission consisted of intelligence gathering. It was accordingly natural that he focused on military topography and as much detail as he was able to gather on the Muscovite order of battle. As for weapons and tactics, Palmquist only mentioned innovations or such peculiarites that were not already commonplace in other European armies. When reading his manuscript, it is obvious that he was not interested in normal muskets, cannons, tactics, and so on. His task was to identify any significant differences between the Muscovite army and those of other European states. It is thus striking that it was the Muscovite artillery which chiefly caught his attention.

170 Palmquist, *Några observationer*, pp.307–9.

171 *Ibid.*, pp.316–17.

172 *Ibid.*, p.321.

173 *Ibid.*, pp.262–4.

4

The North Caucasians in the Muscovite Army

Peoples of the North Caucasus

The steep mountains of the Caucasus range always served as a barrier between the steppes of the north and the more fertile, agricultural areas to the south. Although jagged and bare, and with few real passes from north to south, many narrow and forested, fertile valleys cut through the mountains. There were also major forests and plains in the foothills to the north and south of the mountain range. On the densely wooded Black Sea coastline, terrain was difficult, highways non-existent, and transportation usually far easier by ship or boat than on land. On the side of the Caspian, however, the terrain was somewhat easier, although still rugged, and a major highway followed the coastline from Persia in the south to the steppe empires up north.[1]

The steppes just north of the Caucasus range formed the home of the Noghai Tatars, with whom Ivan III had concluded an alliance around 1475. In the 1550s, the Noghai fragmented, dividing into the Great Horde, the Small Horde, and the Altyul'sk Horde. In 1554, the prince of the Great Noghai Horde pledged loyalty to Ivan IV, as an effect of Muscovy's importance as a market for Noghai horses. However, the Small Noghai Horde in 1560 concluded a treaty with the Crimean Khanate, and many Noghai Tatars took part in the Crimean and Ottoman military expedition against Astrakhan' in 1569 and the Crimean expeditions against Moscow in 1571 and 1572.

Although the highland or alpine regions of the Caucasus are very mountainous, the valleys and foothills are in the ancient period believed to have been populous and agriculturally self-sufficient. These regions were in the sixteenth and seventeenth centuries inhabited by numerous very different ethnic and linguistic groups with a social structure best described as clannish and tribal. The various groups in addition to their other differences professed very different religions. The inhabitants of the central and eastern

---

1   This chapter is based on Michael Fredholm von Essen, 'When Sugar Canes Grow in the Snows: Circassians and Other North Caucasians at War, c. 1500–1722,' *Arquebusier* 29: 6 (2006), pp.2–34.

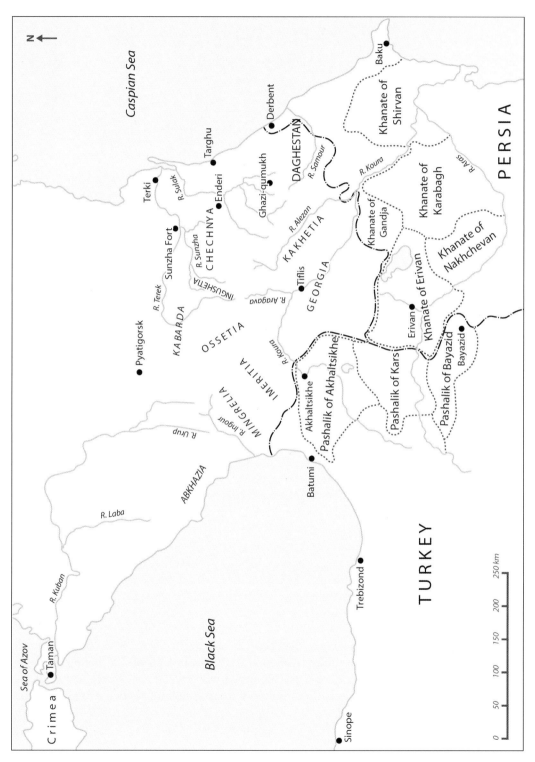

Map 2. The Caucasus

parts of the North Caucasus lived in fortified villages, while those of the western parts of the North Caucasus primarily lived in isolated farmsteads.

The North Caucasus had for long been a backwater in many ways isolated from great power politics elsewhere. By the sixteenth century, however, the climate cooled, the glaciers advanced, and the growing season became shorter. This climatic change caused serious and widespread repercussions for the various tribes that inhabited the alpine regions of the Caucasus range.

There was not only climatic pressure; political and religious pressures were also building up. The population of the North Caucasus had long been polytheists and animists, but by the sixteenth century, Islam was penetrating from the south (from the Ottoman Empire and Safavid Persia) as well as from the Tatars of the Muslim successor states of the Golden Horde in the north. Meanwhile Orthodox Christianity was moving in from the younger but rapidly expanding Muscovite state. Christianity of sorts had, in fact, existed in the Caucasus for centuries and was most common in the western North Caucasus (among the Adyghs and some Kabardians and Ossetians). Islam had taken hold of the east (the various tribes of Daghestan, who lived on jagged bare mountains or in the lowlands near the Caspian), while traditional animism of various kinds remained in between (among the Chechens and Ingush, who lived on the heavily forested hills of the central North Caucasus).

These various tribes, and several others, became collectively and rather loosely known to the Western world as Circassians. The Muscovites instead in most cases called them Tatars, although there were, as noted, also true Tatars in the Caucasus, the aforementioned Noghai Tatars just north of the Caucasus range. The term Circassian (or its Turkic and Russian equivalent, *Cherkes*, which should not be confused with the Ukrainian Cherkassy) in time came broadly to encompass all indigenous peoples of the Caucasus who lived north of the Caucasus Mountains. This is the meaning of the term as it was commonly understood in the past, since the fifteenth century in Russia and from the early sixteenth century in western Europe as well. With regard to Muslim Caucasians at least, the term Circassian or Cherkess is still commonly understood as such in Turkey.

More specifically, however, the term Circassian encompasses only the north-western Caucasians, that is, the Adyghs, Abkhazians, Abazas, and the Ubykhs (extinct as a language since 1992, its speakers having assimilated into the Adygh community) who lived in the forests of the western region of the North Caucasus. At present, many restrict the use of the term Circassian to the Adyghs, who in turn are made up of numerous tribes although they (unlike for instance Abkhazians and Chechens) speak mutually intelligible dialects of Adigabze, the Circassian language. The term Circassian was always used by outsiders and does not constitute a name in the Circassian language.[2] In the period under consideration here, outsiders indeed saw little differences in the culture and lifestyle of the numerous North Caucasian tribes and clans. In this spirit, the term Circassian will here be applied to all indigenous North Caucasians, from the 'true' Circassians of the north-west to the ancestors of the various peoples

---

2   See, e.g., Amjad Jaimoukha, *The Circassians: A Handbook* (New York: Palgrave, 2001), p.11.

who constitute the North Caucasians of today, including Chechens, Daghestanis, and even the Orthodox Christian and linguistically Indo-European Ossetians, who unlike other North Caucasians still regard themselves, and were so regarded by mediaeval European writers, as the linguistic (proven) and ethnic (not quite as proven) descendants of the ancient Alans.

All North Caucasian tribes were warrior societies. War was a way of life in the Caucasus, and blood feuds (often referred to using the Turkic term *kanly*) were and are pursued through several generations. All Circassians were known to raid the neighbouring lowlands. A Persian proverb went, "If the Shah is too mighty, let him only make war on the Caucasus." In Persia, the Caucasus range was known as Sadd-e Iskander, the Wall of Alexander, and was believed to have been fortified by Alexander the Great to keep barbarians out from the civilised world. The Caucasus barrier did not prevent wars, however. A local proverb runs, "When shall blood cease to flow in the mountains? When sugar canes grow in the snows."

The Northern Caucasus was a territory surrounded by powerful states: Muscovy, the Ottoman empire, Safavid Persia, and the Tatar Crimean Khanate. A regional great power was the Shamkhalate of northern Daghestan. Except Muscovy, all were Muslim states. To find other Christians, one would have to search south of the Caucasus, where there lived Christian Georgians and Armenians. To the rear of the Tatar Crimean Khanate was, of course, the Christian Polish-Lithuanian Commonwealth. North Caucasians would in time play usually small but not insignificant roles in the wars of all these various powers.

29. Chechen warrior. (Karl P. Beggrov, 1822)

From 1644 onwards, the first bands of Kalmyks (western Mongols) appeared in the River Terek region, having migrated from the eastern Eurasian steppes. The western Mongols (Oirat, 'confederates', as they called themselves, or as the Turks and accordingly the Muscovites named them, Kalmyks) were traditionally based far to the east, near the uppermost Yenisey south of present-day Tuva. The Kalmyks raided both in the Caucasus and in lands held by Muscovy. The first Kalmyk intrusion was beaten off by an alliance between Kabardians and Noghai Tatars, but already in 1645, the Kalmyk *taishi* (prince), Daichin, entered negotations with Muscovy on an alliance in exchange for grazing rights on the steppe between the lower Volga and the Yaik (Ural) Rivers. The Kalmyks were at the time being pushed out of their eastern territories, thus moving west in increasing numbers. Daichin offered the support of his 20,000 Mongols. By 1650, Muscovy entered into an alliance with the Kalmyks against the Crimean Khanate. From 1655, when Muscovy for political and strategic reasons offered protection to the Kalmyks and the right to grazing along the eastern bank of the Volga as far as Tsaritsyn and along its western bank as far as Samara, relations between

North Caucasians and Kalmyks improved as well. Henceforth, Kalmyks regularly contributed a cavalry force, consisting of several thousands (more in the eighteenth century), when Muscovy went to war against the Crimeans. Kalmyks also occasionally appeared as powerful allies to those Circassians who supported Muscovy, such as against the Crimean Khanate.[3]

Religion was not yet a key factor of allegiance in the North Caucasus and indeed remained a fluid concept in the Caucasus until quite late. By the thirteenth century, the Circassians and most other North Caucasians except the Daghestanis, had still been adherents to their traditional polytheist or animist beliefs or, at least in some cases, converted to Christianity of sorts. They were, for instance, classified as pagans by John of Plano Carpini, who in 1245 was sent as papal envoy to the Mongol Great Khan, but Christians according to John's travel companion Benedict the Pole.[4] In the north-eastern Caucasus, however, Islam was spreading. Southern Daghestan had been conquered and Islamicised at an early stage in the Arab wars of conquest (probably in the eighth century), and Islam had gradually spread into northern Daghestan as well and thence into present-day Chechnya. By the fifteenth century, many, perhaps most of the ancestors of the Chechens were nominally, but only nominally, converted to the new faith. Islam would really not make a greater impact there until by the time of the wars of resistance against Russia from the late eighteenth century onwards. The mountain tribes somewhat further to the west, the ancestors of the Ingush, meanwhile remained adherents to their traditional animist beliefs and would so remain, to a large extent, until the early nineteenth century.[5]

Among the Circassians of the western North Caucasus, the Abkhazians adopted Islam first. This was hardly surprising, since they lived furthest to the south, and in addition along the eastern Black Sea coast where the Ottomans began to establish bases in the sixteenth century. It was also the Ottoman influence that helped to disseminate Sunni Islam among the Abkhazians in the sixteenth and seventeenth centuries. Islam seems to have been introduced from the top down, with noble families converting first for political reasons, followed by the bulk of the population somewhat later. In addition, Muslim traditions and teachings were in many ways only added to the existing mixture of Christian beliefs and traditional animism of the Abkhazians. Most continued, for instance, to eat pork and to celebrate Christian and traditional festivals in addition to the new Muslim ones.[6]

Neither Circassians nor other North Caucasians ever fully united, neither through religion nor ties of kinship. Yet they in the sixteenth to eighteenth centuries clashed frequently with their many and varied neighbours: Crimean Tatars, cossacks, and Muscovites in the north, Ottoman Turks and Mingrelian

---

3 Kasbolat Fitsevich Dzamikhov, *Adygi (cherkesy) v politike Rossii na Kavkaze (1550-e – nachalo 1770-kh gg.)* (Nal'chik: State University of Kabardino-Balkaria, 2001; formerly available at website <www.kbsu.ru/Faculty/Sgi/KOI/index.htm>, ch. 7.2.1; Davies, *Warfare, State and Society*, p.95.

4 Christopher Dawson (ed.), *Mission to Asia* (Toronto: University of Toronto Press, 1980), pp.31, 80. See also Jaimoukha, *Circassians*, pp.148–9.

5 Jaimoukha, *Circassians*, p.151.

6 George Hewitt (ed.), *The Abkhazians: A Handbook* (Richmond, Surrey: Curzon, 1999), p.208.

Georgians in the south, and Daghestanis and to some extent Persians in the east. Caught between the Muslim Tatars, Turks and Daghestanis on the one (spiritual, not geographical) side, and the Orthodox Christian cossacks, Muscovites, and Georgians on the other, religious faith had little role to play among the North Caucasians, who for long would lean towards one or the other depending on current political circumstances. This fluid situation of religiosity would continue until the late eighteenth century, when most North Caucasians adopted Sunni Islam. What had changed? The North Caucasians were by then no longer an active part in the conflict. Whereas they in earlier centuries had raided for profit and played the major powers off one against the other, they now had been decisively forced on the defensive. No longer raiders but fighting for their own survival, they found Islam the one unifying factor that they desperately needed to defend themselves against the seemingly inexhaustible armies of Imperial Russia which eventually, in the mid-nineteenth century, would take control over the region and through more permanent means than previously annex it as a conquered territory.

Principalities and Tribes

The West: The Circassians and the Principality of Kabarda

Although most often ignored by the surrounding great powers, the North Caucasians had in the thirteenth century fallen under the dominion of the Golden Horde.[7] When the Golden Horde dissolved, an opportunity arose for the North Caucasians to recover their independence.

The first mountain-dwellers who did so were the Kabardians, one of the western Circassian tribes. In the probably late fifteenth century (the chronology is uncertain), a Kabardian, Prince Inal Teghen (or Tighwen), who some believe had returned from Mamluk service in Egypt, united many of the Circassian clans. He also appears to have defeated a Georgian army in 1509 (if this indeed was the same Inal).[8] In the sixteenth and seventeenth centuries, a Circassian state existed in the Northern Caucasus under the Kabardian princes. It extended from the Kuban' River in the west to the River Sunzha in the east and from the plains north of present Pyatigorsk and the River Terek in the north to Georgia in the south. Being centred around the Five Mountains (*Pyatygory* in Russian, *Bgiytxw* in Circassian, *Beshtau* in Turkic; present Pyatigorsk), the Principality of Kabarda was at times also known as the Principality of the Five Mountains. Legend states that Inal was succeeded by his five sons, who divided the Circassian state among them.[9] Soon there was no longer any unified leadership among the Circassians, and feudal princes assumed control over the population. Although the

---

7 See, e.g., Lapidus, *History of Islamic Societies*, p.815.

8 See, e.g., W.E.D. Allen (ed.), *Russian Embassies to the Georgian Kings, 1589–1605* (2 vols., Cambridge: Hakluyt Society, Cambridge University Press, 1970), pp.272–3; Dzamikhov, *Adygi*, ch. 4.1.1. Some have suggested that this Inal was confused with the Mamluk Sultan of the same name who lived from 1379–1460, ruled from 1453 onwards, and died in Cairo, but the name Inal was not uncommon among the Mamluks.

9 Dzamikhov, *Adygi*, ch. 4.1.1.

Principality of Kabarda remained strong as compared to the other North Caucasian tribes and maintained diplomatic relations with Muscovy and the Ottoman empire, it remained a backwater. Constantly feuding with each other, the Circassians were unable to unite in the face of external danger.[10] Many Circassians from the Five Mountains went into Muscovite service, as allies or subjects. In 1556, they for the first time joined Muscovy in its war against the Crimean Khanate, attacking the Khanate's eastern border as a loose Muscovite-led coalition of Don cossacks, Lithuanians, and Circassians raided the Kerch straits in light boats, thus for the first time taking the war to the Crimean Khanate itself. Capturing the two towns of Temryuk and Toman, the raid was a success, although the Muscovite conquest of Astrakhan' in the same year arguably was a more lasting victory.[11]

The Kabardian princes (*pshi*, a title originally believed to have denoted 'elder') in many ways corresponded to the feudal barons of Western Europe and the boyars of Muscovy. The child of a couple of princely rank had the honorific title of *mirza*, while the child of a prince and a woman of lower status would receive the lesser noble title of *tuma*. Below the princely families came the gentry composed of their vassals, known as *work* (a term translated by the Muscovites as retainer, *dvoryanin*). This group was divided into two ranks: the *tlakotle* and the *dezhenugo*, as the respective upper and lower rank was called. The key feature of all these nobles was that they enjoyed sovereign status and had the right to change patron at will. Below the nobles came the free farmers, the bonded farmers, and the bondsmen.[12]

If Prince Inal Teghen really had returned from Mamluk service in Egypt, we can expect that he would at least nominally have been a Muslim. Surviving Ottoman documents indeed refer to the Kabardian princes as Muslims. This was surely at least nominally true. The Kabardians had close ties with the Crimean Khanate, and Kabardians often took part in the latter's war as allies of the Crimean Tatars. Those who engaged in the service of the Ottoman Sultan or the Crimean Khan as far as is known all were, or became, Muslims. On the other hand, Russian language sources from the same period make it clear that the Kabardian nobles were superficial about religion. Those who chose to serve the Tsar would convert to Orthodox Christianity. Most noble families would include converts to not only one but both religions. As for the lower classes, they in most cases continued to practice their traditional polytheism or animism which also included traces of Christian belief, which had survived from earlier periods of missionary activity.[13] The fluidity of religious beliefs was clearly shown by the situation in July 1563, when a civil war among the Kabardian princes caused a situation in which Prince Temryuk, a Muslim, acquired the Muscovite Tsar's protection against his two rivals, Princes Siboq and Qanuq of the Beslanays, who (1) were Christians,

10 Jaimoukha, *Circassians*, pp.49–51.

11 Filjushkin, *Ivan the Terrible*, p.114.

12 Chantal Lemercier-Quelquejay, 'Co-optation of the Elites of Kabarda and Daghestan in the Sixteenth Century', Marie Bennigsen Broxup (ed.), *The North Caucasus Barrier: The Russian Advance towards the Muslim World* (London: Hurst & Company, 1992), pp.18–44, on pp.25–6.

13 *Ibid.*, pp.26–7.

(2) hitherto had been in the Tsar's service, and (3) were known in Moscow by their Christian names Aleksei and Gavril. The latter two were forced to flee to Lithuania, whence they entered the service of the Muslim Khan of the Crimean Tatars.[14] So much for religious loyalties.

The Circassians further to the west were considerably more tribal and even more divided than the Kabardians. Two major tribal confederations in the mid-sixteenth century were the Janey (or Zhane) Circassians who inhabited the Taman' peninsula south of the Kuban', and the Beslanays (another Circassian tribe of the Five Mountains which early on had been dominated by the Kabardians but successfully broke away in the fifteenth century[15]), who lived in the middle valley of the Kuban' and its southern tributaries Belaya, Laba, and Urup. There were also various other western Circassian tribes, referred to as 'Free Circassians' in Russian-language documents and 'Unsubdued Circassians' in Ottoman sources. Most probably this should be interpreted as these Circassian being both free and not yet Muslims.

30. Circassian family. (Adam Olearius, 1656)

There were also the Abazas, who had formed a state akin to that of the Kabardians, like them with a social organisation dependant on sovereign princes and great nobles.[16] The Abazas, who like the western Adyghs and the Kabardians would choose and select their allegiance as political conditions dicated between the Crimean Khanate and Islam on the one hand and Muscovy and Orthodox Christianity on the other, could certainly be described as being both free and not yet Muslims.

The Janeys of the Taman' peninsula, due to their proximity to the Crimean Khanate, were the first to come under pressure from the Crimean Tatars. From the early 1490s, major Tatar raids would take place almost every year.[17] The Janeys thus converted to Islam in or soon after the 1560s, but not until it had become clear that Muscovy was unable to gain lasting control over the surrounding territories. Their conversion also illustrates another key aspect of becoming Muslims; in the seventeenth century, an Ottoman document makes it clear that since the Janeys were Muslims, it was no longer permitted to take prisoners among them for the – in the Islamic world – very lucrative trade in Circassian slaves. This restriction did not, however, apply to the Circassian tribes further to the east, which indicates that the majority had not yet converted or were only lukewarm Muslims.[18]

---

14 *Ibid.*, p.27.
15 Already in the eleventh century according to some. Jaimoukha, *Circassians*, pp.47, 53.
16 Lemercier-Quelquejay, 'Co-optation', pp.27–8.
17 Dzamikhov, *Adygi*, ch. 6.1.1.
18 Lemercier-Quelquejay, 'Co-optation', pp.29–30.

That the adoption of Islam did not in any way guarantee peace with more powerful Muslim neighbours was shown on numerous occasions in the seventeenth century[19] and again in 1705–1708, when the Ottoman empire in response to Muscovite pressure at Azov made attempts to occupy Kabarda. Upon the request of the Ottoman Sultan, the Khan of the Crimean Tatars, Qaplan Ghirai, in 1708 led a huge army of some 20,000 to 30,000 men against the Principality of the Five Mountains.[20] The Circassians retreated into the mountains where they either took refuge in existing stone fortifications or erected new ones. Circassian folklore suggests that they thence sallied out in raids against the Tatars. On one occasion, they reportedly inflicted a serious defeat on the Tatar army by rolling heavy stones down the mountainside onto the Tatar camp. The Khan is said to have lost a brother and a son in this battle.[21] In the final battle (the same?) of the campaign, the Circassians routed the Tatar army in a surprise attack on the enemy camp at night. Only some 5,000 Tatars managed to return to the Crimea.[22]

It was a serious defeat, but this did not stop the pressure from the Crimean Tatars. Another huge Crimean Tatar army, reportedly of 40,000 men, devastated Kabarda in 1720.[23] In 1728, the Kabardians again fragmented, this time into two rival factions known as the Kashkadau and Bakhsan after their respective regional bases. The former supported the Ottomans, the latter Russia. As time passed, the Kabardian princes realised that Russia was expanding, while the Ottomans were on the defensive. However, as any Muscovite expansion in their direction by then took place at the expense of Kabardian sovereignty, the Circassians increasingly allied themselves with the Ottomans. The result was a series of wars that began in the late eighteenth century and culminated in the nineteenth century, in which the Circassians were gradually pushed back and eventually had to face the choice of accepting Russian rule or migrate southwards into Ottoman territory. By the end of the nineteenth century, a majority of the Circassians had chosen the latter. It was also by this time, paradoxically, that the Russian invasions and subsequent complete victory pushed almost all remaining Christian Circassians, for pockets of Christianity still existed among the north-western Circassians despite centuries of Muslim influences, into mass conversion to Islam.[24]

---

19 Dzamikhov, *Adygi*, ch. 6.1.2.
20 *Ibid.*, ch. 3.2.1; 6.2.1. The strength of the Crimean army was mentioned in a letter from a contemporary involved in the events, the Kabardian Prince Tatarkhan Bekmurzin. However, this was the reportedly largest Tatar army ever to invade Kabarda, so later or more distant contemporary authors have suggested a strength of from 40,000 to 100,000 men. Dzamikhov suggests a strength of "no less than 40,000 men." However, Prince Tatarkhan Bekmurzin had no reason to deflate the number of invaders. Since this was the largest Crimean army to invade Kabarda, it thus follows that all other figures for invading Crimean armies, as mentioned in this book and elsewhere, may need to be revised downwards accordingly.
21 Jaimoukha, *Circassians*, p.53.
22 Dzamikhov, *Adygi*, ch. 6.2.1.
23 *Ibid.*, ch. 3.2.1; 6.2.1.
24 See, e.g., Jaimoukha, *Circassians*, pp.58–70, 149.

The Inland: Ossetians, Ingush, and Chechens

While the Circassian nobility maintained control over the western parts of the North Caucasus, the situation in the central-eastern parts began to change around the turn of the sixteenth century. These changes, the exact nature of which remains hotly argued by academics, in particular affected the territories of present Ingushetia and Chechnya. These lands seem hitherto to have been under the control of noble clans much like those to the west, but with nobles who in most cases belonged to the Kabardian, Lezghian, Kumyk, and Avar ethnic groups rather than those of the Chechens and Ingush (or, to be precise, the ancestors of these two closely related ethnic groups, the names of which were only recorded from 1708 and 1724, respectively) who actually farmed the land. A few Chechens who moved down into the Terek plains to the north even seem to have entered Muscovite service, commanded by Kabardian nobles.[25]

First, a process began in which the Chechens (who refer to themselves as Nokhchi) and Ingush (who call themselves Ghalghay) seem to have expelled their native as well as foreign nobility. Little is known about what really happened, but Chechen folklore is ripe with stories of how brave commoners struggled against and overthrew ruthless nobles, who until then had exercised almost boundless power from their fortified towers. So much is clear that

31. Ingush or Chechen defensive tower. (Bruno Plaetschke, 1829)

traditional Chechen society, perhaps around this time and definitely before the early eighteenth century, did acquire a for the period unusual level of egalitarian characteristics, which is often taken to be summed up in the Chechen saying, "we are free and equal as the wolves" (which no doubt has more to do with human society than that of wolves). At least from the seventeenth century, leadership became principally a matter of personal achievement and prestige, not descent. The war-leader (*byachcha*) would be elected by the council of elders of the *teip* (clan), and the post was not hereditary in Chechen or Ingush society.

Second, a process began in which in the sixteenth century first the Chechens, then (much later) the Ingush, began to move down into the Terek plains to the north, where they supplanted the Noghai Tatars and other Turkic nomads and in the second half of the sixteenth century encountered the cossacks, who likewise were migrating into the region but from the opposite direction. Strife soon broke out, and the seemingly perpetual struggle between Chechen and cossack began.

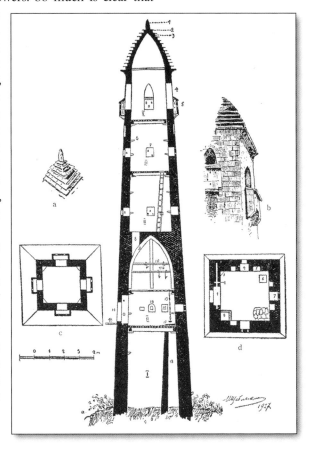

---

25 Dzamikhov, *Adygi*, ch. 5.1.2.

32. Ingush or Chechen *aul* (village) with old defensive towers. (Photo: Kavkas)

Whatever happened to the old nobility, the north-eastern Caucasians, unlike the northwestern Circassians, continued to rely on fortified villages with stone towers. In the north-west, most instead, as noted, lived in isolated farmsteads, although there were also villages of from 40 to 60 houses built into a circle or square with only one gate.[26] Ingush and Chechen residential towers were more or less square in shape. Their walls were 8–10 metres long, and the building was up to 12 metres high. The towers used for defence, however, were up to 20 metres high, tall and narrow. Many walls were decorated with Sarmatian-style symbols (*tamga*) and right- or left-facing swastikas.[27] The front door was often three metres above the ground, and there would be no internal stairway to the next floor. Instead retractable ladders were used for increased security. Each tower would be occupied by a single family.[28]

In the Caucasian inland also lived the often Christian and linguistically Indo-European Ossetians. Being geographically distant from other Christians and by this time of little consequence, they were seldom if ever mentioned in the records. It can be assumed that their way of life was not

26 Jaimoukha, *Circassians*, pp.219–20.

27 Bruno Plaetschke, *Die Tschetschenen: Forschungen zur Völkerkunde des nordöstlichen Kaukasus* (Hamburg: Friederichsen, de Gruyter & Co., 1929; Veröffentlichungen des Geographischen Instituts der Universität Königsberg Pr., Heft 11), pp.39–45.

28 Robert Chenciner, *Daghestan: Tradition & Survival* (Richmond, Surrey: Curzon, 1997), pp.156–7.

that different from other North Caucasians. They were ruled by their own nobles who themselves were dependent on the Kabardian princes.[29]

The East: Daghestan

Different sources give very different information on the religious beliefs common in Daghestan. This is hardly surprising since the country was inhabited by a large number of very different tribes. Arab geographers indeed referred to the Caucasus as Jabal al-Alsine, 'Mountain of Languages'. By this time, Daghestan was divided into at least three principalities. Most sources agree that Daghestan, or at least the lowlands on the Caspian seashore, had been converted to Islam by Arabs probably already in the eighth century. On the other hand, the geographer Abu'l-Qâsim Ibn Hawqal in c.960 or 976 found this country entirely Christian, which would seem to indicate that the last traces of Christianity may have disappeared by the end of the tenth century or soon thereafter. The status of Islam was also reinforced by the Seljuq migrations south of the Caucasus in the eleventh century.[30]

So much is in any case clear that before the sixteenth century, a Caucasian ethnic group known as Qumukhs extended their dominion from their highland settlement of Qumukh down to the Caspian coastland. In the lowlands, they gained control over the Kumyks, pastoralists speaking a Turkic language who lived down in the plains and who may indeed have adopted their name only as a Turkic pronunciation of Qumukh. The Qumukhs, however, referred to themselves as Lak or Lakz, which for complex linguistic reasons also caused them to be known (by the Muscovites and subsequently most others) as Lezghians.[31] The Lezghians took control over the entire northern part of Daghestan. There they had established a state known as the Shamkhalate, after the title, Shamkhal (or Shevkal), of its ruler (many believed that the title derived from the Arabic name *Sham*, 'Syria', because these rulers claimed Arab descent; however, the title, like several others used in Daghestan, was probably of local origin).[32]

Until the end of the fifteenth century, the capital of the Shamkhalate was located at Ghazi-Qumukh (known as Kazi-Kumukh to the Muscovites). In the early sixteenth century, the capital was moved to Targhu (known by the Muscovites as Tarku), a key caravan centre at the crossroads of the two highways connecting Derbent with Astrakhan' and Derbent with Taman'.[33]

At the head of the Shamkhalate was the Shamkhal and his clan in the form of princes, khans, and their relatives (with titles such as *mirza*, *beg*, and *bey*). Below them came nobles of middle rank (*chanka*). The vassals of the Shamkhal formed the third rank of nobles (*uzden'*), which in itself was divided in various ranks. Below them followed the free farmers, serfs, and slaves, respectively. The Shamkhalate remained unified until 1574, after which this state gradually disintegrated until it by the end of the seventeenth century had lost its control

29 Allen, *Russian Embassies*, pp.30–31.
30 Lapidus, *History of Islamic Societies*, p.815.
31 Allen, *Russian Embassies*, pp.37–9.
32 *Ibid.*, p.39.
33 Lemercier-Quelquejay, 'Co-optation', p.32.

over the Daghestani highlands.[34] In 1599, the Shamkhalate and its allies could raise some 5,000 cavalry in all. Should the Kumyks, Circassians, and other North Caucasians have been able to unite, a native guide employed by the Muscovites then estimated, they would have been able to raise about 15,000 cavalry in addition to soldiers on foot.[35] This was close to the mark; in 1605 the Shamkhalate, even though in decline, managed to raise a military force as large as 13,000 cavalry, including allies. However, the Shamkhalate dissolved into a number of very small Kumyk principalities, the limited size of which is shown by the number of cavalry each could muster: the Shamkhal of Targhu, 200 men; Ghazi-Qumukh, 500; Enderi, 200; Erpeli, 400; Kafir-Qumukh, 150; and so on.[36] In 1712, the Shamkhalate had been reduced to the principality of Targhu, but this did not prevent the Shamkhal, Adil Ghirai, together with another small Kumyk principality, from going to war with Kabarda in 1712. Soon afterwards, he also claimed overlordship over all Muslims in the Russian town on the Terek. A much reduced Shamkhalate survived to claim Russian protection in 1750–1751.[37]

In the high mountains of Daghestan lived various non-Turkic tribes such as Avars, Darghins, Lezghians, and others. They were little known by outsiders, reportedly ruled by elders, and no doubt led a way of life not very different from the Chechens further to the west. With the decline of the Shamkhalate, the Avar Khanate became the most powerful principality of Daghestan. Its ruler no longer recognised the right of the elders to elect his successor, instead turning the lordship of the khanate into a hereditary title. Even so, the Avar Khanate could not assume control over the main trade routes as the Shamkhalate had done earlier.[38] The Avar Khan asked for Russian citizenship in 1753[39] and the Khanate survived until its ruling family was wiped out in 1834 by the renowned religious leader Imam Shamil.[40]

To the south of the Avars was the little but wealthy principality of Kaytak, which was ruled by a prince with the title of Utsmi (of unknown derivation), somehow elected by the tribal elders, and which was inhabited by a heterogeneous population of tribes such as Darghins, Kaytaks, Lezghians, and others. This principality controlled Kubachi, which was a famous centre for metalwork including the production of weaponry. The principality also controlled an important part of the coastal Targhu-Derbent highway along the Caspian. At the beginning of the sixteenth century, the principality of Kaytak could raise 500 cavalry and about 1,000 foot.[41]

---

34 *Ibid.*, pp.30–33.

35 Allen, *Russian Embassies*, pp.522, 556–60.

36 Lemercier-Quelquejay, 'Co-optation', p.43 n.21. The numbers given to a large extent correspond to a more detailed list from 1599 by the already mentioned native guide employed by the Russians. Allen, *Russian Embassies*, pp.559–60.

37 Dzamikhov, *Adygi*, ch. 5.1.1.

38 Allen, *Russian Embassies*, pp.40–42; Lemercier-Quelquejay, 'Co-optation', pp.33–4.

39 Dzamikhov, *Adygi*, ch. 5.1.1.

40 Moshe Gammer, *Muslim Resistance to the Tsar: Shamil and the Conquest of Chechnia and Daghestan* (London: Frank Cass, 1994), pp.62–3.

41 Allen, *Russian Embassies*, p.39; Lemercier-Quelquejay, 'Co-optation', p.34.

The south of Daghestan consisted of the likewise small principality of Tabasaran, with a population of Lezghians, Tabasarans, and various mountain tribes such as Tsakhurs, Rutuls, and Aguls. The principality's importance was its closeness to the highway from Shirvan to Derbent. In 1599, Tabasaran could raise 500 cavalry.[42]

North Caucasians in the Muscovite, Ottoman, and Safavid Wars

The first Muscovite outpost in the Caspian region beyond Astrakhan' was probably established in the Terek River delta by the time of the first Muscovite military expedition into Daghestan in 1560 (see below). At first a mere wooden stockade (*ostrog*), soon a town, variously known as Terki, Terka, and Terskiy Gorod, grew up adjacent to the fort. Incidentally, the fort blocked the line of communications and trade between the Ottoman fortress at Azov and Derbent, which was an Ottoman fortress on the Caspian. By 1636, the town had become an important centre for trade and was generally regarded as the most distant Muscovite town in the Caucasus.[43] By the 1670s, the town was greatly improved and hosted a garrison of 2,000 streltsy and a strong artillery force.[44]

By then, the region was also a hub for cossack activity. As noted, small bands of cossacks had crossed the Caspian and sailed up the Terek River, settling in the delta as the Terek cossacks in about 1578. The Terek cossacks soon engaged in frontier warfare with the various peoples of the Caucasus: Kabardians, Circassians, Chechens, and Noghai. When in 1586, Muscovite regular troops again arrived at the mouth of the Terek, the Terek cossacks continued their activities but henceforth they did so in the service of Moscow. Their Orthodox religion set them apart from the neighbouring Caucasian tribes, but hardly anything else. As noted, the Terek cossacks were soon joined by the Greben' cossacks (cossacks of the 'mountain ridge'), who settled in the foothills of the Caucasus range.

The Muscovite expansion into the Caspian region began early. Following Ivan IV's victories against the Tatar khanates of Kazan' and Astrakhan' in 1552 and 1556, respectively, many Circassians (primarily Adjars and Kabardians in the Kuban' region) submitted to Muscovy, embracing Christianity in the process. In 1555, the western Circassians sent an embassy to Moscow which formally submitted to the Muscovite Tsar – in the same way that they also submitted to all other neighbouring great powers. The Circassians presumably felt the pressure from the Crimean Khanate. Indeed, some Kabardian princes chose to ally themselves strongly to the Muscovite cause. One influential Kabardian, the Muslim Prince Temryuk, in 1557 entered into an alliance with Tsar Ivan, in which Temryuk accepted Muscovite protection, in particular against the Shamkhal of Daghestan, who indeed was allied to the Khan of the Crimea. A

42   Allen, *Russian Embassies*, pp.39, 560. See also Lemercier-Quelquejay, 'Co-optation', p.34.
43   Adam Olearius, *Moskowitische und Persische Reise: Die Holsteinische Gesandtschaft beim Schah 1633–1639* (Stuttgart: Thienemann, Edition Erdmann, 1986), p.154.
44   Palmquist, *Några observationer*, p.278.

curious factor in the equation was that an embassy from the Shamkhalate had arrived in Moscow the previous year due to the Shamkhal's need to defend his country against the Kabardians. In 1557, Moscow also reportedly received a vow of alliance or vassalage from another Muslim ruler named Ismail Bey (d. 1563), the Khan of the Great Noghai Horde. While noteworthy, the Great Noghai Horde was already in decline, with key Noghai leaders leaving to establish separate Noghai Hordes. In 1560, Muscovy nonetheless approached Ismail Bey for a joint Muscovite-Kabardian-Noghai alliance against the Crimean Khanate and its protector, the Ottoman empire.[45]

These diplomatic maneuvres clarified the strategic environment. Muscovy and the Crimean Khanate remained the key regional adversaries. The Crimea was under the protection of the Ottoman empire and itself supported the Shamkhalate. Muscovy thus offered protection to Kabarda (and from 1589, to the Georgian kingdom of Kakheti), and allied with the Noghai Tatars (an alliance that did not survive the death of Ismail Bey but which in time was replaced by a more enduring alliance with the Kalmyks). As for the other major powers, the Polish-Lithuanian Commonwealth, following the principle of the enemy of my enemy being my friend, offered limited support to the Crimean Khanate.

Combined Muscovite-Kabardian operations against the Crimean Tatars took place in the Don and Azov region in 1560–1561. In 1560, a Muscovite army under Ivan Cheremisinov-Karaulov was also dispatched against Daghestan in support of Kabarda in its war against the Shamkhalate. Cheremisinov, it will be remembered, had previously been the head of one of the first streltsy regiments. He had also participated in the conquests of Kazan' and Astrakhan'.[46] The Shamkhal's army was defeated, and the Shamkhal himself had to take refuge in the mountains. In 1561, Tsar Ivan (following the death in the previous year of his first wife, Anastasia) betrothed and then married Gwashcheney, the daughter of the Muslim Kabardian ruler, who for this purpose was baptised Mariya Temryukovna. One of Prince Temryuk's sons, Sulht'anqwl (known to the Muscovites as Salnuk or Saltanuk), had already in 1558 gone to the Muscovite court as part of the alliance concluded a year earlier. In Moscow, he became known under his new baptised name, Prince Mikhail Temryukovich Cherkasskiy.[47] Several members of his clan, known as Cherkasskiy in Muscovy, took up positions as senior military commanders in the Muscovite army. In about 1580, for instance, Prince Boris Kanbulatovich Cherkasskiy entered Muscovite service. In 1582–1583 and 1588–1589, he commanded the Muscovite forces in Novgorod, and in 1585–1586 and again in the winter of 1591–1592, he served as overall commander on the southern border.[48] Their descendants continued to serve Russia in influential positions for generations. Among many notable members of this clan was Prince Alexander Bekovich-Cherkasskiy, who commanded the first

45 Dzamikhov, *Adygi*, ch. 3.1.1; 6.1.1.
46 V.V. Penskoy, '*Tsenturiony' Ivana Groznogo 1: Ivan Semenov syn Cheremisinov* (Milhist.info, 2012; available at website <www.milhist.info/2012/11/19/penskoy_2>, accessed on 25 January 2018).
47 Dzamikhov, *Adygi*, ch. 3.1.1; 6.1.1.
48 Berry and Crummey, *Rude & Barbarous Kingdom*, p.331 n.19.

Russian expeditionary force against the Uzbeks of the Khanate of Khiva in Central Asia in 1717; the expedition ended in disaster and most of his men died together with their commander.[49]

Another example of the complexity of the strategic environment at the time was that in 1560, when joint Muscovite-Kabardian operations against the Crimean Tatars took place in the Don and Azov region, the King of Poland and ruler of the Grand Duchy of Lithuania, Sigismund II Augustus, wrote to the Muslim Crimean Khan, Davlat Ghirai, to warn him of the dangers of the Muscovite-Kabardian alliance.[50]

In 1563–1566, a civil war was fought in Kabarda between Temryuk and other princes. In 1565, Temryuk asked for, and received, Muscovite assistance in putting down his rivals. In 1567, he also requested that Muscovy establish a garrison on the Terek River close to his borders (presumably on the spot already in use by Muscovites). However, by closely allying himself to Muscovy, Temryuk had made enemies with the Crimean Tatars. In 1570 (following the outbreak of the first war between the Khan's Ottoman protector and Muscovy in 1569), a Khan of the Tatars, presumably Davlat Ghirai, ordered an attack on the Five Mountains. The Circassians had no help to expect from Muscovy, which until this year had been engaged in wars in Livonia against Lithuania and, in 1570 chose to attack the Swedish forces in present-day Estonia. Temryuk faced the Tatar army, led by the Tatar Khan's son Aldi Ghirai, with a combined army of Kabardians and Beslanays on the banks of the middle Kuban'. However, the Tatars won a resounding victory. Temryuk himself was wounded, and his two sons fell into Tatar captivity. As a result of the Tatar victory, the Khan forced many Circassians to convert (or at least to conform better) to Islam and resettle on the banks of the Kuban', which henceforth became Circassia's northern frontier. Another result of the Tatar victory was that the Crimean Khan henceforth could concentrate his efforts on Muscovy; in 1571, as noted, Davlat Ghirai led an army of 40,000 (consisting of Crimean Tatars, Tatars of the Great and Small Noghai Hordes, and several contingents from the North Caucasus) which broke through the Oka border and continued to the outskirts of Moscow. As a result of this major setback, Muscovy in 1571 or 1572 temporarily abandoned its fort on the Terek and for the time being withdrew its remaining forces.[51] From this time it was not uncommon for the same Circassian family to have some members who were Orthodox Christians and others who were Muslims. Some might even still be adherents to the traditional polytheist and animist cults.[52]

The Muscovite Expeditions against the Shamkhalate

Even so, the Muscovite interest in the Caucasus continued. Muscovites resumed control of the fort on the Terek in 1578. By 1586, Muscovite regular troops had returned, too, and by 1588, a Muscovite garrison was established

---

49 Dzamikhov, *Adygi*, ch. 4.2.2.
50 *Ibid.*, ch. 6.1.1.
51 *Ibid.*, ch. 6.1.2.
52 On these wars, see also Jaimoukha, *Circassians*, pp.51–2; Dzamikhov, *Adygi*, ch. 5.1.2.

in the fort.[53] In 1589, Muscovy agreed to take the King of Kakheti (who ruled part of the eastern territory of present-day Georgia) under its protection, and in 1594, Tsar Fyodor I (1557–1598; r. 1584–1598) sent an army of 7,000 men (including 2,500 streltsy and Terek cossacks[54]) under Prince Andrey Ivanovich Khvorostinin against the Shamkhal's capital, Targhu. Prince Andrey Khvorostinin was a brother of Dmitriy Khvorostinin, who had fought at the battle of Molodi. The Muscovites captured the capital, but the Muscovite army was subsequently destroyed on the banks of the Sulak River in Daghestan.

In 1604, Tsar Boris Godunov (c.1551–1605; r. 1598–1605), who had functioned as regent for Tsar Fyodor, despatched another army, this time of 10,000 men, against the Shamkhal, This was a joint expedition of the respective forces from Kazan' and Astrakhan'. Ivan Mikhailovich Buturlin, the commander from Kazan', served as overall commander, with the commander from Astrakhan', Pleshcheyev, as his second-in-command. The Muscovite army again included streltsy and was supported by Terek and Greben' cossacks. The Muscovites for the second time captured Targhu. However, Buturlin's army was in 1605 besieged in Targhu by a combined force of the Shamkhal and the Ottoman empire, led by a Daghestani commander, Sultan Mahmud of Enderi. The latter had at his disposal 13,000 Daghestani cavalry, raised from the Kumyks, Noghai Tatars, Avars, and Lezghians, in addition to several thousand soldiers on foot raised from the mountain tribes. His army also included Ottoman janissaries and artillery from Derbent. The Muscovites could not withstand the artillery bombardment and the Ottoman mining operations, which collapsed a bastion and buried over 100 Muscovites. Terms of withdrawal were agreed, but during the withdrawal, the Muscovites were attacked by Avars and Kumyks who disregarded the treaty due to the toxic combination of drunkenness with the fiery exhortations against the infidels of their mullahs. Sultan Mahmud attempted to maintain order but failed. Some 7,000 Muscovite troops were killed in the ensuing chaos, including Buturlin and Pleshcheyev, Buturlin's son, and the two sons of Pleshcheyev. The confused nature of the massacre is shown by the fact that among the dead were also Sultan Mahmud and a young boy, reportedly his son, whom he had given to Buturlin as a hostage. Seeing that all was lost, Buturlin killed the boy as the tribesmen attacked.[55]

Muscovy for the time being had to abandon its thrust into the Caucasus and would not make another attempt until Tsar Peter in 1722 led an expedition down the Caspian coast against Derbent, which was then controlled by Persia. By then, all of Daghestan had fallen under at least nominal Persian rule. According to the peace treaty of 1723, Persia had to cede to Russia the districts of Daghestan, Shirvan, Ghilan, and Mazanderan.[56] Two Muslim Kabardian princes, Arslanbek Kaytukin and Aslanbek Kelemetov (as they were known to the Russians) chose to join Tsar Peter on the expedition with their military

---

53 Davies, *Warfare, State and Society*, p.209 n.15.

54 Lemercier-Quelquejay, 'Co-optation', p.40.

55 *Ibid.*, pp.40, 43 n.21; Allen, *Russian Embassies*, pp.549–50.

56 George Vernadsky, *Political and Diplomatic History of Russia* (Boston: Little, Brown, and Co., 1936), p.240.

forces. Another Kabardian prince, El'murza Bekovich-Cherkasskiy from Moscow, commanded one of the regular Russian army units.[57]

The campaign was successful against Persia, but it still turned out to be the final Russian expedition to the Caucasus for a considerable time. While in Daghestan, Tsar Peter sent a Russian cavalry force into the forests of eastern Chechnya. There the Russians were repulsed with serious losses by the local Chechens. In Kabarda, Prince Arslanbek Kaytukin had already entered into a dynastic union with the Crimean Khan, Davlat Ghirai II (r. 1709–1713), thus preparing for the weakening of Kabarda's links with Moscow.[58] Russia was not yet ready to extend its power deep into the Caucasus and would not be so until the end of the century.

However, this did not put an end to the traditional practice of North Caucasians serving in Muscovite and Russian armies. As late as in the second half of the seventeenth century, some Muscovite officers in the south signed the military registers in Arabic script instead of Russian or any West European language. Although some have suggested that these officers were of Ottoman or Crimean origin, and this certainly remains possible, it is even more likely that they were North Caucasians.[59]

North Caucasians and Cossacks

Moreover, the Greben' and Terek cossacks remained behind in their by then traditional territories. This posed special problems and opportunities with regard to the Chechens and other North Caucasians. Chechens and cossacks did not only fight each other; they also adopted aspects of each other's culture and at times even adopted each other into their respective Chechen *teips* (clans) and cossack communities. The cossacks acquired the same relationship with the western Circassians, from whom the cossacks espoused many of their laws, their method of warfare, military equipment and arms, and specialised skills such as the *dzhigitovka* (from Circassian *djighit*, cavalryman), a kind of military acrobatics on horseback. As one historian pointed out, "the Cossacks of that day were probably at most the equals in civilisation of the Chechens and Kumyks, and certainly the inferiors of the Adyghs, to whom belonged the Kabardian princes and people."[60] At least at first, religion was not a strong factor in these wars, which mainly seem to have been concerned with such fundamentals as herds, women, and territory. The Chechens and Ingush in any case did not, as noted, adopt Islam except nominally or on an individual basis until the late eighteenth century, when, faced with strong Russian pressure, Sufi Islam finally managed to take hold of most non-Slavic North Caucasians.

---

57 Dzamikhov, *Adygi*, ch. 3.2.1; 5.1.1.
58 *Ibid.*, ch. 3.2.1.
59 Stevens, *Russia's Wars of Emergence*, p.191 with note.
60 John F. Baddeley, *The Russian Conquest of the Caucasus* (London: Longmans, Green and Co., 1908), p.11. Spelling of names slightly altered.

The Petyhortsy

In 1561, a number of Kabardian princes opposed to Muscovy and, more importantly, their Circassian rivals who had allied with Muscovy, left the Five Mountains for Poland to petition for help. The Polish king granted the Circassians refuge in Poland, so in 1562, five Kabardian princes (known in Poland as Onyszko/Aleksander Kudadek, Kassim and Gawrila Kambulatowicz, and Kudadek's relatives Solgien and Temruk Szymkowicz) moved permanently to Poland with their families and 300 men. Most were, or became, Christians but a number remained believers in the old animist religion. Since they came from the Five Mountains, they became known in Poland as Petyhortsy, which was the Polish pronunciation of the Russian name of their home. These men formed the backbone of a number of special *Petyhorcy* cavalry regiments in Polish service, which for decades regularly came to receive fresh volunteers from the Five Mountains Circassians.[61]

Not all Petyhortsy Circassians who went to Poland ended up in Polish service. As noted, some also served in Crimean Tatar armies from the sixteenth century onwards. Others forgot their earlier animosity and went into Muscovite service. Yet others appear to have ended up in Muscovite service despite first subjecting themselves to Poland, since, as noted, Fletcher mentioned 4,000 of them as being in the service of Muscovy. In either case, the Petyhortsy retained their traditional dress (red and grey caftans with shaggy fur cloaks) and weapons, primarily lance, bow, and chain mail.

North Caucasians in the Ottoman-Safavid Wars

Although not of as great importance as in the Muscovite-Ottoman wars, many North Caucasians also took part in the sixteenth- and seventeenth-century intra-Muslim wars between the Ottoman empire and Safavid Persia. The key role of the North Caucasus was the option to use the territory as a staging area for the troops of the Crimean Khanate to move south along the Derbent highway to join their Ottoman allies against the Persians. One Kabardian prince, Kazyy Psheapshokov (as he was known to the Russians; the first name may be the Muslim title Ghazi, meaning frontier warrior for the faith), actively supported the Ottomans, and plans for Crimean Tatar troops to move south through Kabardian territory were made in 1606, 1608, 1616, 1629, and 1637. The attempt was never made, due to the opposition of other Kabardian princes and the Muscovite forces in the region, so the Ottomans every time had to bring in their Crimean Tatar allies by ship to Sinope in northern Anatolia instead. This particular prince was without doubt a Muslim, he even named one of his sons Islam.[62]

Being somewhat remote from the main theatre of operations, most North Caucasian princes who took part in these wars did so in the capacity of mercenaries or very minor allies. An example was the Kabardian prince Mudar Alkasov (as known to the Muscovites), whose domains included the Daryal Gorge that connected the North Caucasus with Georgia. He rode

---

61 See, e.g., Jaimoukha, *Circassians*, pp.117–18.
62 Dzamikhov, *Adygi*, ch. 3.1.2, 4.2.1.

down to Persia in 1614–1615 where he entered the service of Shah Abbas. Other Kabardians such as Prince Kazyy, meanwhile, continued to oppose the Persians and through their forces, perhaps, ensured that the Persian ruler, Shah Abbas, never contemplated an offensive in their direction. Their importance should not be overstated, however, since a chronicle noted that "the Shah never found the road to Kabarda" – presumably because he had no reason to go there.[63]

Armies of the North Caucasian Principalities

How many troops were usually fielded by the North Caucasian tribes and principalities? There is no clear evidence on this point, but it should be noted that due to the fragmented and somewhat feudal structure of the Circassian tribes, each noble would bring and command his own men. There were no national armies. Some princes controlled no more than a small village or two, while even the most powerful princes in Kabarda held sway over only a few thousand subjects. Two examples from the seventeenth century illustrate this. Prince Sanjalay commanded 400 men in his own settlement and a further 600 Tatars in another settlement. The noble brothers Oleguk and Hatikuk, who controlled more than 50 villages, could still call out only around 1,000 cavalrymen although they could also levy more than 2,000 serfs as infantry.[64] By 1723, a Circassian ambassador to Russia, Prince Magomed Atazhukin, noted that there were 800 Abaza farmsteads on the left side of the River Baksan, and that these altogether could raise 2,000 soldiers.[65] Kabarda was the most densely populated region of the North Caucasus. It has been suggested that Kabarda could mobilise 1,500 cavalry in the sixteenth century. Russian sources indicate that much later, in 1775, the Kabardian lords could raise as many as 15,000 cavalry.[66]

Circassian princes in Muscovite service tended to bring only small retinues. When the Kabardian Prince Kasbulat Mutsalovich Cherkasskiy (as he was known in Russia) in 1674 was put in command of a joint expedition against Azov on behalf of the Muscovite Tsar, he himself brought only 150 retainers. The Kalmyk leader, Ayuuki Khan, supplied 5,000 Kalmyk cavalry, while the Tsar sent 3,000 Muscovites and Don cossacks.[67]

In the seventeenth century, certain Chechen clans could field 1,000 warriors.[68] As noted, in 1605 the Daghestani commander, Sultan Mahmud of Enderi, commanded 13,000 Daghestani cavalry, raised from the Kumyks, Noghai Tatars, Avars, and Lezghians, in addition to several thousand soldiers on foot raised from the mountain tribes and Ottoman allies. On the other hand, we have also seen that the small Kumyk principalities that succeeded the Shamkhalate could only muster from 150 to 500 men each, and that the

---

63 *Ibid.*, ch. 3.1.2.
64 Jaimoukha, *Circassians*, p.159.
65 Dzamikhov, *Adygi*, ch. 5.1.2.
66 Lemercier-Quelquejay, 'Co-optation', p.25, 42 n.4
67 Dzamikhov, *Adygi*, ch. 7.2.1.
68 Lemercier-Quelquejay, 'Co-optation', p.35.

principality of Kaytak at the beginning of the sixteenth century could raise 500 cavalry and about 1,000 foot, while the principality of Tabasaran could raise only 500 cavalry. The manpower available to the North Caucasian war leaders was thus limited, which helps to explain the lack of truly devastating wars before the end of the eighteenth century.

Troop Types

Cavalry

Circassians were master horsemen, riding small but strong and fiery Kabardin horses. The North Caucasian cavalrymen (*djighits*) were famous for their skills, as displayed in the *dzhigitovka* eventually adopted by the cossacks. Cavalry was always common among the North Caucasians, although not all warriors would have access to horses. Those who did certainly included the retinues of fully armoured men of the Circassian princes and other powerful nobles. If we dare to extrapolate from the prevalent tactics of the nineteenth-century Chechens, North Caucasian cavalry would charge furiously at tremendous speed, firing their muskets (or in earlier periods, bows) at 20 paces while holding the reins in their teeth. Then, swinging back their missile weapons and drawing their *shashkas* (swords), they would continue into contact with the enemy.

Circassian horsemen did not use spurs. Instead, following the Inner Asian style of horsemanship, they relied on a short whip, just like Mongols and Muscovites.[69]

The Kabarda in particular was famous for horse breeding. The major nobles would maintain their own stud farms, and each horse would be branded on the left flank with the particular mark, *tamga*, of the clan that bred him. Kabardian horses, Kabardins, were exported not only to other parts of the North Caucasus and to Georgia but also to places as far away as Muscovy, the Crimea, Lithuania, and Poland.[70]

The Kabardin horse, with a body height of about 15 hands (153–155 cm) today and perhaps somewhat less in the period under consideration here, is believed to derive from the horses of the steppe nomads crossed with various Persian and Turkmen breeds. The Kabardin horse is known as a mountain breed, reared for survival in mountainous terrain at high altitude under harsh conditions such as the Caucasian winter. It was, and is, seldom shod.

Like all Circassian leatherwork, saddles and other horse gear were lined with red and black leather and decorated with silver plates.

Infantry

There is little or no evidence on the tactics and fighting styles of the infantry fielded by the various North Caucasian tribes and principalities in the period under consideration here. Most, it should be remembered, were poor farmers or even slaves, so it is unlikely that they would have been very enthusiastic,

---

69 Jaimoukha, *Circassians*, p.217.

70 On Kabardin horses, see, e.g., the website <www.equiworld.net/horses/horsecare/Breeds/ kabardin/index.htm>, accessed on 25 January 2018. See also Allen, *Russian Embassies*, pp.322–4.

well trained, or even well armed as warriors.

However, it was, of course, quite common for the noble cavalry to dismount, if the tactical or topographical situation so required. During raids, one might expect that most (if not all) of any infantry deployed would in fact consist of dismounted cavalry, as it is unlikely that poor farmers or agricultural slaves were brought along on such expeditions. The one possible exception would be skirmishers, who as in other warrior societies might have consisted of young men not yet able to afford a horse and proper gear.

During the religiously inspired wars of the nineteenth century, Circassians often fought the infidel Russians to the last man and sometimes lashed themselves together with their sword belts for a last stand. They especially hated cossacks, who, although Russians and Orthodox Christians, had adopted the same lifestyle as the Circassians. While such hatred certainly arose from time to time also in earlier centuries, as the fate of Buturlin's army in 1605 proved, one should remember that the religious feelings that inspired such self-sacrifice and fanaticism had generally not yet developed, and would not do so until the Russian invasions from the late eighteenth century onwards. In the period under consideration here, any North Caucasian combat units would be much more likely to cut their losses and withdraw if the battle was not going their way.

Navy

Some Circassian tribes, in particular the Ubykhs and Abkhazians, lived close to the Black Sea and were known to operate as pirates, setting out in boats and small ships to attack shipping close to the shore. The same vessels were used for trade with the Ottoman empire and no doubt the Crimean Khanate. The Circassian ships were equipped with both sails and oars. The latter appear to have been the main means of propulsion. At least in the early nineteenth century (and presumably before) a typical vessel could hold 60–70 men. There were also larger ships that could take up to 140 men. One eyewitness, Edmund Spencer, in 1837 described the vessels as:

> Flat-bottomed, lightly built, and narrow, each rowed by from eighteen to twenty-four men … Near the helm was a species of deck, on which three or four men were seated; and the prow of each was adorned with a figure, rudely carved, representing, it might be, the head of a deer, a goat, or a ram: most probably the latter.

Spencer also pointed out that under oars, the boats "were propelled with great velocity" and that "these boats are built large enough to contain from fifty to eighty men, when they are propelled, in addition to rowing, by an angular sail."[71] Others have indicated that the boats did not have a keel but came with a rudder and a small square sail. The oars were very short and "fixed to rowlocks of enormous length with the transverse cross-bars for the

---

71 Edmund Spencer, *Travels in Circassia, Krim Tartary, &c.: Including a Steam Voyage Down the Danube, From Vienna to Constantinople and Round the Black Sea* (2 vols.; London: Henry Colburn, 1837).

hands of rowers." Some Circassian ships were armed with light cannon as well.[72] From surviving descriptions of these ships, they sound very similar to the *chaykas* used by cossacks for riverine transport and on the Black Sea.

Dress, Weapons, and Armour

From the point of view of weapons technology, the North Caucasus was a backward place. Firearms came late to the region, and suits of armour remained in common use into the nineteenth century.

At least since the early sixteenth century, and presumably before, Circassian men shaved their foreheads but retained a long lock of hair behind the crown of the head. It was also not uncommon, in particular among religious leaders, to stain one's beard and the palms of one's hands with the dark orange of henna.[73]

In the early sixteenth century, the Circassians reportedly wore an outer garment of white felt akin to a poncho. Underneath, they wore trousers and other clothes of silk (if they could afford it) or linen.[74] The felt cloak was not, however, what would become known as the classic Caucasian garment. This was instead the Caucasian warrior's dress called, after the people who wore it, the *cherkesska* (the Russian term for what the Circassians in at least some languages referred to as *tsey*), a long, tight-fitting, narrow-waisted outer garment with wide sleeves. It was made of cloth that fanned out in the lower part until it reached the knees. It was furthermore distinguished by being barred across the chest by double rows of from 14 to 20 usually white silver or wooden cartridge cases (*hezir*). The *cherkesska* was usually grey (unsurprisingly the most common colour according to Adam Olearius who twice passed through the North Caucasus in the 1630s[75]), brown, or black, although it in a few limited cases among the nobles came in white or other bright colours.[76] Red and grey such garments were mentioned among the Petyhortsy in Poland, and since these colours were commonplace in Circassian art and handicraft, such colours no doubt existed among the other North Caucasian tribes as well.

The *cherkesska* in its final form, as described above, was a fairly late development, perhaps first seen in the eighteenth century. It is for instance unlikely that the cartridge cases, which became the most recognisable characteristic of the *cherkesska*, were added before this time, since cartridges as far as is known were simply not used earlier, although wooden tubes for measured gunpowder charges were. The *cherkesska* derived from the simpler caftan used in previous centuries. The ultimate origin of the garment was the caftan worn in Inner Asia by the eighth century which reached Europe with the Magyars in the ninth century (and, incidentally, ultimately was

72 A.Y. Chirg, *Circassian Navy during Russian-Caucasian War* (n.d.), on the website <http://adygi.ru/index.php?newsid=663>, accessed on 25 January 2018.
73 See, e.g., Jaimoukha, *Circassians*, p.193.
74 Mathias de Miechow, *Traktat von baiden Sarmatien und anderen anstossenden landen in Asia und Europa von sitten und gepräuchender völker, so darinnen wonen: Ain anders von den landen Scithia und den innwonern des selben lands genannt die Ciarchassi* (Augsburg, 1518).
75 Olearius, *Moskowitische und Persische Reise*, p.329.
76 See, e.g., Jaimoukha, *Circassians*, pp.192–3.

the origin also of the eighteenth and nineteenth century West European hussar uniforms). This type of caftan existed in the Caucasus even before the Magyars reached Europe. A very small but well preserved such caftan found in a child's grave in Moshchevaya Balka in present Krasnodar Territory has been dated to the eighth or ninth century. This garment in every way looks like that of an adult, except that it only has three rows of simple buttons to close in front (from neck to waist; the garment is simply too small for additional rows of buttons).[77]

A good caftan or *cherkesska* would only have been worn by those who could afford it. Most Caucasian mountain-dwellers would not belong to this group. As late as in 1822, the Latvia-born artist Karl Petrovich Beggrov painted a Chechen who wore a far more humble caftan-like coat of greenish hue, perhaps made of felt. He also wears a very simple form of the goat's-hair felt cloak known as *burka* (see below). As armament, he carries a flintlock musket and the double-edged sword known as a *kindjal*.

Most Circassians indeed seem to have dressed for war in a rather disreputable way, and they had a reputation for wearing clothes in tatters. A nineteenth-century observer commented that "in general the Circassians, when taking to the field, put on the worst and coarsest attire they can find; but many of their young heroes, out of emulation, a spirit of bravado or aspiring to the honours of martyrdom, render themselves conspicuous by wearing an entari of the gayest colour."[78]

Over the caftan or *cherkesska* was worn, hung by a strap from the shoulders, the shaggy, sleeveless *sch'ak'we* or (in Turkic) *burka*, a black goat's-hair felt cloak with wide square shoulders which is believed to derive from a pre-Islamic ritual dress.[79] While black *burkas* were used for everyday wear, white *burkas* were used for festivities.[80] If poor, the North Caucasians instead wore what was described as wretched felt cloaks. Some cloaks were hooded. A seventeenth-century version of an everyday *burka* of what must have been a very common (that is, not noble) style was illustrated by Adam Olearius, who also described this garment.[81] It certainly appears to fulfill the epithet of wretched, even though the garment illustrated clearly was a fur cloak. This illustration, incidentally, seems to be the only contemporary depiction anywhere of North Caucasians from the period under discussion here.

The *burka* may, in fact, be the oldest survival of Caucasian dress types. Some claim to recognise the *burka* in a description of the fifth-century Armenian historian, Movses Khorenats'i, who noted that the "leader of a savage group of Caucasian mountain-men, invading Armenia from the north-east, was covered in a spear-proof felt armour."[82]

---

77 B.B. Piotrovskij (ed.), *Tesori d'Eurasia: 2000 anni di Storia in 70 anni di Archeologia Sovietica* (Milan: Arnoldo Mondadori, 1987), p.172.

78 John Augustus Longworth, *A Year among the Circassians* (2 vols.; London: Henry Colburn, 1840), vol. 2, p.51.

79 Jaimoukha, *Circassians*, pp.192–3.

80 Chenciner, *Daghestan*, p.180.

81 Olearius, *Moskowitische und Persische Reise*, p.327.

82 Chenciner, *Daghestan*, pp.180–81.

At least by the nineteenth century, and probably in earlier centuries as well, a North Caucasian covered his head with a pointed heavy black sheepskin hat, known as *papakha*, or alternatively a turban, green for those who had completed the *hajj* pilgrimage to Mecca. Religious leaders wore lambskin caps enhanced by a turban, in the well-known nineteenth-century leader Imam Shamil's case large and red-tasselled. A Circassian would wear a commonly black or grey wide-brimmed felt hat or a caracul cap made of astrakhan fur (*adige pi'e* or *kalpak*). There was also a shaggy woollen cap (*bashlyk, axta,* or *yr'pa*) which consisted of a strip of woollen cloth bound up in a particular way. On their feet, Circassians wore high, soft leather boots.[83]

A man's measure was often valued in the number of severed enemy heads and hands he had taken. A young Circassian warrior often wore severed hands from his saddle-bow. Only right hands were taken. In addition, sliced-off ears were often strung along the whip thong.

As for the Circassian women, they had a reputation for beauty both in Russia and the Islamic lands to the south. This was of course not only an advantage; many thousands of them ended up being captured and sold as slaves further south in the Islamic world.

Weapons used by the North Caucasians included bows and arrows, lances and spears, a set of darts or javelins (*djid*), swords, and daggers. Firearms were introduced in the sixteenth century, but they became widespread only in the eighteenth century.[84]

Circassian swords in the fifteenth and sixteenth centuries were primarily used by cavalry, being sabre-like weapons with cross-guards to protect the hand and pointed tips, by some believed to have been intended for piercing chain mail armour. These weapons were commonly some 105 to 115 cm long.

In probably the seventeenth century, a new type of cavalry sword emerged. This was the *shashka* (Kabardian: *seshkhue*), another but only slightly curved sabre-like weapon with a forked hilt without knuckle guards. The oldest known such weapon is dated to 1713 and belongs to the Moscow History Museum, but it is unlikely to have been the first ever made since this particular blade was imported from Western Europe. The *shashka* was carried in a shoulder strap with its cutting edge generally upwards. Many blades for *shashka* swords were from the eighteenth century onwards imported from Italy, Germany, and Hungary through the ports of the Black Sea.

In the nineteenth-century religiously inspired wars, a favourite Chechen tactic was to harass the Russian soldiers with sniper fire from cover, then when the Russians deployed their own skirmishers, to ambush these with wild cavalry *shashka* charges. Similar tactics may have been used earlier as well.

In the seventeenth century another new kind of sword also appears to have become common in the North Caucasus, although it certainly had existed in the general region of the Caucasus for centuries. This was the

---

83 Jaimoukha, *Circassians*, pp.192–3.
84 *Ibid.*, pp.214–15. On Circassian weapons, see Yurij A. Miller, *Caucasian Arms from the State Hermitage Museum, St. Petersburg: The Art of Weaponry in Caucasus and Transcaucasia in the 18th and 19th Centuries/Kaukasiske Våben fra Eremitagemuseet, Skt. Petersborg* (Odense: Danish Arms and Armour Society/Våbenhistorisk Selskap, n.d.).

kindjal, a long double-edged dagger or short sword without a hand guard. It was almost always straight, although occasionally slightly curved, and may have derived from the fundamentally identical *qama* of Georgia. However, similar weapons have been used by a variety of peoples in the region ever since the first millennium BC. The *kindjal*, grooved and tapering to a fine point, was suitable for the penetration of chain mail armour. It was worn on a leather strap across the left groin. However, the *kindjal* was also often used as a mere utility knife.

The Circassian nobility used exquisitely ornamented weapons with hilts of horn or, even better, silver. The latter was often decorated with a special niello alloy composed of silver, copper, lead, and sulphur. The scabbard, meanwhile, was made of wood often covered with velvet. Scabbards were usually made by women for the members of their family.

Archery was very important among the Circassians, who employed composite bows of the Inner Asian type. In the fifteenth century, it was noted that all Circassians, even members of the nobility, every day would make their own arrows. The arrows supposedly were of very high quality, with excellently tempered arrowheads. Indeed, the Crimean Tatars and Noghai Tatars were known to buy large numbers of Circassian arrows, which in the light of the famed Tatar skill in archery would seem to confirm their inherent quality. As with sword scabbards, bowcases and quivers were made by the Circassian women for members of their family out of red or black leather, edged with coloured strips of the same material.[85]

In the poorer and less developed parts of the North Caucasus, in particular, it was also common to use bows that fired small round stones instead of arrows. The stones were carried in a shoulder bag. The Ingush and Chechens were still hunting birds with such weapons early in the twentieth century. In earlier centuries, such weapons were also used for war in Daghestan and presumably all over the North Caucasus.[86]

Lances and javelins were commonly employed by North Caucasian cavalry. Some infantry no doubt used spears, but the sources are silent on this point.

Firearms were, as noted, introduced to the North Caucasus in the sixteenth century. They became common only in the eighteenth century, although they for the rest of the century co-existed with bows and arrows. A few Circassians continued to use composite bows as late as in the nineteenth century. Most but not all firearms were imported from the Crimea or Kubachi in Daghestan. The muskets were long and made in Ottoman Turkish style. Many Circassians used stands to support their muskets while firing. The musket was often protected from the weather and dust by a sheepskin covering.

As noted, the North Caucasians did not hesitate to fire their muskets from horseback just before they engaged the enemy. On foot, they had a reputation for expert marksmanship, resting their guns on twisted twig tripods. If cornered, they were known, at least in the religiously inspired wars of the later periods, to prepare a last stand by killing their horses to make a rampart

85 Zihia, *Circassian Weaponry* (2003/2004), published at the website <www.zihia.narod.ru/ing/weaponry.htm>, accessed on 25 January 2018.
86 Chenciner, *Daghestan*, p.32.

33. Circassian shields.
(Viskovatov, 1841)

of their bodies, digging themselves a trench with their *kindjals*, and then firing from across their saddle-bows until they ran out of bullets.

Not so long after the introduction of firearms came the use of measured gunpowder charges kept in wooden tubes. These tubes, closed with ornamented silver caps, came to be carried in special pockets on the breast of the Circassian caftan, thus giving rise to the birth of the characteristic Circassian *cherkesska*. In addition, high-quality gunpowder for use in the pan of a musket was kept in powder flasks made of wood, horn, or bone, frequently adorned with silver plates.

The Circassians fielded fully armoured cavalry in the form of the Circassian nobility. Most members of the nobility and their retinues were armoured, wearing steel helmets of the Turco-Persian type (in Russian, as noted, known as *misyurka*), either of the tall, conical (or occasionally pyramidal) type with a pointed crest or a spike on top (*kulah-khud*) or the low variety with a small, round plate that only covered the crown of the skull (*kulah-zirah*). Either type came with a long chain mail coif or neckguard. The Circassian nobles also wore chain mail and splint mail armour with vambraces throughout the period, as already the Polish scholar Mathias de Miechow (1457–1523) noted in the early sixteenth century.[87] They continued to do so well into the nineteenth century. In addition, the Circassian nobles wore leather gloves with round wrist protections, secured to the hand by straps of red or black leather with lengths of mail attached and decorated with gold or silver threads.

Armed with bows and spears, in addition to swords and even firearms, they also occasionally carried small, round targets or hand-shields made of wood or hard leather and bound with iron. The latter came to be most typical of the Ossetians in and around the Truso and Daryal Gorges.[88]

Circassian suits of armour were of good quality and well known in the region; in the sixteenth century the Ottomans exacted tribute from the Circassians in slaves, horses, and suits of armour. Kabardian armourers also worked in Muscovy, in Astrakhan' already by 1660. In 1661, the Tsar indeed ordered the Kabardian armourers there to move to Moscow so as to continue to manufacture suits of armour and sabres in the capital.[89]

---

87 Mathias de Miechow, *Traktat von baiden Sarmatien und anderen anstossenden landen in Asia und Europa von sitten und gepräuchender völker, so darinnen wonen: Ain anders von den landen Scithia und den innwonern des selben lands genannt die Ciarchassi* (Augsburg, 1518).

88 Allen, *Russian Embassies*, pp.367–8.

89 Dzamikhov, *Adygi*, ch. 3.1.2.

5

The Muscovite Penetration into Siberia

Peoples of Siberia

East of the Urals, Siberia constituted a yet more vast territory than the European parts of what would become Russia. From the Ural range, the land descended into the wide western Siberian plain, which formed the basin of the River Ob' and its tributary, the Irtysh, both of which flowed slowly from the southern Altai mountains into the Arctic Ocean. This was the coniferous forest known as *taiga*, the home of numerous fur-bearing animals including the stoat or ermine and the sable, the furs of which were highly praised and provided substantial income to whoever could control the fur trade. In fact, revenues from the fur trade constituted a key reason, possibly the only reason, for Muscovite expansion into Siberia at the time when it took place.

East of the western Siberian plain was the central Siberian upland, with rapid rivers such as the Yenisey running northwards into the Arctic. In the south-east, the uplands ended with the Lake Baikal, the deepest lake in the world. East of the Baikal, the River Lena flowed northwards through Yakutia into the Arctic. This was the mountains and plateaus of the Far East, the Pacific region of Siberia which had warmer summers and more rain because of its vicinity to the Pacific Ocean.

Siberia was by no means an uninhabited land when the Muscovites began to advance across the Urals. In the Urals, the Ostyaks (Khanty) and Voguls (Mansi) were tribal peoples divided into separate clans with hereditary chieftains. Armed with longbows, spears, and coats of mail and helmets made of iron, which they themselves extracted and forged (then a rare skill in Siberia), or alternatively layers of elk antler, they lived in fortified winter settlements consisting of log huts and shelters covered with earth surrounded by stockades and earth ramparts. However, they were few in numbers and divided in clans, which meant that in the long term, they were unable to resist the Muscovites who moved into their territories. They were also semi-nomadic, living chiefly by hunting and fishing and spending the active season based in temporary shelters of poles and birch bark. In winter, they moved by ski, and in summer, by dugout or birchbark canoe. Both Khanty and Mansi

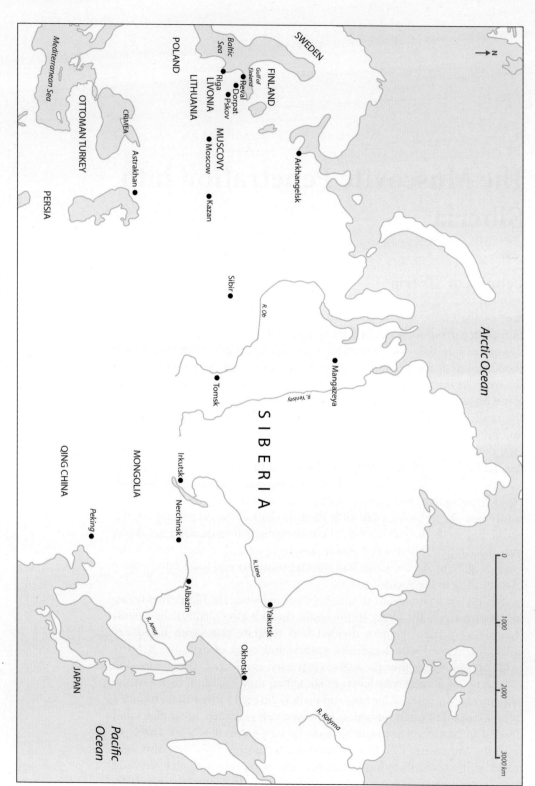

Map 3. Muscovy's expansion to the west, south, and east across Siberia.

wore fur-trimmed skin clothing, richly embroidered shirts made from nettle or hemp fibres, thigh-length hose of reindeer leather, and deer or elk-skin moccasins. Many were extensively tattooed, and those who could afford it adorned themselves with glass beads and metal ornaments acquired by trade.

Beyond the Khanty, in the south-eastern part of western Siberia, lived the Ostyak-Samoyeds (Selkup). Even fewer in numbers, their way of life was very similar to the Khanty and Mansi and based on fishing and hunting.

However, the chief power in the forests of western Siberia was the Siberian Turks, that is, the descendants of the Bashkirs and Tatars who had once formed part of the Mongol Empire but subsequently fragmented and constituted parts of the the Noghai Horde, the Khanate of Kazan', and the Khanate of Sibir'.

The Tatar Khanate of Sibir' emerged at the disintegration of the Golden Horde as the chief power of the forestlands of western Siberia. Eventually establishing a capital at Qashliq (also known as Isker or Sibir', near present-day Tobol'sk), the Khanate of Sibir' played a prominent role in the wars on the steppe, despite being based in the forestlands. In fact, the forestlands provided a key source of income, since the Khanate extracted tribute (*yasak*) from the Khanty, Mansi, Selkup, and Bashkirs in the form of furs and other forest products. Settled or semi-settled in nature, the Khanate of Sibir' consisted of several towns, of which Sibir' was the chief and eventually gave Siberia its name. The Tatar nobility was nominally Muslims, but most of the population, like the Khanty, Mansi, Selkup, and other Siberian forest tribes, adhered to ancestor cults, the worship of nature spirits, and shamanism. Their main weapon was the composite bow, and their military system was much like that of other Tatars. By the mid-sixteenth century, they are believed to have been 5,000 in numbers, with possibly 30,000 subjects from other tribes.[1]

Yet further beyond, central and north-eastern Siberia was dominated by the Tungus, who lived in small clans throughout the whole of southeastern Siberia, northern Mongolia, and Manchuria. The Tungus, travelling on foot or on skis with their domesticated reindeer, lived in conical tents of reindeer skins or birch bark sheets. Dressed in deerskin coats, with loincloths, leggings, moccasins or soft boots, and reindeer-skin caps, they, too, were frequently tattooed. Armed with bows, swords, and glaives (a 40–50 cm long, heavy one-edged knife mounted on a pole, known as *pal'ma*), some also wore simple armour of wooden or bone plates. Tungus clans moved seasonally, only gathering in camps in summer, and even then, they were few in numbers. Their religious beliefs were dominated by shamanism.

The Buryat Mongols controlled the territories around Lake Baikal. Led by a hereditary aristocracy of clan chiefs, the Buryats were nomads, and already collected *yasak* from Tungus, Samoyeds, and other tribes in their territory. The Buryat Mongols owed allegiance to the khans of Mongolia. Dressed in the traditional Mongol wrap-over fur or cloth coat and soft leather boots with thick felt soles, their culture was little different from that of Mongols

---

1   Terence Armstrong (ed.), *Yermak's Campaign in Siberia* (London: Hakluyt Society, 1975), pp.20–22.

34. Left: Siberian cossack holding anchor (left) and Siberian Tatar with bowcase and quiver (right) presenting fur tribute. (Semyon Remezov, 1701)

35. Left: Samoyed with typical knife (left) and Ostyak (right) in characteristic headdress presenting fur tribute. (Semyon Remezov, 1701)

elsewhere. Having no firearms, they were armed and fought much like Mongols had done for centuries.

The Yakuts, a Turkic people, dominated the territory on the River Lena. The Yakuts still retained vestiges of the aristocratic and tribal structure of other Turkic-speaking tribes on the steppe, with elaborate titles and clans. This was also the source of their undoing, since there was much rivalry between clans.[2] The northern Yakuts were primarily hunters, fishermen, and reindeer herders, while the southern Yakuts raised cattle and horses. The Yakuts moved seasonally, with their horses and oxen, from scattered settlements consisting of log cabins in winter to somewhat larger summer camps, consisting of large conical buildings covered with sheets of birch bark. In times of war, they occasionally built defensive stockades around their settlements. They not only forged iron, the also produced iron from ore. In winter, the Yakuts wore long fur hats and long fur coats decorated with fur trimmings and appliqué designs, and were fond of silver or other metal ornaments in the form of belts, necklaces, and so on. They used bows and glaives, and some wore helmets and coats of mail.

In the Arctic north, in the tundra region that encompassed the northern reaches on both sides of the Urals, lived the Samoyeds (Nenets). They were nomads who relied on semi-domesticated reindeer and hunting for their livelihood. At times of war, they were armed with bows and spears.

Finally, and most distant, in the region of forest, tundra, and high mountains in north-eastern Siberia, lived the Yukagirs, Chukchis, Koraks, and Eskimos. None of these ethnic groups was particularly numerous, and none used metals. In effect, they lived in an environment little changed since the Ice Age. They lived in semi-subterranean huts in winter and large reindeer skin or sealskin tents in summer. Clothing, too, was made of reindeer skin or sealskin, and many were tattooed. An Eskimo man wore labrets (round plugs of bone) inserted in his lips at the corners of his mouth. However, they were warlike. The Chukchis and Koraks wore armour, helmets, and shields of bone-plated seal hide, and their bone-tipped arrows and hunting spears made formidable weapons.

The Stroganov Family and Yermak

The Muscovite penetration into Siberia was technically an advance overland; however, just like in the European side of what would become Russia, due to the difficult terrain the advance primarily took place by river.

The first Muscovite move into Siberia came already at the time of Ivan III, and it took place in the northern Urals, where the Komi of Perm' had been conquered already in 1472, and Komi auxiliaries were used to raid their eastern Mansi and Khanty neighbours. However, more convenient access to Siberia existed further to the south, beyond Kazan'. The Khanate of Sibir'

---

2   Aleksei P. Okladnikov, *Yakutia before Its Incorporation into the Russian State* (Montreal: McGill-Queens University press, 1970), pp.409–11, 417.

36. Left: Yermak and his company, armed with musket, spear, berdysh, and shield, subdue several Vogul communities and receive fur tribute; right: Yermak and his company, with a spearman in West European armour and dress in a prominent position, defeat the Siberian Tatars at Tyumen'. (Both Semyon Remezov, c.1700)

claimed overlordship over the Mansi west of the Urals in this region, and it was there that Muscovy first came into armed conflict with the Khanate.[3]

In 1558, Grigoriy Stroganov (c.1533–1577), of a Novgorod merchant family, applied to Ivan IV for and received a charter that allowed him to colonise a large territory on both banks of the Kama River, in Perm'. The concession was to be used for agriculture and salt works. The rights and privileges granted by the charter, including immunity from taxation and customs duties for 20 years and permits to build fortified towns and raise troops armed with firearms, were so broad that Stroganov in practical terms became the governor of the territory. Stroganov was also obligated to protect the new frontier from Tatar raids.[4] To do so was also in his own interest, in order to safeguard his investments.

This being on the Siberian frontier, Stroganov built a fort, called Kankor. In 1564, he obtained permission to build a second fort, Kergedan, on the Oryol River. Since the territory was subject to raiding by Cheremis, Bashkirs, and others, Ivan permitted the arming of the Stroganov family's cossacks, who went on to subjugate the Khanty for defensive purposes.

The Stroganovs were of obscure background, being neither boyars nor servicemen. They were fundamentally merchants. Yet they enjoyed

3   Forsyth, *History of the Peoples of Siberia*, p.29.
4   Armstrong, *Yermak's Campaign*, pp.281–4.

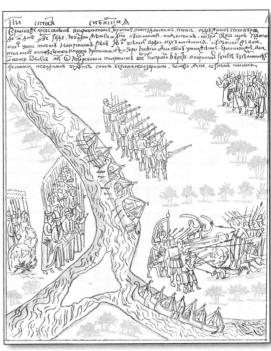

37. Left: Siberian Tatars, Samoyeds in typical dress and armed with their characteristic knives, and other Siberians (possibly Ostyaks) present fur tribute to the Khan of Sibir'; right: Yermak's company line up against the Siberian Tatars, who are deployed on both sides of the river. (Both Semyon Remezov, c.1700)

considerable privileges, answering only to the Tsar. They built towns and fortresses, formed an army that included artillery, established a cannon foundry of their own, and traded, untaxed, with the Asian territories. Hardly any other non-princely family owned considerable wealth. Yet the state concessions granted to the Stroganovs resulted in them acquiring huge landed properties which employed thousands of labourers.

When Ivan in 1565 formed the *oprichnina* as a personal power base, many ambitious individuals were drawn to it as a source of power and careers. Among them was the Stroganov family which saw advantages in doing so and accordingly were among those who offered their estates to Ivan, adding their properties to the Tsar's *oprichnina* already in 1566.

By then, a Tatar Khan, Kuchum (r. 1563–1598, d. 1601), had gained control of Sibir' and the Khanate of Sibir' with the support of the Noghais. Kuchum, who was related to the Shaybanid Uzbek khan of Bukhara (in present-day Uzbekistan), had initiated the conversion of the Siberian Tatars to Islam and also received a number of exile Muslims from Kazan' to strengthen his forces. Moreover, Kuchum hoped that his Islamic zeal would result in military support from the Crimean Khanate and the Ottoman empire against the Muscovites.

Hostilities between Kuchum and the Stroganovs began in 1572. Kuchum sent an army of Mansi, Khanty, Bashkirs, and Cheremis to raid the Stroganov lands on the Chusovaya River in Perm'. He also encouraged the native tribes under Stroganov rule to revolt against the Muscovites. The frontier war continued for the next 10 years. In 1574, Ivan granted the Stroganovs yet

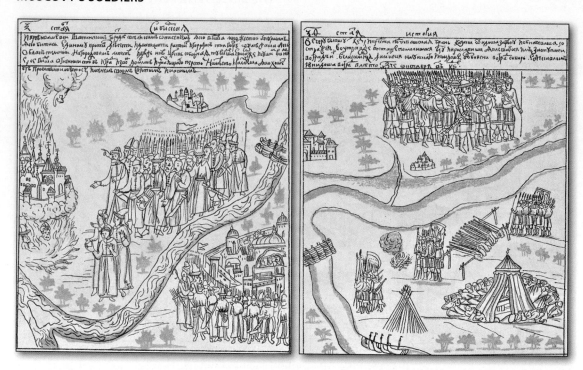

38. Left: Yermak's company, armed with spears and bows and, judging from the men's dress, reinforced by quite a number of Siberian Tatars, perceive divine visions of future Siberian cities and burning infidels; right: Yermak's camp, on the way to Qashliq, capital of the Khanate of Sibir'. This being October, the men sleep close together around Yermak's tent, and spears and muskets are neatly stacked in the appropriate locations. Yermak (top) wears **zertsalo** ('mirror') armour, while his men are armed and equipped in a variety of styles, often without visible armour. (Both Semyon Remezov, c.1700)

more territory, this time beyond the Ural range.[5] The Stroganovs then turned to the Don cossacks. With Ivan's permission, the Stroganovs hired 640 Don cossacks to defend their lands, commanded by two former river pirates. One was Yermak Timofeyevich (c.1532–1585), the other Yermak's lieutenant Ivan Kol'tso (d. 1584). Armed by the Stroganovs with firearms, cannons, and some personal armour, the cossacks soon pursued their enemies across the Ural and onwards into Siberia. The defensive force rapidly transformed itself into aggressors, which, based on Ivan's 1574 charter, may have been the Stroganovs' intention all along. In 1581, the cossacks, reinforced by a detachment of the Stroganov family's contract soldiers (Muscovites, Lithuanians, Tatars, and 'Germans') – in total some 840 men, 540 cossacks and 300 of Stroganov's men – under Yermak's command began to push into Siberia to attack Kuchum on his own territory.[6]

Yermak's men had a huge advantage in their firearms. The Siberian Tatars had little experience of such weapons. Yermak's expedition looted several villages and, in October 1582, forced Kuchum to abandon his capital after a battle on the Irtysh. Yermak sent Kol'tso with the good news to the Stroganovs and the Tsar. Ivan reciprocated with money and gifts, then sent two of his commanders,

---

5   *Ibid.*, pp.39, 289–92.
6   *Ibid.*, p.42.

Prince Semyon Bolkhovskiy (who soon died of natural causes) and his voivode, Ivan Glukhov, to take possession of the newly conquered lands.

However, despite their advantage in firearms, the Muscovites were few in numbers and suffered from shortages of supplies, particularly in winter. Many died in ambushes, including Kol'tso in 1584. Finally, Yermak, too, with most of his men were killed in a night attack in 1585. Yermak's remaining lieutenant, Matvey Meshcheryak (whose name suggests a Finno-Ugrian origin), and the voivode Ivan Glukhov had to abandon Sibir' with the about 150 survivors of the expeditionary force.[7]

Onwards into Siberia

Despite the setback of Yermak's death, Muscovy did not surrender its attempts to gain control over the territory of the Khanate of Sibir'. Henceforth, Moscow sent large numbers of servicemen, cossacks, and streltsy into Siberia. The Muscovite expansion eastwards was often justified as a means of recovering territories that the Muscovites regarded as having been previously lost to the Mongols.[8] Further expeditions against the natives took place from 1586 to 1598, when Kuchum was finally defeated, after years of resistance. As before during Muscovy's expansion, any local chief who agreed to go inte Muscovite service was allowed to retain his position, in exchange for providing soldiers for the continued conquest and the collection of *yasak*. Becoming known as 'Tatar servicemen' (*sluzhilyye tatary*) or 'Ostyak servicemen', they became of key importance because of their local knowledge, since despite the Muscovites eventually gaining the upper hand, Tatar resistance continued, especially on the southern steppe frontier, until the 1670s. In fact, the Muscovites were at first not eager to push on into the steppes, since there were no fur-bearing animals there.

In Siberia, the military system that developed was close to that of the southern border, which indeed was another active frontier. Troops served in garrisons (even though this was not referred to as 'town service' which, as noted, was the common term employed elsewhere). The region fielded no campaign service troops. After the defeat of the Khanate of Sibir', military activities in most cases consisted of small-scale war, more raiding and pillaging than battles or sieges. The *ostrog* (pl. *ostrogi*) type of wooden fortified posts became a key means of control during the conquest of Siberia. Such a fort could be built in a few weeks. It could then be expanded further. Many Siberian wooden forts grew into towns. Since Siberian tribes lacked artillery, they often found the wooden fortifications difficult to breach, as long as the outposts were manned by determined soldiers.

In the outlying ranges of the Altai mountains, the Muscovites established a bridgehead in the Tom River valley, where the local Tatar chief, Toyan (probably a title not a name), accepted to enter Muscovite service. The town of Tomsk was founded in 1604 and, in 1618, so was the town of Kuznetsk,

---

7   *Ibid.*, pp.8, 57.
8   Lapidus, *History of Islamic Societies*, pp.416–17, pp.420–23; Forsyth, *History of the Peoples of Siberia*, pp.26–35.

named after the 'blacksmith Turks' (*kuznetskiye tatary*) who were among few Siberian tribes who worked iron. By 1620, a Muscovite enclave had been established in the region. The annexation of western Siberia was fundamentally completed. Although subjected to frequent raids throughout the seventeenth and early eighteenth centuries and long having the characteristics of a frontier outpost, Muscovite rule had come to stay.

By then, Muscovite fur traders had also moved into the Arctic. In 1600, Prince Miron Mikhailovich Shakhovskoy (d. 1632) led a first expedition of cossacks and Finno-Ugrian Komi auxiliaries beyond the Ob' into Samoyed territory. Establishing the town of Mangazeya among the Samoyeds, with a garrison that eventually consisted of streltsy, cossacks, and 'Lithuanians', the Muscovites found themselves under siege by Samoyed tribes armed with bows and spears in 1604, 1606, and at least four times in the 1640s. Samoyed opposition to the Muscovite activities, which made the wildlife extinct and included the indiscriminate pillaging of tribal settlements, grew increasingly serious in the winter of 1662–1663. Then the Samoyeds attacked Mangazeya and two Muscovite forts, killing many Muscovites and wiping out the defenders of one fort, Pustozyorsk. Although the better armed Muscovite forces subsequently retaliated against the Samoyeds, the latter attacked again in 1666, 1667, 1668, and 1669. As a result, the Muscovites abandoned Mangazeya in 1672. Even so, violence continued whenever Muscovite *yasak* collectors entered the territory.[9]

The Tungus, too, resisted the Muscovites. *Yasak* collectors moved east into the southern territories of central Siberia before 1610. Considerable fighting with the Tungus took place, in particular from 1617 to 1622, until 1633, when the southern Tungus clans finally had been defeated, typically with the help of auxiliaries from other, rival ethnic groups. However, from the 1620s to 1640, *yasak* collectors regularly imposed their demands on all northern Tungus clans.

Muscovite fur traders and explorers ranged widely across Siberia. The country was rich in sables, and the Muscovites frequently clashed with local tribes who regarded the Muscovites as poachers. They also occasionaly clashed with each other. The Tsar commonly appointed military governors – voivodes – in pair, with the intention that they should control each other, thus not being overly rapacious in their activities. Yet, any newly opened hunting grounds were soon exhausted. As the sables were hunted into extinction, the Muscovites had to continue moving. In fact, this was the push factor that made the Muscovites continue onwards with such rapidity. Since the *yasak* was the key reason for moving into Siberia, it made no sense to remain settled down when the supply of sable diminished.

The movement east was spearheaded by cossacks. The Siberian cossacks were in Moscow's employ, serving as soldiers and tax-collectors. They were also frontiersmen, colonisers, traders, and bandits. The cossacks in Siberia were a heterogeneous group of hunters, peasants, exiles, vagabonds, river pirates, and common adventurers from many countries, including

---

9   Forsyth, *History of the Peoples of Siberia*, pp.45–7.

mercenaries and former prisoners-of-war of Lithuanian, Polish, White Russian, Ukrainian, Swedish, German, and Danish extraction. In time, most of them settled as town cossacks in the newly built towns. In 1639, a new type of cossack community emerged, the Trans-Baikal cossacks.

However, the Baikal region was dominated by the Buryat Mongols, and like other steppe nomads, they were more of a problem for Muscovite *yasak* collectors and troops to deal with than the forest tribes. The Muscovites first heard of the Buryats in 1625. However, the Buryats, supported by their Tungus dependents, remained unconquered until 1655. Even then, resistance did not end. In 1695–1696, the Buryats again rose in rebellion, laying siege to Irkutsk in the process. It would take time before Muscovy made significant advances beyond the edge of the Siberian forest and into the steppes, where Mongols and Kazakhs would continue to resist Muscovite expeditions well into the eighteenth century and, in some cases, until the late nineteenth century.

The Yakuts, too, resisted the Muscovites, from their first encounters and particularly when in 1632 cossacks from Yeniseysk build a fort in their territory, first named Lensk, later renamed Yakutsk. However, the Yakuts were divided, which assisted the Muscovite victory. Yakut resistance continued until at least 1684.

Most Muscovite soldiers in Siberia, as elsewhere, depended on the supply of grain from the state for their upkeep. They were also supposed to receive regular wages, but in Siberia, such were paid out infrequently or not at all. Even the hereditary servicemen depended on grain supplies, even if these technically should come from their own land grants. However, the cost of sending grain to Siberia was prohibitive, and the time for supplies to reach their destination made the concept of grain supplies uncertain to say the least. Moreover, grain was a key commodity for the production of vodka. This was not only a popular drink with the troops, it was also a valuable commodity that could be traded for fur with the natives. That the vodka trade no doubt also made the natives vulnerable, through drunkenness and addiction, was no doubt a lucrative side effect. So grain was needed both to sustain the troops and to achieve additional profits.

To solve the grain supply problem, Moscow decided to send peasants into Siberia to make the settlements self-supporting. Some were sent by the state, but considerable numbers set out on their own, just like the situation on the southern border. A Siberian chancellery was established to supervise the forts and garrisons that marked Muscovite rule in the region.

Problems with the grain supply still persisted, however. In northern Siberia, no crops could be grown. The old system of distributing grain for bread to the troops persisted. However, the production of vodka was such a profitable business that many voivodes diverted the grain supplies for the purpose of distilling vodka, which was then sold for the voivode's personal profit.

The frequent failure to pay and supply the troops, as well the heavy-handed means employed by most voivodes to maintain discipline, resulted in a number of cossack uprisings. Some cossacks even departed for China, entering into Manchu service (more on which below). The worst of these uprisings took place in 1695–1698, when cossack uprisings took place throughout south-eastern Siberia, from the Yenisey to Nerchinsk, on the border with China.

With colonisation came yet another threat to the native tribes. Like in the Americas, the Europeans brought diseases which resulted in epidemics that ravaged the natives. Smallpox, in particular, which previously was unknown in Siberia, from 1630 onwards wiped out numerous native communities.[10]

The central and eastern parts of Siberia remained far away from Moscow. In the seventeenth century, riverine travel (the only feasible means of travel) from Moscow to Yakutsk took more than a year, which included an interruption of several months during the winter. A round trip might take anything from three to four years, again for reasons of the climate.[11]

Beyond the Yakuts, in north-eastern Siberia, Muscovite explorers in 1633–1638 sailed downriver to the mouth of the Lena to explore the Arctic coast. From 1635 to the 1650s, forts were built as far east as the Kolyma and Anadyr Rivers. Like the Yakuts, the Yukagirs, too, were divided, and the Muscovite *yasak* collectors would take advantage of the prevalent clan rivalry to suppress the natives. Yet, sporadic uprisings took place up to the 1670s.

In 1639, an expedition of cossacks under Ivan Moskvitin reached the Pacific coast. A few years later, the explorers built the fort of Okhotsk, which henceforth became a key base on the Pacific. Here, too, the Tungus displayed fierce opposition to the Muscovite presence. Okhotsk was stormed and destroyed in 1654. Yet more uprisings took place in 1665 and 1677. But like elsewhere, the natives were too few, and militarily too weak, to turn the tide. Yet more Muscovites arrived, in larger numbers, until resistance ended.

In 1644, the Muscovites first met the Chukchis. The Chukchis, despite their Ice Age culture, was possibly the most warlike of all the Siberian tribes. From the time of the first encounter, Muscovites spent 120 years attempting to subdue the Chukchis, without success. The Koraks were encountered in 1669. Almost equally warlike as the Chukchis, the Koraks, too, resisted the Muscovites and wiped out one of the first cossack expeditions sent against them. However, again intertribal rivalry facilitated the Muscovite conquest. The Muscovites hired Yukagirs and Tungus against the Koraks. Even so, fighting continued into the mid-eighteenth century.

Muscovy and the Manchu Empire

However, the biggest challenge to Muscovite colonisation in the east was the Manchu empire, which by then had taken control over China. Muscovite fur traders and explorers eventually also moved into the Amur valley north of Manchuria. The country was rich in sables, and the Muscovites frequently clashed with local tribes who regarded the Muscovites as poachers. As a result, by the mid-seventeenth-century, two vigorous, young empires – the Muscovite and the Manchu – found themselves confronting each other at the Amur River.[12] Most of their forces in the region remained small, but nonetheless a number of small, vicious wars were fought between Muscovites and Manchus.

---

10 *Ibid.*, p.58.
11 *Ibid.*, p.66.
12 Mark Mancall, *Russia and China: Their Diplomatic Relations to 1728* (Cambridge, Massachusetts: Harvard University Press, 1971), pp.21–32; John J. Stephan, *The Russian Far East: A History*

Most Muscovite military units were small, and largely made up of cossacks and hereditary servicemen.[13] Armament consisted primarily of muskets, but many forts had up to a dozen cannons. The one difference between the Muscovites' armament and equipment as compared to those at the time being used in Europe was that in Siberia, armour was still in widespread use, at least among those who could afford it. Even shields, which had disappeared in European Muscovy a century ago, remained in use. This was not necessarily a sign of backwardness; most native opponents, including the Manchus, relied heavily on archery, and the Muscovites may have argued that armour and shields still provided reasonable protection against arrows.

Muscovites had been exploring the Amur River and also conducted raids into the outer reaches of Manchuria since the early 1640s. Other Muscovites, among them the aforementioned Ivan Moskvitin and, soon after, the brutal Vasiliy Poyarkov, penetrated to the Okhotsk coast around the same time, building the wooden fort there which later became Okhotsk. They, too, assumed control over territory claimed by the Manchus. In 1650, a ruthless former peasant named Yerofey Khabarov led a large-scale raid of cossacks supported by several small sledge-mounted cannons and a unit of 21 Muscovite regular soldiers into the outer reaches of Manchuria. In 1651, Khabarov built a fort on the Amur, called Achansk, where his force spent the winter. Reinforcements had now increased Khabarov's party to over 200. However, this territory already had not only native owners, as the others over whom the Muscovites had imposed their rule, but also a far more powerful overlord, the Manchu ruler of Qing China. The Manchus under Nurgaci had formed a budding empire in 1616, conquered Peking and key regions of China in 1644, and then continued to make China its largest and most wealthy imperial possession under the dynastic name of Qing.[14] But the Manchus had not forgotten their possessions to the north.

The savagely oppressed natives of the Amur region accordingly requested Manchu assistance, and a Qing army was despatched towards the Muscovite position. The Muscovites, who in the light of later events may have exaggerated, claimed that it was 2,000 men strong. On 24 March 1652, the Qing army attacked Achansk and broke its walls with artillery fire. Khabarov and his men managed to drive off the Qing with moderate losses (if Khabarov's somewhat exaggerated report is to be trusted, the Muscovites gained the victory and killed 676 Manchus, against a mere 10 Muscovite dead). The Qing had orders to take the Muscovites alive, which for obvious reasons precluded aggressive tactics. However, Khabarov realised that the Manchu artillery was superior to his own, and the few firearms the Manchus carried (called 'rapid-firing' matchlocks in one report) surpassed the Muscovite guns

---

(Stanford, California: Stanford University Press, 1994), pp.21, 28; Forsyth, *History of the Peoples of Siberia*, pp.104–5.

13   This section is in part based on Michael Fredholm von Essen, 'Cossacks against the Manchu Empire, 1651–1689', *Arquebusier* 23: 6 (1997), pp.3–5.

14   Fredholm von Essen, *Eight Banners and Green Flag*.

in firepower.[15] Khabarov wisely chose to retreat, pursued by an army of 6,000 Manchu troops and natives who had rallied against the Muscovite invaders.

Although by then an increasing number of Muscovite regular troops were being sent to the Far East, this had little effect on the Amur conflict. The Amur was too far away for them to reach. Besides, the outbreak of the Thirteen Years War in 1654 obliged the Tsar to recall most of the Siberian reinforcements to Europe. The Qing maintained a small temporary garrison at Ningguta (in present-day Jilin province), but this was by no means large enough to secure the frontier. In 1654 a clash occurred between Manchu regulars (bannermen) from the Ninguta garrison and Muscovite soldiers based at the fortified stockade at Kumarsk, overlooking the River Kumar just north of the Amur. The next year the banner troops unsuccessfully tried to take the Muscovite fort.[16] Many Muscovites operated as river pirates, and much of the movement was by ship on the Amur. The Muscovites primarily raided to get supplies, mainly grain, as well as tribute. The Qing at first responded by forcibly resettling some local tribes out of reach of the Muscovites. Nonetheless, Khabarov and his successor Onufriy Stepanov continued to raid the Amur region with their fleet of ships for several years. In 1657, the Qing accordingly established Ningguta as a permanent garrison.

In 1658, the Manchu garrison commander appointed in the previous year, Šarhûda (d. 1659), led a large Qing fleet armed with artillery that caught up with Stepanov, killing him and capturing over 200 of his about 500 cossacks. Šarhûda was upon his death the following year succeeded by his son, Bahai, who continued his father's strategy. Manchu forces actively sought out and destroyed Muscovite stockades along the Amur. In 1660, Bahai defeated a Muscovite expedition at the juncture of the Sungari and Amur Rivers. Bahai reported to Peking:

> We concealed our warships along both banks of the river. When the enemy boats arrived, we came out of our hiding and the enemy immediately retreated. Our troops pursued them and the enemy deserted their ships and attempted to flee along the shore. We beheaded more than sixty of the enemy and a great number of them drowned. Forty-seven women were captured. We also took firearms, shields, armour, and other implements of war.

The women captured were probably those unfortunates from Siberian tribes who had previously been encountered and captured by cossacks. Due to these defeats, official Muscovite involvement in the region came to a halt, and only outlaws and renegade cossacks remained on the Amur.[17]

---

15 Basil Dmytryshyn, E.A.P. Crownhart-Vaughan, and Thomas Vaughan, *To Siberia and Russian America: Three Centuries of Russian Eastward Expansion 1: Russia's Conquest of Siberia – A Documentary Record, 1558–1700* (Portland: Oregon Historical Society Press, 1985), pp.269–73.

16 *Ibid.*, pp.308–13.

17 Stephan, *Russian Far East*, pp.29–30; Forsyth, *History*, p.105; Robert B. Oxnam, *Ruling from Horseback: Manchu Politics in the Oboi Regency, 1661–1669* (Chicago: University of Chicago Press, 1975), p.163 (which includes Bahai's report); Pamela Kyle Crossley, *The Manchus* (Oxford: Blackwell, 1997), p.102.

In 1662, Bahai was appointed military governor at Ningguta, a position that he would retain until 1682. He took major steps to ensure that northern Manchuria was brought firmly under Qing rule. Under him, the Qing enlarged the garrison at Ningguta, which henceforth came to serve as a base from which to control the various tribes in the region (Bahai incorporated some of them into the Manchu banner system) and monitor Muscovite activities. In 1665 and 1668, Bahai led garrison troops from Ningguta up the Sungari and Amur Rivers where he defeated bands of cossacks.[18]

In 1672, Muscovite troops returned to the region. Renewed hostilities broke out between Muscovites and natives tributary to the Qing. Manchu expeditionary forces were sent to the Okhotsk coast to assert Qing sovereignty. In the years between 1676 and 1684, the Manchu Kangxi emperor sent large numbers of additional troops to the region. He established a new military command at Jilin (Kirin), to the west of Ningguta and complete with shipyard facilities for the construction of war junks, many of which were now being built for use on the Amur. The new fleet was then being trained for river warfare. From 1680, the Qing also established a line of fortifications around the Manchurian borders. A new town was constructed at Aihun (known to the Muscovites as Aygun), and used as a base of operations. The Muscovites were successfully cleared out, and their three forts on the Zeya, Selemya, and Tugur Rivers were destroyed in 1683–1684.[19]

The Muscovites had also built and fortified a settlement named Albazin (earlier known as Yaksa) at the most northerly point on the great curve of the Amur. The wooden fort, perhaps originally founded by Khabarov in 1651 and subsequently occupied by mutinous but soon pardoned cossacks in 1665, had been unsuccessfully attacked by Manchu forces already in 1670. In 1684, Moscow dispatched 2,000 men to Albazin, held by the voivode Aleksei Larionovich Tolbuzin (d. 1686). The wooden fort at Albazin had both artillery towers and a moat, outside which was another palisade and various other defences such as pits with hidden iron stakes.[20]

By then Qing military engineers had developed a naval infrastructure with boats and junks for troop transportation and grain supplies, teams of draft animals, and troops trained in riverine warfare (and indeed ice-skating), which in 1684 enabled the Manchus to bring up a large army from Peking, probably 5,000 but reputedly no less than 15,000 men with 200 guns under the command of a banner commander named Sabsu. On the frontier, the Manchu army was joined by tribal Mongols. The Muscovites were overawed. In 1685, after a siege of four days, the Muscovites complied with Manchu demands, surrendered their arms, and evacuated the fort. The Manchu impact had indeed been so strong that 45 cossacks with families instead defected to

18   Oxnam, *Ruling from Horseback*, pp.164–5.

19   Crossley, *Manchus*, pp.103, 108; Oxnam, *Ruling from Horseback*, p.165; Pamela Kyle Crossley, *A Translucent Mirror: History and Identity in Qing Imperial Ideology* (Berkeley: University of California Press, 1999), p.296.

20   On Albazin and subsequent events, see, e.g., Stephan, *Russian Far East*, pp.30–31; Willard J. Peterson (ed.), *The Cambridge History of China* 9:1: *The Ch'ing Empire to 1800* (Cambridge: Cambridge University Press, 2002), pp.150–53; Forsyth, *History*, pp.106–8; Mancall, *Russia and China*, pp.115–40.

join the Manchu banner troops. The Manchus accepted their defection, and the cossacks provided the core for a new banner unit henceforth known as the Albazinian bannermen. Yet it was not for their military prowess that the Manchus had accepted them. The Qing had vainly hoped to find somebody qualified to teach Russian; however, all proved illiterate, and many of the new bannermen were probably Inner Asians in Muscovite service.[21] The Manchus then destroyed Albazin. However, as soon as the Manchu forces were gone Tolbuzin and 800 to 900 Muscovites returned with a dozen cannons, more than two tonnes of gunpowder, and supplies to last a year to rebuild the fort with more modern defences, including earthen ramparts.

In 1686, another Manchu expedition of 5,000 men and perhaps as many as 40 cannons returned to Albazin, killed Tolbuzin who fell while leading a sortie, and after a siege of several months retook the fort, which was again destroyed. By then it was winter and barely 70 defenders remained alive, half of whom soon succumbed to disease and starvation.[22] Negotiations followed on Muscovite territory, held there between the Manchu Prince Songgotu with the linguistic support of the Jesuits Jean-François Gerbillon and Tomé Pereira from the Qing capital and the Muscovite emissary Fyodor A. Golovin, and under the ominous threat of a strong Manchu army (12,000 Qing troops supported by at least 2,000 Buryat and Onggut Mongols) with 50 cannons. In 1689, the negotiations resulted in the Nerchinsk treaty. Muscovy had to abandon the Amur region to the Manchus. This treaty, together with the later treaty of Kyakhta, signed in 1727, delimited and with the exception of a single allowed trade route (through Kyakhta) closed the Manchu-Muscovite border. An agent of the tsar as well as a Muscovite ecclesiastical mission were allowed to settle in the Qing capital, and Muscovite caravans regularly visited Peking. Relations were from this time generally peaceful, as Muscovy did not have the resources to match Qing military power in the region.

21 Crossley, *Manchus*, pp.81, 102, 104, 213–14; Evelyn S. Rawski, *The Last Emperors: A Social History of Qing Imperial Institutions* (Berkeley: University of California Press, 1998), p.242; Mancall, Russia and China, p.133.

22 Dmytryshyn, Crownhart-Vaughan, and Vaughan, *To Siberia*, pp.482–3.

6

Conclusion: The Muscovite Army on the Eve of Tsar Peter's Reforms

By the end of the seventeenth century, the Muscovite army operated in the south, east, and west. It also carried out limited operations in the Arctic north. The Muscovite army had already transformed itself into a Western army, although it still contained troops and military traditions from the East, which was the origin of the Muscovite military system. These traditions included a combined arms approach, of eastern origin but improved and refined by Muscovy, with a focus on cavalry operations with significant infantry and artillery support. Tsar Peter's subsequent reforms, although decisive, accordingly rested on a legacy of previous reforms, including the introduction of regiments organised in the West European style earlier in the century. It is obvious from the examples of, in particular, Prince Golitsyn's campaigns, that Tsar Peter did not inherit an obsolete or old-style army. The military reform that led to the introduction of a European military system was already well underway. Yet, links with North Caucasus and Siberia had brought further Oriental influences into the Muscovite military system. These elements did not disappear with Tsar Peter's reforms. Cossacks, Circassians, and Kalmyk Mongols continued to serve in Russian armies well beyond the time of Tsar Peter and indeed into the present.

A recurring problem was always logistics, caused by the vast size of Muscovy's theatres of operation, the lack of proper highways and roads, and climate conditions. However, this was a known problem, and something that the Muscovites improved over time. The one key issue that the Muscovite army fundamentally failed to address was the need for continuous training, both for existing and new units. The hereditary servicemen, including a significant number of those who eventually served in the new formation cavalry units, were not only intended to be self-supported financially and logistically, they were also fundamentally self-trained. This meant that the men's personal, martial capacity varied considerably, with those of a military bent being far more proficient than those who merely served to uphold family tradition and safeguard their land grant. Moreover, neither would be proficient in operating as a unit, since they hardly ever trained in formation. There were no training depots for new recruits, nor did Muscovy have the financial resources to raise, arm, and train such recruits during an ongoing campaign. Mobilising an army was an effort in itself, and there was no system, and indeed no available resources, for raising additional, untrained men, when replacements were needed. While the need for a permanently standing army had been understood since the days of Ivan IV, the Muscovite economy had never really been able to sustain a large, standing army. As a result, each time a standing force was created (the streltsy in the sixteenth century, the new formation regiments in the seventeenth century), the persistent lack of funding meant that the men had to be effectively demobilised when no longer needed, and then switched to individual trades or farming to support themselves. With few exceptions, the standing units were standing on paper only. They could be mobilised, but to prepare them for campaign duties, training often would have to start all over again, at least if they were expected to operate at full capacity. As for tactical exercises and manoeuvres, such training measures essentially did not take place until Tsar Peter introduced them.

Muscovy had created a centralised administrative and military system. The Muscovite administration aimed to control all aspects of military life and had good records of officers, soldiers, supplies, and arsenals. There was also a focus on Moscow itself. Yet, as the expansion to the south, into the Caucasus, and to the east, into Siberia, shows, a study of surviving Russian-language documents alone may be insufficient fully to understand the Muscovite army, since these documents, due to most having been issued in Moscow, have an institutional bias towards centralisation. As has been demonstrated, Moscow could not control every move taken by its commanders and armies on distant frontiers, and there were documented differences between the regions in how the military system developed and was utilised. The Muscovite state was not quite as highly centralised and fixated on Moscow as traditional scholarship, focused on surviving records from first churchmen and the court, then the military administration, may have made us believe. There were regional differences, and life on the frontier was both more free and more entrepreneurial than life in Moscow.

Yet, the trend in Muscovy, as well as in Western Europe, went in the direction of increased state power and a monopoly of violence in the hands of the government. But an absolutist government system could not emerge before the creation of a permanent standing army divorced from ties to rival centres of power. The old-style army, led by the nobility, was despite the nobles' dependence on land grants not eager to be manipulated by an absolutist government in Moscow and could not be trusted never to challenge the Tsar's power. Neither were the streltsy, who grew increasingly linked, in thought and family relationships, with the townspeople among whom they lived, always the tool needed for an absolutist government to enforce its will. The frequent uprisings in the second half of the seventeenth century demonstrated that they, too, despite their role in policing and internal security were somewhat less than pawns in the hands of the government. The cossacks might be loyal when they had to, but as events in Siberia showed, they frequently cared considerably more for their own interests and profits than for those of a distant government. This left the new formation regiments, dependent on the treasury for wages and supplies and frequently commanded by foreign officers. This was the standing army needed for a ruler such as Tsar Peter to transform the military and society into an absolutist form of government. Tsars such as Ivan IV might have been autocratic rulers within their court but they could seldom rule uncontested, which Ivan's experiment with the *oprichnina* showed. It was only Tsar Peter who managed to turn himself into an absolute monarch, and he did so on the basis of the new formation army, which in turn depended on the continuing supply of conscripts from the lower orders, primarily peasants, who were both hardy in face of adverse service conditions and left without recourse to other options due to a lack of education combined with a strong belief in the societal order sustained by the church.

But the new army was expensive, and although Muscovy had natural resources, the vast distances and relatively small population meant that these were not always easily exploited. Muscovy was perhaps not exceptional in this regard in the period under consideration here; however, the economic poverty of the state and low population density, in particular in comparison to Western Europe, caused difficulties that were not of Muscovy's own making.

A recurring Muscovite need was for strong investments in manpower and defense spending to secure the long, open frontiers in the south and east. Not only did these essentially open borders generate a certain frontier spirit, they also put heavy demands on the state and its system for taxation and provisioning of border troops. Although the system of border defences improved considerably over time, and there were few major Tatar raids that penetrated the defensive lines after 1660, previous centuries had seen considerable turmoil. Moreover, the successful fortification of the southern border caused economic distress and radical social changes, in particular in the stature of the hereditary servicemen but also in the enserfment of peasants in the settled agricultural regions.

The southern border in particular, but also much of the rest of Muscovy, consisted of vast areas and sparsely populated, or even unhabited, open terrain. Even when Muscovy aimed to emulate Western European military practices, such as with the introduction of new formation regiments, the Muscovite army always consisted of a larger proportion of cavalry than was common in Western Europe. The Muscovites were not alone in this; the Lithuanians, Poles, and Swedes also included significant numbers of cavalry within their armed forces. The reason was that cavalry was needed in Eastern Europe, and was essential for operations on the steppe. Only cavalry forces had the mobility needed for intelligence, reconnaissance, and foraging across the sparsely populated expanses that constituted the Muscovite army's regular theatres of operation. Cavalry patrols also had defensive tasks, including patrolling to locate enemy invasion forces and guarding crops in the field.

It is difficult to estimate the total manpower available to Muscovy. We have only estimates for the total population. Allowing for territorial changes, the population is believed to have grown from about 5.8 million in 1500 to perhaps some 9–10 million in 1550. The population may have declined during the 1550s, only recovering by the end of the century. From the turn of the seventeenth century until the time of Tsar Peter, the population is estimated at around some 11–12 million.[1] Both contemporary and modern observers have assessed the potential maximum size of the Muscovite armed forces at the end of the sixteenth century as being probably around 110,000, of which somewhat more than 40,000 might serve in any given campaign season. Modern observers estimate that by the 1680s, the potential size of the armed forces was some 200,000, of whom about half could be fielded in any given campaign season. The rest, in both the sixteenth and seventeenth centuries, would still be available for garrison service.[2] However, we have seen that the contemporary observer Palmquist in 1674 estimated the total number of men available for military purposes in Muscovy to be 300,000, of which a third, somewhat more than 100,000 men, might serve on active duty in any given campaign season. Moreover, Palmquist's estimate seems to have been fairly accurate. These were significant numbers, far higher than could be raised by most neighbouring states except the Ottoman empire, and it can be assumed that this high level of military mobilisation carried negative repercussions for the economic development of the Muscovite state.

The Muscovites were good soldiers, and they functioned well in conditions of adversity, which indeed were common. Perhaps the greatest tribute to the Muscovite army at the time came from its enemies. A sixteenth-century assessment of the Muscovite army can be found in the Chronicle of Balthasar Rüssow (1536–1600), a Livonian German. Rüssow noted both the admirable personal characteristics of the Muscovite soldiers and the domestic reasons which also kept them fighting under adverse circumstances:

> The Russians are good soldiers in fortresses. This is due to the following reason. Firstly, the Russians are an industrious people. When circumstances require it a Russian can work tirelessly, day and night, amidst all dangers, and he prays to God that he may die righteously for his sovereign. Secondly, the Russian is accustomed from early youth to keep the fasts and to be content with meagre fare. As long as he has water, flour, salt and vodka, he can subsist on these for quite a long time, whereas a German cannot. Thirdly, if the Russians voluntarily surrender a fortress, however small, they dare not return home, for they are put to a shameful death. In foreign lands they hold a fortress to the last man and prefer to perish to the last man rather than be led under escort to a foreign land. To a German it makes no difference whatever where he lives, as long as he has enough to eat and drink. Fourthly, the Russians regard it not only as a disgrace but also as a mortal sin to surrender a fortress.[3]

In other words, the Orthodox ideology of the Chosen People of the New Israel and Muscovy as the bulwark of Christendom served as a psychological stimulus for the Muscovite soldier in hard times.

A century later, Palmquist, who, although he visited Muscovy for purposes of intelligence collection and hoped that his work would be used for a future

---

1   Keep, *Soldiers of the Tsar*, p.88.
2   *Ibid.*, pp.87–8.
3   Cited in Wipper, *Ivan Grozny*, pp.225–6.

invasion, had no personal experience of the fighting qualities, or lack thereof, of Muscovite soldiers, still noted that a typical Russian was "very strong of body and limb" and "needs little by way of tools, or by way of food … for a wandering merchant or a soldier may carry with him no more than a sack of oatmeal. He takes a few spoonfuls of this for each meal and mixes it with water or kvass [a sour kind of light beer], and this mixture provides all his food and drink."[4] These qualities no doubt contributed to the formation of hardy soldiers.

Hardiness and stubborn resilience may, indeed, have characterised the majority of Muscovy's soldiers. The merits described by Rüssow and Palmquist were passive virtues, their strength being in defence and endurance. Yet, the Russian soldier also displayed an offensive capability, proven by the persistent push into Livonia and the west, into the south, and into Siberia all the way to the Pacific. These activities were not linked to any religiously inspired crusading spirit, only a very real wish for pushing out from the centre, for going beyond the borders in search of new lands, fortune, and fame, but also for the freedom that in a centralised state such as Muscovy only could be found on the frontier.

Quite a few Muscovite soldiers displayed an entrepreneurial spirit, and not only in the trading activities that many engaged in to support themselves. At home, this was evident from the technical innovations that emerged within the Muscovite army. On the frontier, this spirit led to Cheremisinov's and Buturlin's expeditions into the Caucasus in 1560 and 1605, Tolbuzin's repeated attempts to hold the Amur in 1684 and 1686, and Golitsyn's marches to the Crimea in 1687 and 1689. While some of these commanders ultimately failed in their attempts, their actions established the foundation for an enterprise the result of which remains visible in the external borders of present-day Russia.

---

4   Palmquist, *Några observationer*, pp.98–99.

Colour Plate Commentaries

Artwork by Maksim Borisov

Cover: Origins of the Muscovite Army, Sixteenth Century to Mid Seventeenth Century

Mounted Archer

The early Muscovite army consisted almost exclusively of cavalry, organised along Mongol lines. This mounted archer carries a composite bow, which like the accompanying bowcase and quiver, both suspended from the belt, is of Mongol type. In sixteenth- and seventeenth-century Muscovy, a complete set of cavalryman's armaments, including a bow in its bowcase and a quiver full of arrows, was known as a *saadak*. The fabric-covered bowcase and quiver are decorated with embroidery or in appliqué. In addition to the bow, the man is armed with a sabre and a dagger.

Like most Muscovite cavalrymen, he wears a short-sleeved, high-collared, densely padded hemp coat (*tegilyay*, from the corresponding Mongol term). Sometimes the *tegilyay* included iron bands or even armour plate fastened inside. In addition, he wears an Oriental-style helmet and vambraces.

The man's superior-quality arms, armour, and equipment indicate that he is either a hereditary serviceman or a serving man from the retinue of a wealthy noble.

He rides in the Mongol style, with a saddle and short stirrups, and uses a Mongol-style short whip (*nagayka*) instead of spurs. Hereditary servicemen and serving men of this type continued to serve in Muscovite armies until the very end of the seventeenth century. From 1643 until the old-style cavalry was abolished in 1701, they were required to add a pair of pistols (typically wheellocks) and a musket to their armament. However, those who still considered the bow their primary weapon could instead choose to have either a pistol or a carbine as auxiliary firearm. Serving men were still allowed to be armed with bows only.

Plate 1: The Southern Front

Voivode

A voivode was in the Muscovite cavalry army the title used for the commander or deputy commander of a division. Selected from high-ranking princes and boyars, voivodes could afford elaborate mail or scale armour of traditional

Turco-Mongol type, with metal plates, joined by straps, to protect the chest, back, arms, and legs, a suit of armour of this type being known as *zertsalo* ('mirror'). Such armour, in part often covered in silk brocade or velvet, was regularly used in battle by voivodes and old-style cavalry until the end of the seventeenth century. At other times, voivodes wore the traditional garments of the wealthy aristocracy, which like most clothes worn by Muscovites at the time were of Inner Asian origin, including the caftan, a long narrow gown, and high, soft boots. Unsurprisingly, the noblemen's clothes were lavish and of high quality, often including silks and expensive furs.

In addition to his sabre, a voivode would typically carry a mace as a symbol of command. He would also bring a pair of pistols in saddle holsters on his horse.

Tatar Cavalryman

Many Tatars fought within the Muscovite army, since a number of Tatar enclaves existed within the Muscovite state. Most Tatar soldiers were expert horsemen and often operated in conjunction with cossack cavalry, since their style of fighting was very similar. The main difference between the Tatar troops and other Muscovite forces was that the former less frequently carried firearms and accordingly were limited to the light cavalry role. Yet, light cavalry was vital for patrolling the southern border, which frequently was under threat from the Crimean Tatars.

This Tatar cavalryman carries a composite bow in its bowcase and a quiver, as well as a dagger and the customary whip. There is little to distinguish him from a Russian light horse archer. He is well-to-do, since he wears a short-sleeved green coat over his caftan, but he has in part stripped to his shirt for easier movement when using the lariat. Yet, he may not have been able to afford a sabre.

In contrast to this cavalryman, the Tatar military elite wore lavish arms and armour, often of the same type as used by the Muscovite boyars and the wealthiest hereditary servicemen.

Plate 2: Expansion to the East

Cossack

There were several types of cossacks, ranging from the town cossacks who were voluntary recruits who served as infantry in exchange for payment to the free cossacks who lived in distinct communities along primarily the Don, Volga, and Dniepr rivers and, until the mid seventeenth century, often technically were not subjects of the Tsar but were paid money, weapons, cloth, and grain in return for their support in protecting the border against incursions by Crimean and occasionally Ottoman invaders. They were not all horsemen; many were expert boatmen since the communications lines usually followed the major rivers. Cossacks were also hired for service elsewhere and played a prominent role in the expansion into Siberia. This cossack infantryman, armed with a flintlock musket and dressed in a civilian woollen coat, fur hat, and peasant-style footwear, is typical of the seventeenth-century Siberian cossacks. His sash is tied at the back. This cossack carries a bullet pouch, suspended from a leather bandolier, and a powder-flask, in addition to whatever other personal equipment he needs.

Noble Officer

This noble or wealthy hereditary serviceman in civilian dress may be an officer or, in the time of Ivan IV, an *oprichnik*, a member of Ivan's personal corps that was established to maintain internal order and destroy his domestic enemies. His black, fur-lined woollen coat suggests the latter. The officer also wears a caftan and the high-heeled, hob-nailed boots that became common among the nobility. He is armed with a sabre and the customary dagger.

In battle, he would likely serve on horseback, carry a composite bow or a set of pistols, and then wear some kind of armour, because of his wealth probably similar in style, although not quite as lavish, as the types customarily worn by voivodes, high-ranking princes, and boyars. However, officers of this this type also served on foot, as commanders of infantry.

Infantryman

While it is known that Muscovy early on established a standing corps of infantry, the streltsy, most evidence of what they looked like actually derive from the seventeenth century. This early musketeer represents a Muscovite soldier either from the time before West European-style powder-flasks and wooden powder cartouches (individual flasks each with a measured charge of powder) were introduced in the first half of the seventeenth century, or from a provincial unit which had not yet adopted such equipment. He carries a bullet pouch, suspended from a leather bandolier, a powder-flask, and a Y-shaped priming flask for the operation of his musket, which is an early flintlock type. In addition, he carries a sabre and the ubiquitous knife. He wears the usual caftan as well as the high, soft boots of Inner Asian origin that were originally used on horseback but by this time had grown increasingly common among Muscovites. This soldier might be an early strelets or a town cossack, or even the type of soldier that occasionally appears in the service registers under the label mounted cossack arquebusier.

It is conceivable that sixteenth-century streltsy used helmets and possibly even armour when on campaign, if so probably of the densely padded hemp coat (*tegilyay*) type already described for the mounted archer, some combination of chain mail and plate, or brigandine (*kuyak*) armour. There is no known archive document that confirms that armour was ever issued to the streltsy; however, it should be remembered that there is indeed no confirmed evidence at all on what they then actually looked like while on campaign duty. It would be surprising if the Tsar's selected infantry would not be issued with helmets and some kind of armour under those circumstances. Sixteenth-century illustrated chronicles depict Muscovite matchlockmen wearing armour and helmets at the siege of Kazan'; however, we do not know if these depictions were taken from real life or merely mirrored the legacy of Byzantine religious art.

Plate 3: Garrison Duty, Mid to Late Seventeenth Century

Artilleryman

Artillerymen dressed similarly to the infantry, although their caftans and headgear commonly were red or reddish brown. In addition, Moscow artillerymen had a parade uniform the primary item of which was a disc-shaped breastplate (*alam*). This consisted of a pair of discs of steel or copper hung on chest and back. This particular disc is embossed with a double-headed eagle, the initially Byzantine symbol adopted by Ivan III to signal that Moscow was the spiritual heir of Constantinople. The double-headed eagle also appears on the decorated linstock that this soldier carries while on ceremonial duty.

Dragoon

The dragoon regiments, first raised in 1632, effectively functioned as mounted infantry. They were regarded as the lowest type of new formation troops and were mainly raised on the southern frontier. Dragoons were not intended to fight as cavalry, so at first, they were dressed and armed just like infantry, with muskets. As a result, they had to dismount to fire. By the time of the Thirteen Years War (1654–1667), many dragoons were re-armed with carbines, which enabled them to operate more like cavalry, which was particularly useful on the southern border. This dragoon also carries a West European rapier as a sidearm. Other dragoons might be armed with an axe or even a *berdysh* pole-axe in addition to the musket or carbine. The dragoon regiments played a major role in Muscovy's wars, not least because they were cheap to raise, but were abolished at the beginning of the 1680s.

Strelets

The streltsy ('shooters') formed the solid backbone of the Muscovite army from the time of Ivan IV well into the seventeenth century. The Moscow-ranked streltsy were the most important, even though streltsy were raised in provincial towns as well. The colour of the uniform of this strelets shows that he belongs to Colonel Davyd Grigor'yevich Vorontsov's regiment of Moscow streltsy, as illustrated by Erik Palmquist in 1674. By this time, most streltsy had been re-armed with flintlock muskets. However, some of them retained their old matchlock muskets into the 1670s, including this soldier, who has protected his musket's gunlock with a dedicated gunlock cover, made of fulled woollen fabric and decorated in appliqué in a pattern of stylised flowers. Such gunlocks were common among Muscovite troops. He carries a bullet pouch, a West European powder-flask, and a set of West European-style powder cartouches, suspended from a leather bandolier, on which he also has attached a spare match. In addition to his musket, the soldier carries a *berdysh* poleaxe which he used as a musket rest as well as for hand-to-hand combat, in particular against cavalry. In addition to these weapons, a strelets would also carry a sabre or rapier.

This particular strelets is an experienced soldier, which is proven by the golden kopek coin, which he displays fastened to his hat. Such a coin was awarded for bravery, like a medal, and was then displayed attached to a sleeve or set in the hat.

Plate 4: The Western Front, Mid to Late Seventeenth Century

New Formation Musketeer

The introduction of the new formation regiments in the early 1630s was a means to adopt West European military innovations in the Muscovite army. However, until the outbreak of the Thirteen Years War in 1654, there were still no permanent new formation regiments. Each regiment would disband at the end of the campaign season. This problem was to some extent overcome in 1656–1657, when two new formation infantry regiments were raised that became known as the 'selected regiments'. To some extent, they became a standing force, which enabled them to retain their fighting skills and thus grow in importance.

In the new formation regiments, organisation, arms, equipment, and tactics aimed to follow European standards. This, however, did not necessarily apply to uniforms. Most Muscovite infantry, unlike the foreign officers who often commanded the new formation regiments, were dressed similarly to the streltsy, in caftans and high, soft boots.

The colour of the uniform of this private soldier, a musketeer, shows that he belongs to the second 'thousand' of the first selected regiment, commanded by Colonel Aggey Alekseyev syn Shepelyov, in 1661. As a new recruit, he still wears peasant shoes instead of boots. However, he has been issued the full outfit of matchlock musket, a bullet pouch, a West European powder-flask, and a set of West European-style powder cartouches, suspended from a leather bandolier on which he also has attached a spare match, and a West European rapier. In addition, he carries a swinefeather (elsewhere also known as Swedish feather), which was a short pike with an attachment for resting the musket barrel that could be used as protection against cavalry. A unit of musketeers with swinefeathers firmly planted in the ground in front of them would give the appearance of a wall of spear points. Moreover, with the addition of logs to link them together, several swinefeathers could be arranged into a *cheval-de-frise*, an anti-cavalry obstacle that was positioned in front of the infantry ranks so as to provide protection against a cavalry charge.

Reiter

The first new formation cavalry regiment was a reiter regiment raised in 1632. Originally a German troop type, reiters were mounted pistoleers protected by an iron helmet and half-armour, that is, plate armour covering the upper body and, at times, arms. In actual practice, this meant that Muscovite reiters typically wore a helmet and a West European-style cuirass. Most Muscovite reiters were sons of hereditary servicemen, and just like their fathers in the old-style cavalry, each reiter was expected to equip himself, at his own expense. Each reiter was required to muster with a horse, a musket (later carbine), a pair of pistols, a rapier or sabre, West European-style half-armour, and a suitable helmet. Reiters wore Muscovite dress – caftan and boots – under their West European-style cuirass. The focus was on new organisation and armaments, not re-training, so the difference between a reiter and an old-style cavalryman might, at first, not have been that great. In 1680, weaponry was standardised. Henceforth, each reiter was required to bring a carbine and a pair of pistols.

This reiter is reloading his wheellock carbine. He wears the standard, West European-style set of arms and armour, but with a sabre, not a rapier. He still rides in the Mongol style, with short stirrups, and uses the customary short whip (*nagayka*) instead of spurs.

New Formation Pikeman

The colour of the uniform of this private soldier, a pikeman, shows that he belongs to the second 'thousand' of the second selected regiment, commanded by Colonel Yakov Maksimov syn Kolyubakin, in 1661. This regiment settled in Butyrki, a Moscow suburb, after which it eventually was named, becoming known as the Butyrsk regiment.

Like other new formation infantrymen, he is armed in the West European style, with a long pike, rapier, and West European half-armour. He has also been issued a helmet of the morion type. Unlike the new formation cavalry, new formation infantrymen were issued uniforms, arms, and equipment from state arsenals.

Plate 5: The Eastern Front

Kalmyk Cavalryman

From 1644 onwards, the first bands of Kalmyks (western Mongols) appeared in the River Terek region north of the Caucasus range. The Kalmyks were traditionally based far to the east, near the uppermost River Yenisey. Within a few years, Muscovy entered into an alliance with the Kalmyks and gave them grazing rights. Henceforth, Kalmyks regularly contributed cavalry when Muscovy went to war.

This Kalmyk cavalryman carries a Mongol-type matchlock musket with an attached forked, A-shaped rest. Inner Asian muskets were often so long that typically, such a rest was attached to the stock for greater ease in firing. This rest, about 0.5 metres long, was pivoted to a projection on the lower side of the stock. Many Kalmyk nobles were crack shots, since this was a skill useful in hunting, even though the traditional composite bow remained in widespread use and indeed was regarded as the more dangerous weapon. Somehow, some Kalmyks even learnt how to fire the matchlock from horseback while at full gallop, in a similar way to the bow.

It was not unusual to see Kalmyks armed with both spear, matchlock (carried on the back, as here, or between the saddle and the horse, under one's leg), sword, and bow. This Kalmyk cavalryman carries a captured sabre instead of his traditional sword and has also added an axe to his weapons pack. In addition, he wears a chain mail and plate cuirass over a quilted coat, a helmet of traditional Mongol design, and vambraces. The metal reinforcements on his quilted coat suggests that it may consist of brigandine armour (*kuyak*), a garment of cloth or leather reinforced with metal plates from both sides, of the type commonly used by Mongols and adopted from them by the Muscovites. Naturally, this Kalmyk rides in in the Mongol style, with short stirrups, and has not neglected to bring his short whip (*nagayka*).

Ostyak or Vogul auxiliary

Siberia, like the Urals that linked Europe with Asia, was inhabited by a variety of tribal peoples when the Muscovites began to advance into the east. Among the first encountered were the Khanty and Mansi. The Muscovites referred to them as Ostyaks and Voguls, respectively. Divided into a variety of separate clans, many Khanty and Mansi chieftains agreed to enter into Muscovite service as a means to retain their positions. In return, they provided auxiliary soldiers who because of their local knowledge often were of prime importance for the continued conquest. Quite a few of those who entered into Muscovite service became formally contracted to serve in exchange for payment, as Ostyak servicemen, and some gained a measure of standing in Muscovite society.

This auxiliary, who might be either an Ostyak or Vogul, is dressed and armed in the traditional manner when campaigning under winter conditions. He wears fur-trimmed skin clothing decorated in appliqué, which hides a richly embroidered shirt made from nettle or hemp fibres and thigh-length hose of reindeer leather. This being winter, he wears boots made of skin, while in summer deer or elk-skin moccasins would be sufficient.

He is armed with a laminated (not composite) longbow and carries a quiver of arrows on his back. He might also carry a spear. This auxiliary has no better armour than a breastplate made from layers of elk antler, but his chief might wear a coat of mail and an iron helmet. Those who could afford it adorned themselves with glass beads and metal ornaments acquired by trade. This man's knife sheath is made in typical Khanty and Mansi style. Both Khanty and Mansi were in most cases extensively tattooed, but this man appears to have avoided this custom.

Plate 6: Eastern and Western Influences

Circassian Noble Cavalryman

From the time of Ivan IV, many Circassian nobles from the North Caucasus entered into Muscovite service, as individuals or in small groups. Being master horsemen, Circassian nobles served as fully armoured cavalry. They wore chain-mail and splint-mail armour with vambraces throughout the period under consideration here and well beyond. Circassian suits of armour were of good quality and enjoyed a reputation far beyond the Caucasus. Nobles wore steel helmets of the Turco-Persian type, either the tall, conical variety with a pointed crest or a spike on top (*kulah-khud*) or, as this noble cavalryman, the low variety with a small, round plate that only covered the crown of the skull (*kulah-zirah*). Either type came with a long chain-mail coif or neckguard. Most would also carry a small, round shield made of wood or hard leather and bound with iron.

This noble carries a composite bow of the Inner Asian type, stored in a bowcase and with a quiver suspended from his belt, as well as a sword. This might have been a sabre with cross-guard. In the seventeenth century, however, the *shashka*, another sabre-like weapon with a forked hilt without knuckle guards, became more common. The *shashka* was typically carried in a shoulder strap with its cutting edge generally upwards. In addition to his main sidearm, this noble also carries a *kindjal*, a long double-edged dagger or short sword without a hand guard. It was almost always straight, although occasionally slightly curved. A *kindjal* was worn on a leather strap across the left groin. This cavalryman might also carry a lance and a set of darts or javelins (*djid*).

The Circassian nobility used exquisitely ornamented weapons with hilts of horn or, even better, silver. The latter was often decorated with a special niello alloy composed of silver, copper, lead, and sulphur. Scabbards, bowcases, and quivers were usually made out of red or black leather, edged with coloured strips of the same material, or covered with velvet.

However, from the point of view of weapons technology, the North Caucasus was a backward place. Firearms were introduced only in the sixteenth century, and they became widespread no earlier than in the eighteenth century, which explains why this noble cavalryman does not carry one.

Hussar

The hussars were the last type of new formation cavalry to be formed in Muscovy. The first, small hussar regiment was raised in 1662, under Lieutenant Colonel Nikifor Karaulov. Styled on the famous Polish winged hussars, who on several occasions had been used with devastating effect against Muscovite units, the Muscovite hussars, too, were armed with long, probably lightweight lances. For protection, they carried helmets, half-armour, and vambraces.

All hussars were wealthy hereditary servicemen or boyars from the northwestern parts of Muscovy. Considering themselves an elite formation, like their Polish counterparts, they never served on the southern or eastern border. Like any other hereditary serviceman, a hussar was expected to equip himself, at his own expense. Being rich, his equipment would be costly and of better quality than what was available to most others or was issued by the state arsenals. This hussar is armed with a lance, sabre, and a pair of pistols, left in the saddle holsters on his horse. In addition, he carries a Polish-style war-hammer. His arms and armour are not the only evidence of Polish influences. By this time, spurs began to be used by those Muscovites who were exposed to European practices. The hussar has adopted certain other types of European fashion as well, including shaving off his beard but retaining a smart moustache. Otherwise, he retains Muscovite clothing, including the ubiquitous caftan. His costly cloak would consist of a panther, tiger, or at least a lynx skin.

Bibliography

Abramov, Aleksey, 'Reforma sluzhilogo plat'ya, 1680', *Zeughaus* 45 (2012): pp.2–11.

Adrianova-Peretts, V.P. (ed.), *Poslaniya Ivana Groznogo* (St. Petersburg: Nauka, 2005).

Allen, W.E.D. (ed.). *Russian Embassies to the Georgian Kings, 1589–1605.* 2 vols., Cambridge: Hakluyt Society, Cambridge University Press, 1970.

Armstrong, Terence (ed.), *Yermak's Campaign in Siberia* (London: Hakluyt Society, 1975).

Attius Sohlman, Margareta (ed.), *Stora oredans Ryssland: Petrus Petrejus ögonvittnesskildring från 1608* (Stockholm: Carlssons, 1997).

Babulin, Igor' B., *Bitva pod Konotopom, 28 iyunya 1659 goda* (Moscow: Zeughaus, 2009).

Belyayev, I.D., *O russkom voyske v tsarstvovaniye Mikhaila Feodorovicha i posle ego, do preobrazovaniy, sdelannykh Petrom Velikim: Istoricheskoye izsledovaniye* (Moscow: Universitetskaya tipografiya, 1846).

Berry, Lloyd E.; and Robert O. Crummey (eds.), *Rude & Barbarous Kingdom: Russia in the Accounts of Sixteenth-Century English Voyagers* (Madison: University of Wisconsin Press, 1968).

Birgegård, Ulla (ed.), *J.G. Sparwenfeld's Diary of a Journey to Russia 1684-87* (Stockholm: Kungl. Vitterhets Historie och Antikvitets Akademien, Slavica suecana Series A, Vol. 1, 2002).

Chernov, A.V., 'Obrazovanie streletskogo voyska', *Istoricheskiye zapiski*, t.38 (Moscow, 1951): 281–90.

Chernov, A.V., *Vooruzhennye sily Russkogo gosudarstva v XV-XVII vv.: S obrazovaniya tsentralizovannogo gosudarstva do reform pri Petre I* (Moscow: Voyennoye Izdatel'stvo Ministerstva Oborony Soyuza SSR, 1954).

Cotossichin [Kotoshikhin], Grigori Carpofsson, *Beskrifning om muschofsche rijkets staat* (Stockholm: Ljus, 1908).

Danchenko, Vladimir Georgievich, 'The Production, Heraldic Programme and Artistic Design of Standards in Seventeenth Century Russia', Fred Sandstedt, Lena Engquist Sandstedt, Martin Skoog, and Karin Tetteris (eds), *In Hoc Signo Vinces: A Presentation of The Swedish State Trophy Collection* (Stockholm: The National Swedish Museums of Military History, 2006).

Danielsson, Arne, 'Utländska fälttecken utställda i Trofékammaren', *Meddelande från Kungl. Armémuseum* XXV (Stockholm: Kungl. Armémuseum, 1964).

Danielsson, Arne, *Catalogue of Foreign Colours, Standards, Guidons Exhibited in the Trophy Room of the Royal Army Museum, Stockholm.* n.d. A translation of the above, but without illustrations and without mention of the author's name.

Davies, Brian L., *Warfare, State and Society on the Black Sea Steppe, 1500–1700* (London: Routledge, 2007).

Dmytryshyn, Basil (ed.), *Medieval Russia: A Sourcebook, 900–1700* (Hinsdale, Illinois: The Dryden Press, 2nd edn 1973).

Dmytryshyn, Basil; E.A.P. Crownhart-Vaughan; and Thomas Vaughan, *To Siberia and Russian America: Three Centuries of Russian Eastward Expansion 1: Russia's Conquest of Siberia – A Documentary Record, 1558–1700* (Portland: Oregon Historical Society Press, 1985).

Dzamikhov, Kasbolat Fitsevich. *Adygi (cherkesy) v politike Rossii na Kavkaze (1550-e – nachalo 1770-kh gg.)*, (Nal'chik: State University of Kabardino-Balkaria, 2001).

Epstein, Fritz T. (ed.), *Heinrich von Staden: Aufzeichnungen über den Moskauer Staat* (Hamburg: Cram, de Gruyter & Co., 1964).

Fennell, J.L I. (ed.). *Prince A. M. Kurbsky's History of Ivan IV* (Cambridge: Cambridge University Press, 1965).

Fennell, J.L.I. (ed.), *The Correspondence between Prince A.M. Kurbsky and Tsar Ivan IV of Russia 1564–1579* (Cambridge: Cambridge University Press, 1955).

Filjushkin [Filyushkin], Alexander, *Ivan the Terrible: A Military History* (London: Frontline Books, 2008).

Filyushkin, A.I., *Russko-litovskaya voyna 1561–1570 i datsko-shvedskaya voyna 1563–1570 gg.* (St. Petersburg: Milhist.info, 2015).

Fredholm von Essen, Michael, *Nomad Empires and Nomad Grand Strategy: The Rise and Fall of Nomad Military Power, c.1000 BC–AD 1500* (Stockholm: Stockholm University, Asian Cultures and Modernity 9, 2005).

Frost, Robert I., *The Northern Wars: War, State and Society in Northeastern Europe, 1558–1721* (Harlow, Essex: Pearson Education. 2000).

Fuller, William C., Jr., *Strategy and Power in Russia 1600–1914* (New York: The Free Press, 1992).

Gaziński, Radosław. 'Die Kaperflotte von Iwan IV. dem schrecklichen im Lichte von Akten des Herzoglich Stettiner Archivs', *Studia Maritima* 26 (2013): 29–38.

Gorelik. Mikhael V., *Warriors of Eurasia From the VIII Century BC to the XVII Century AD.* (Stockport: Montvert, 1995).

Gush, George, *Renaissance Armies 1480–1650* (Cambridge: Patrick Stephens, 1975).

Hakluyt, Richard, *The Discovery of Muscovy: From the Collections of Richard Hakluyt – With The Voyages of Ohthere and Wulfstan from King Alfred's Orosius* (London: Cassell & Company, 1889).

Hakluyt, Richard, *Voyages and Discoveries: The Principal Navigations, Voyages, Traffiques and Discoveries of the English Nation* (Harmondsworth: Penguin, 1972).

Hewitt, George (ed.). *The Abkhazians: A Handbook* (Richmond, Surrey: Curzon, 1999).

Höglund, Lars-Eric; Åke Sallnäs; and Alexander Bespalow, *Stora Nordiska Kriget 1700–1721*, Vol. 3: *Ryssland, Sachsen, Preussen och Hannover – Fanor och uniformer* (Karlstad: Acedia Press, 2004).

Jaimoukha, Amjad, *The Circassians: A Handbook* (New York: Palgrave, 2001).

Kappeler, Andreas, *Ivan Groznyj im Spiegel der ausländischen Druckschriften seiner Zeit: Ein Beitrag zur Geschichte des westlichen Russlandbildes* (Bern: Herbert Lang, 1972).

Khrenov, M.M.; R.T. Zubov; I.F. Konovalov; G.N. Nesterov-Komarov; and M.A. Terovkin, *Voyennaya odezhda russkoy armii* (Moscow: Voyennoye izdatel'stvo, 1994).

Keep, John L.H., *Soldiers of the Tsar: Army and Society in Russia, 1462–1874* (Oxford: Clarendon, 1985.

Krylov, V.M. et al., *The Military-Historical Museum of Artillery, Engineer and Signal Corps: The Guide* (St. Petersburg: The Military-Historical Museum of Artillery, Engineer and Signal Corps, 2008).

Kurbatov, Oleg A., *Tikhvinskoye osadnoye sidenie 1613* (Moscow: Zeughaus, 2006).

Lemercier-Quelquejay, Chantal. 'Co-optation of the Elites of Kabarda and Daghestan in the Sixteenth Century', Marie Bennigsen Broxup (ed.), *The North Caucasus Barrier: The Russian Advance towards the Muslim World* (London: Hurst & Company, 1992).

Le Vasseur, Guillaume, sieur de Beauplan, *La description d'Ukranie de Guillaume Le Vasseur de Beauplan* (Ottawa: Les Presses de l'Université d'Ottawa, 1990). Edited by Dennis F. Essar and Andrew B. Pernal.

Lyutov, A.M., *Edged Weapons in the Collection of the Russian Museum of Ethnography* (St. Petersburg: Russian Museum of Ethnography, 2006).

Malov, Aleksandr, 'Gosudarevy vybornyye Moskovskiye polki soldatskogo stroya: Kratkiy ocherk istorii i organizatsii', *Zeughaus* 13 (2001): pp.2–7.

Malov, Aleksandr, 'Gosudarevy vybornyye Moskovskiye polki soldatskogo stroya: Komandiry vybornykh polkov', *Zeughaus* 14 (2001): pp.2–7.

Malov, Aleksandr, 'Znamena polkov novogo stroya', *Zeughaus* 15 (2001): pp.6–10.

Malov, Aleksandr, 'Znamena polkov novogo stroya: Simvolika kresta', *Zeughaus* 16 (2001): pp.2–7.

Malov, Aleksandr, 'Russkaya pekhota XVII veka: Gosudarevo zhalovan'ye-sluzhiloye plat'ye', *Zeughaus* 17 (2002): pp.10–16.

Malov, Aleksandr, " 'Konnost', lyudnost' i oruzhnost' sluzhilogo 'goroda' pered Smolenskoy voynoy: Na materiale Velikikh Luk", *Zeughaus* 18 (2002): pp.12–15.

Malov, Aleksandr, 'Gosudarev vybornyy polk Aggeya Shepeleva: Pervoye soldatskoye sluzhiloye plat'ye', *Zeughaus* 20 (2002): pp.10–13.

Malov, Aleksandr, 'Garnizon Borisoglebskoy kreposti: Gosudarevo sluzhiloye plat'ye, 1666', *Zeughaus* 21 (2003): pp.3–7.

Malov, Aleksandr, 'Gosudarevo sluzhiloye plat'ye Pervogo vybornogo polka 1661 g', *Zeughaus* 22 (2006): pp.6–9.

Malov, Aleksandr, 'Gosudarevo sluzhiloye plat'ye Vtorogo vybornogo polka v kontse 1650-kh – nachale 1660-kh gg', *Zeughaus* 24 (2007): pp.5–7.

Malov, Aleksandr V., *Russko-pol'skaya voyna 1654–1667* (Moscow: Zeughaus, 2006).

Mancall, Mark, *Russia and China: Their Diplomatic Relations to 1728* (Cambridge, Massachusetts: Harvard University Press, 1971).

Margeret, Jacques, *The Russian Empire and Grand Duchy of Muscovy: A 17th-Century French Account* (Pittsburgh: University of Pittsburgh Press, 1983). Translated by Chester S.L. Dunning. First published as *Estat de l'empire de Russie, et grande duché de Moscovie*.

Massa, Issac, *A Short History of the Beginnings and Origins of These Present Present Wars in Moscow under the Reign of Various Sovereigns down to the Year 1610* (Toronto: University of Toronto Press, 1982). Translated by G. Edward Orchard.

Miller, Yurij A., *Caucasian Arms from the State Hermitage Museum, St. Petersburg: The Art of Weaponry in Caucasus and Transcaucasia in the 18th and 19th Centuries/Kaukasiske Våben fra Eremitagemuseet, Skt. Petersborg* (Odense: Danish Arms and Armour Society/Våbenhistorisk Selskap, n.d.).

Nossov, Konstantin, *Russian Fortresses 1480–1682*. Oxford: Osprey Fortress Series 39, 2006.

Okladnikov, Aleksei P., *Yakutia before Its Incorporation into the Russian State* (Montreal: McGill-Queens University press, 1970).

Olearius, Adam, *Moskowitische und Persische Reise: Die Holsteinische Gesandtschaft beim Schah 1633-1639* (Stuttgart: Thienemann, Edition Erdmann, 1986).

Olearius, Adam, *The Travels of Olearius in Seventeenth-Century Russia* (Stanford: Stanford University Press, 1967). Translated by Samuel H. Baron.

Ostrowski, Donald, *Muscovy and the Mongols: Cross-Cultural Influences on the Steppe Frontier, 1304–1589* (Cambridge: Cambridge University Press, 1998).

Palacios-Fernandez, Roberto, 'Moskovskiye strel'tsy', *Zeughaus* 1 (1992): pp.8–15.

Palacios-Fernandez, Roberto, 'O proiskhozhdenii tsvetov petrovskoy leyb-gvardii', *Zeughaus* 5 (1996): pp.4–7.

Palacios-Fernandez, Roberto, 'Moskovskiye pushkari', *Zeughaus* 6 (1997): pp.5–11.

Palacios-Fernandez, Roberto, 'Muzykanty vybornykh moskovskikh soldatskikh polkov', *Zeughaus* 7 (1998): pp.7–9.

Palmquist, Erik, *Några observationer angående Ryssland, sammanfattade av Erik Palmquist år 1674*. (Moscow: Lomonosov, 2012).

Penskoy, V.V., *Srazheniye pri Molodyakh 28 iyulya – 3 avgusta 1572 g* (Milhist.info, 2012).

Penskoy, V.V., *'Tsenturiony Ivana Groznogo 1: Ivan Semenov syn Cheremisinov* (Milhist.info, 2012).

Plaetschke, Bruno, *Die Tschetschenen: Forschungen zur Völkerkunde des nordöstlichen Kaukasus* (Hamburg: Friederichsen, de Gruyter & Co., 1929); Veröffentlichungen des Geographischen Instituts der Universität Königsberg Pr., Heft 11.

Poe, Marshall, 'Herberstein and Origin of the European Image of Muscovite Government', Frank Kämpfer (ed.), *450 Jahre Sigismund von Herbersteins Rerum Moscoviticarum Commentarii: 1549–1999* (Wiesbaden: Harrassowitz, 2002).

Poe, Marshall, 'Muscovite Personnel Records, 1475–1550: New Light on the Early Evolution of Russian Bureaucracy', *Jahrbücher für Geschichte Osteuropas* 45:3 (1997): pp.361–78.

Porfiriev, I.E., *Peter I: Grundläggare av den ryska reguljära arméns och flottans krigskonst* (Stockholm: Hörsta, 1958). Originally published in the Soviet Union in 1952.

Pouncy, Carolyn Johnston (ed.), *The Domostroi: Rules For Russian Households in the Time of Ivan the Terrible* (Ithaca: Cornell University Press, 1994).

Rakhimzyanov, Bulat R., 'The Debatable Questions of the Early Kasimov Khanate (1437–1462)', *Russian History* 37: 2 (2010): pp.83–101.

Sandstedt, Fred; Lena Engquist Sandstedt; Martin Skoog; and Karin Tetteris (eds.), *In Hoc Signo Vinces: A Presentation of The Swedish State Trophy Collection* (Stockholm: The National Swedish Museums of Military History, 2006).

Shpakovsky, Viacheslav; and David Nicolle, *Armies of Ivan the Terrible: Russian Troops 1505–1700* (Oxford: Osprey Men-at-Arms 427, 2006).

Staden, Heinrich von, *The Land and Government of Muscovy: A Sixteenth-Century Account* (Stanford: Stanford University Press, 1967). Translated by Thomas Esper.

Stevens, Carol Belkin, *Russia's Wars of Emergence 1460–1730* (London: Routledge, 2013).

Stevens, Carol Belkin, *Soldiers on the Steppe: Army Reform and Social Change in Early Modern Russia* (DeKalb: Northern Illinois University Press, 1995).

Velikanov, Vladimir. " 'Salatskiye trofei': Polkovoye imushchestvo streletskikh polkov Nechayeva i Protopopova, poteryannoye v srazhenii pri Salatakh, 1703", *Zeughaus* 52 (2013): pp.3–13.

Vernadsky, George, *The Mongols and Russia* (New Haven: Yale University Press, 1953).

Viljanti, Arvo, *Gustav Vasas ryska krig 1554–1557* (Stockholm: Kungl. Vitterhets Historie och Antikvitets Akademiens Handlingar, Historiska serien 2:2, 1957).

Viskovatov, Aleksandr Vasil'yevich, *Istoricheskoye opisaniye odezhdy i vooruzheniya rossiyskikh" voysk"*, vol. 1 (St. Petersburg: Voyennaya tipografiya, 1841).

Viskovatov, Aleksandr Vasilevich [Vasil'yevich], *Uniforms of the Russian Army in the Era of Ancient Tzar: From the Reign of Vasili IV to Michael I, Alexis, Feodor III during the XVIIth Century (From Viskovatov's Historical Description of the Clothing and Arms of the Russian Army).* (Zanica: Soldiershop Publishing, 2017). Translation of the above.

Zvegintsov, V.V., *Russkaya armiya 1: 1700–1763gg*, Typescript, 1967. Translated into German by Oscar Urbonas. Army Museum archive, Stockholm. F 18 BI, Vol. 1.